DIGITAL
ENABLEMENT

The Consumerizational and Transformational
Effects of Digital Technology

DIGITAL
ENABLEMENT

The Consumerizational and Transformational
Effects of Digital Technology

Editors

Shan Ling Pan
M S Sandeep

University of New South Wales, Australia

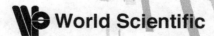

World Scientific

NEW JERSEY · LONDON · SINGAPORE · BEIJING · SHANGHAI · HONG KONG · TAIPEI · CHENNAI · TOKYO

Published by

World Scientific Publishing Co. Pte. Ltd.
5 Toh Tuck Link, Singapore 596224
USA office: 27 Warren Street, Suite 401-402, Hackensack, NJ 07601
UK office: 57 Shelton Street, Covent Garden, London WC2H 9HE

Library of Congress Cataloging-in-Publication Data
Names: Pan, Shan-Ling. | M.S. Sandeep, editors.
Title: Digital enablement : the consumerizational and transformational effects of digital technology /
    edited by Shan Ling Pan (University of New South Wales, Australia),
    M.S. Sandeep (University of New South Wales, Australia).
Description: New Jersey : World Scientific, [2017] | Includes bibliographical references and index.
Identifiers: LCCN 2017002296 | ISBN 9789813209121
Subjects: LCSH: Information technology--Economic aspects. |
    Information technology--Social aspects.
Classification: LCC HC79.I55

British Library Cataloguing-in-Publication Data
A catalogue record for this book is available from the British Library.

For any available supplementary material, please visit
http://www.worldscientific.com/worldscibooks/10.1142/10424#t=suppl

Desk Editor: Shreya Gopi

Typeset by Stallion Press
Email: enquiries@stallionpress.com

Printed in Singapore

Contents

Acknowledgment

The editors would like to acknowledge the following grants: National Natural Science Foundation of China (NSFC): 71529001 and 71632003.

Chapter 1

Digital Entrepreneurship Ecosystem as a New Form of Organizing: A Case of Zhongguancun

Wenyu Du

Management Science and Engineering Department
School of Business, Renmin University of China
duwenyu@rbs.org.cn

Wenjie Li

Management Science and Engineering Department
School of Business, Renmin University of China
lwjcolin@ruc.edu.cn

Abstract

Digital entrepreneurship ecosystem (DEE) plays a significant role for generating digital innovations because it contains variable resources and facilitates the collective collaborations. Many regions have established the DEE to support digital innovations in order to improve their economic environment. However, researches on digital innovation at ecosystem level are limited. In addition, the knowledge about "how to organize DEE" is inadequate. To unveil the organizing forms of DEE, we consider DEE as a "new" form of organizing for the absence of traditional organizing elements such as hierarchy and formal authority. Through this theoretical lens, DEE can be analyzed as an organization, rather than a combination of actors. Empirically, we conducted a case study of Zhongguancun (ZGC), a successful DEE in China, and interviewed 51 heterogeneous people. We found that eight activities compose the organizing form of DEE.

Keywords: Digital entrepreneurship, Ecosystem, New forms of organizing.

Introduction

Since digital innovation becomes a critical factor to gain firms' competition, it is common that digital innovations mainly take place within firms, rather than in competitive market (Autio *et al.*, 2015). However, digital innovation also takes place outside the boundary of firms through collective collaboration, which complements the resources limitation of single firm (Adner and Kapoor, 2010). Thus, we need to treat digital innovations at the ecosystem level, which could provide a platform to aggregate various resources and facilitates such collaboration (Lindgren *et al.*, 2008). In practice, digital entrepreneurship ecosystem (DEE) has already been complimented to accelerate digital innovations, such as Silicon Valley. Many regions also started to establish DEEs to support digital innovations as a means to revive local economy, such as London, Berlin, Paris, Tel Aviv in Israel, Singapore, and China (Herrmann *et al.*, 2015; McKinsey Global Institution, 2015; Yip, 2015).

Therefore, DEE plays an important role as an accelerator for creating digital start-ups. Currently, however, researches on digital innovation at the ecosystem level are limited, which hampers our understanding of DEEs (Shen *et al.*, 2015). To illustrate, existing research on digital innovation mainly focuses on individual, organizational, and industrial levels (Bharadwaj *et al.*, 2013; Sambamurthy *et al.*, 2003; Yoo *et al.*, 2010). Even those research in the ecosystem context has mainly addressed organizational or industrial activities within the ecosystem (Lee and Berente, 2011; Selander *et al.*, 2010). Given this urgent, *Information System Journal* (ISJ), the top journal in IS literature, calls for papers on unveiling the characteristics of digital entrepreneurship in a wide context (Shen *et al.*, 2015, p. 1).

Contrary to the traditional thinking of organizing, many DEEs can organize variable actors well without formal authority. However, the knowledge about "how does DEE organize" is inadequate, posing a great knowledge gap for both scholars and practitioners. Different from traditional organizations, actors in DEE do not share the same goal and are free to make their decision based on their own goals and benefits, which may lead to the conflicts rather than collaboration. For example, the actors may prefer to drain the value within the ecosystem for maximum of their benefit, rather than share it with other actors. Therefore, exploring the details of organizing processes that facilitate inter-organizational coordination and collaboration is a worthy research point (Gulati *et al.*, 2012).

Thus, our study aims to analyze the DEE as a whole to answer the question "how does a DEE organize to support digital innovations." In order to answer this question, we adopt the theoretical lens of forms of organizing (Puranam *et al.*, 2014), in which the four universal problems — problems of task division, task allocation, reward distribution, and information flow — have to be addressed. Since DEE is different from the traditional form of organizing for lack of traditional organizing elements such as formal authority, the solutions to these four problems may be novel (Puranam *et al.*, 2014). Thus, the organizing process of DEE is relatively novel and we can treat DEE as a "new" form of organizing. This theoretical lens enables us to analyze DEE as an organization rather than a pure combination of actors. These universal problems of organizing provide us with an operational framework to analyze the organizing activities in DEEs.

We conducted a case study on Zhongguancun (ZGC), a successful DEE known as the Silicon Valley of China. Analyzing data collected from 51 interviewees with high heterogeneity, we find eight activities to achieve the organizing form of DEE. Our chapter has three contributions. First, we contribute by extending the research on digital innovation from individual or organizational level to an ecosystem level by analyzing the DEE as a whole (Shen *et al.*, 2015). This is because the DEE is conducive to digital innovation exploitation since it aggregates various resources and facilitates inter-firm collaboration. Second, our chapter makes contributions by complementing the design study of organization through the case exhibition of DEE as a new form of organizing (Gulati *et al.*, 2012; Puranam *et al.*, 2014). Finally, our chapter contributes to the entrepreneurship literature by unveiling the organizing processes of an entrepreneurial ecosystem (Autio *et al.*, 2015).

Literature review

Digital innovation and DEE

According to the Yoo *et al.* (2010), digital innovation can be defined as the implementation of new combinations of digital and non-digital components to produce novel products and processes. Due to the limitation of resource and knowledge available within individual organizations, many firms seek to leverage external resources to generate digital innovations (Selander *et al.*, 2010). Meanwhile, the collaboration networks of inter-firms (Schilling and Phelps, 2007) and boundary-spinning practices (Lindgren *et al.*, 2008) have significant effect on innovations. Thus, digital innovation typically involves multiple actors and interactions. In other words, ecosystem which contains variable resources and information is significant for digital innovations.

Innovation and entrepreneurship are inherent (Bessant and Tidd, 2007) since many digital entrepreneurships are based on digital innovations and also create digital innovations. Meanwhile, the DEE is important for the success of digital entrepreneurship for the integration of resource and supportive element beyond the firm level (Spigel, 2015). Yet, research on digital entrepreneurship at the ecosystem level is limited. Most of them focus on individual and organizational levels, in which entrepreneurial process and context are the main research points (Shane and Venkataraman, 2000; Zahra *et al.*, 2014). Other researches on digital entrepreneurship at a wide context are clusters (Delgado *et al.*, 2010) and networks (Nambisan and Sawhney, 2011). Although these researches have different perspectives, they share a common ground that a macro scope is needed to understand the strategy of digital entrepreneurship (Spigel, 2015). Thus, the term "ecosystem" became popular in the digital entrepreneurship literatures.

For the underdevelopment and undertheorization of ecosystem, a tool or framework is needed to analyze the ecosystem structurally (Autio *et al.*, 2015; Spigel, 2015). Because agents within the ecosystem are legally independent entities, it is straight to consider ecosystem as a multi-organizational problem, as most researches did. Nonetheless, the conception of "meta-organization", in which firms or individuals are not bound by formal authority, based on employment relationships (Gulati *et al.*, 2012), enables us to involve the framework of organization theory to analyze ecosystem. In order to unveil the black box of DEE's organizing process, we adopt the framework of form of organizing. Details will be shown in the next section.

Forms of organizing

There are two fundamental problems of organizing: the division of labor and the integration of effort (Puranam *et al.*, 2014). According to the research of Puranam *et al.* (2014), the problem "division of labor" can be divided into two sub-problems: task division and task allocation; the problem "integration of effort" can also be described as reward provision and information flow (summarized in Table 1).

Task division refers to *the problem of mapping the goals of the organization into tasks and subtasks* (Puranam *et al.*, 2014, p. 165). It describes the problem of how to breakdown the system goal into contributory subtasks in an organization. In other words, it decides what jobs the system has. For task division, Puranam *et al.* (2014) argued that the following three principles should be relevant: excluding members who do not fit in the system goal, no essential tasks remaining incomplete, and little redundancy among subtasks. These principles can be achieved by the initial design (MacCormack *et al.*, 2006), the participation and contribution by members (Puranam *et al.*, 2014), co-specialization of members (Thomas and Autio, 2012) and the transparency of task division (Baldwin and Clark, 2006).

Task allocation refers to *the problems of mapping the tasks obtained through task division to individual agents* (Puranam *et al.*, 2014, p. 165). It describes the problem of how to allocate a job to the right one. The common mechanisms of task allocation are assignment (Hackman and Oldham, 1976) and self-selection based on capability, resource, and preference (Puranam *et al.*, 2014). The process of self-selection can be

Digital Enablement

Table 1. Summary of Forms of Organizing

Fundamental Problems	Description	Example of Solutions
Task Division	The problem of mapping the goals of the organization into tasks and subtasks	✓ Initial structure designed by founder (MacCormack *et al.*, 2006) ✓ Participation and contribution by other members (Puranam *et al.*, 2014) ✓ Transparency of task division (Baldwin and Clark, 2006)
Task Allocation	The problems of mapping the tasks obtained through task division to individual agents	✓ Assignment (Hackman and Oldham, 1976) ✓ Self-selection based on internal factors (Puranam *et al.*, 2014) ✓ Self-selection based on external factors such as competition
Reward Distribution	The problem of mapping a set of rewards to the agents in the organization and motivating the agents to cooperate	✓ Compensations (Prendergast, 1999) ✓ Intrinsic motivation (Hackman and Oldham, 1976) ✓ Social norms (Shah, 2006); ✓ Value creation (Thomas and Autio, 2012) ✓ Culture as a tool kit (Spigel, 2015)
Information Flow	The problem that an organization's agents have the information needed to execute their tasks and coordinate actions with others	✓ Physical collocation (Puranam *et al.*, 2014) ✓ Virtual tools (Puranam *et al.*, 2014) ✓ Conference (Garud, 2008)

considered as decision making, which can be influenced by both internal and external factors. Competition is an external factor for an organization, but it is also a critical factor for a successful ecosystem (Moore, 1993; Peltoniemi and Vuori, 2004). Therefore, the self-selection based on competition is also a pattern of task allocation.

The distribution of rewards refers to *the problem of mapping a set of rewards to the agents in the organization — in order to motivate the agents to cooperate by taking costly actions toward executing the tasks they have been allocated* (Puranam *et al.*, 2014, p. 165). It mainly solves the problem of how to motivate agents to enter in and pay effort to achieve tasks. Under the employment contract, compensation is the main mechanism of reward distribution (Prendergast, 1999). As for the motivation problem, intrinsic motivation is also important for motivating employees to pay effort on tasks (Hackman and Oldham, 1976), especially in the new forms of organization where the employment contract is missing. The value logic of ecosystem provides agents in ecosystem with opportunities to capture and co-create values (Thomas and Autio, 2012). This value creation attracts agents to join into the ecosystem and ensures the fair distribution of rewards. Reward distribution can also be enhanced by social norms (Shah, 2006) and culture (Spigel, 2015; Swidler, 1986).

The information flow refers to *the problem that an organization's agents have the information needed to execute their tasks and coordinate actions with others* (Puranam *et al.*, 2014, p. 166). It constructs the linkages among agents to the integration of their efforts. Physical collocation and virtual tools are the common channels to achieve information flow (Puranam *et al.*, 2014). For a community, a conference plays a significant role as the prime venue for information exchange and interaction (Garud, 2008).

Methodology

ZGC is selected as the case to research because it is a successful DEE and data collection is relatively convenient for geographic proximity. Since establishment in June, 2014, ZGC has attracted about 40 service providers to join in, including venture capitals, accelerators, universities, and mentors. In addition, about 400 third-party organizations provide service to support digital entrepreneurship. More than 2,000 entrepreneurial teams were incubated in ZGC and some of them have grown to big companies whose value was estimated to be more than 10 billion.

This study follows the interpretive case study methodology (Klein and Myers, 1999). Our analysis unit is the DEE. Three phases were conducted in this study.

The first phase was the preparation part, which started in December 2014. In this phase, second data about ZGC and entrepreneurship development in China were widely obtained and analyzed (for detail information, refer to Appendix B, Table B.1). Then some elite interviews were conducted. We fortunately got the interview permission of the deputy head of Zhongguancun Administrative Committee (ZAC). ZAC is a government department in charge of development and construction of ZGC. Later, interviews were conducted among some main accelerators. After analyzing the data, a big picture was shown about the ZGC and its contexts of China's digital entrepreneurship boom. This analysis also revealed some details about the construction and relationship of members in ZGC. Organizations and individuals were independent legally, which means that there was no employment relationship among them. This finding is also confirmed in the next phase of study.

The second phase was extensive data collection, which started in April 2015. In the phase, semi-structured interviews were extensively conducted in ZGC. After excluding some low-quality interviews (such as irrelative interviews, and stopping in the early stage because of contingency), 51 unique interviews were conducted in total, including digital entrepreneurs, infrastructure managers, government officers, accelerator staffs, venture investors, and service providers (for more information, refer to Appendix A, Table A.1). Each interview lasted more than 45 minutes and was conducted by at least two researchers. These interviews yielded 472 pages of transcripts and notes. In order to get a deep understanding of ZGC and access more interviewees, one of our researchers joined in an accelerator as an intern for 4 months (form May to August 2015).

The third phase was data analysis, which started in August 2015. The techniques of open coding and selective coding were used to systematically analyze data (Corbin and Strauss, 1990). Combining literature review, the findings are identified and supported.

To ensure reliability and validity of data collection and analysis, some methods were applied simultaneously. To achieve reliability in data collection, data were implemented and triangulated by interview variety members from system architect to individual participant. Combining secondary data (such as news, websites, and government documents) and interview data also enhanced the reliability of data and findings. In order to achieve validity, atleast two researchers were involved during both data collection and analysis. We present our analyzing process and findings to other researchers to get feedback and consequently enhance the validity of our findings.

Task division

In the ZGC, task division is accomplished through (1) the category design by architect and (2) co-specialization within participants.

In the early stage of ZGC, the main tasks are designed by the architect, which is considered as high-centralized process (Gulati *et al.*, 2012). When designing the DEE, a system-level goal is essential. This goal is a kind of guidance for the system. Tasks divided into details have to support to achieve this goal. As the team of architects of ZGC has experience in establishing an entrepreneurial accelerator in Silicon Valley, the structure of Silicon Valley as a DEE was imitated and imported into ZGC. Thus, the main categories of jobs were designed such as acceleration centers, venture capitals, entrepreneurial mentors, education resources, and physical infrastructures (including collocation places, telecommunication facilities, transportation infrastructure, and security protection). As an officer who participated in the designing process of ZGC stated, *"in the initial stage of this project, we design the main structure of ZGC, in which some specific members are necessary, such as accelerate centers, venture capitals, collocation places and so on."*

This high-centralized process of design decides what kinds of work ZGC as a DEE provides. The visibility of the system goal and category makes it possible to attract agents who own ability to achieve it (Baldwin and Clark, 2006). To some extent, the irrelevant members are excluded through the visibility and definition of categories of ZGC. For example, agents who aim to work for entrepreneurship would be attracted by the visible goal, while others unrelated with entrepreneurship would not be interested in ZGC.

Therefore, task division is achieved through *category design by an architect.*

Although the architect has the ability to design the main category of task in the early stage, the details of the subtask division in ZGC still need to be explored. *"Although we have experience on entrepreneurial service in Silicon Valley, the detail structure of the entrepreneurship system is still needed to be explored. Meanwhile, because the context of ZGC is quite different form Silicon Valley, we cannot copy the pattern of Silicon Valley directly"*, an officer participating in the design work of ZGC stated. But with more and more participation and contributions, the task division can be elaborated and developed by itself (Puranam *et al.*, 2014). Therefore, after designing the main category of tasks, the architect imported heterogeneous agents into ZGC through some reward distributions such as subsidies to enable the complementariness of task division (Thomas and Autio, 2012), which was a low-centralized process.

At this stage, heterogeneous agents with specialized resources and abilities cooperate, which overcome the lack of resource limitation of individuals and also complement the subtask division by achieving the demands of others. These subtasks are not designed by an architect. For instance, some agents find that some entrepreneurs have a problem to convert the innovation idea to entrepreneurship business, and thus they established a small industry to solve this problem. These agents have specific experience and ability to solve this problem but lack innovation ideas, while entrepreneurs have innovations, some of them lack the ability to achieve them. Therefore, co-specialization within participants complements the subtasks which are not designed and enhances the completeness of task division.

Thus, task division is achieved through *co-specialization within participants*.

Task allocation

The pattern of task allocation is close to the task division because it has to solve the allocation problem based on the task division (Puranam *et al.*, 2014). In the early stage of ZGC, category design is the main method of task division. Correspondingly, methods of task allocation should suit the design process, similar to the co-specialization process. In ZGC case, we found that task allocation is accomplished through (1) captain assignment by architect and (2) self-selection based on competition, which correspond to the methods of task division.

At the early stage of ZGC, in order to get the premium and appropriate resources, a competitive bidding mechanism was involved to select and allocate elite members. In this mechanism, the tasks were assigned to the members who owned adequate and appropriate resources to achieve the tasks.

Agents that are assigned to certain tasks or categories can be considered as project leaders, or board managers in an open community. In the ZGC, we call them "captains." Because these captains have premium resources and social reputations, they can build their own authority and manage this category well to support the system-level goal. For instance, a big IT company in China is assigned to be the captain of category of hardware-related entrepreneurship. This company leverages both internal and external resources to build an environment that facilitates the hardware-related innovation and entrepreneurship. These innovations and entrepreneurships are also beneficial for this company because they are related to the industry of this company and also enhance the agility of company through the accessible innovation from outside. As we can see, these captains have the ability to manage their category well and are also beneficial with the development of category (which solve the motivation problem). This high-centralized process of assignment ensures the main tasks (or categories) to be allocated to the right agent to achieve them.

Therefore, task allocation is achieved through *captain assignment by architect.*

In the second phase, when captain members have been confirmed, self-selection becomes the dominating factor of task allocation. Self-selection is based on the task division of co-specialization, which is a low-centralized process. Heterogeneous agents cooperating to achieve co-specialization have to base on the willingness of each other, in which any other high-centralized allocation processes (such as assignment) are not involved. Meanwhile, for the self-organizing nature of ecosystem (Moore, 1993), the main method of task allocation in ZGC as a DEE is self-selection (Gulati *et al.*, 2012; Puranam *et al.*, 2014). As one of the entrepreneurs stated, "*most service providers in ZGC are open to everyone, and we can choose them based on our interests and willingness.*

To the contrary, these service providers also have right to choose you based on their interests."

Therefore, task allocation is achieved through *self-selection based on competition.*

Reward distribution

Reward distribution solves the problem of motivation to join in the system and to take effort to achieve the tasks. In ZGC case, the motivation problem is achieved through (1) value co-creation and (2) entrepreneurial culture as a toolkit.

Many tangible rewards are found to attract agents to join in ZGC, such as subsidies from government, low renting fee, and other policies. These tangible rewards may have positive effects on attraction members, but according to our investigation, these tangible rewards are not the main reason to attract people to join in. As an entrepreneur who is an overseas returnee stated, *"Subsidies in ZGC are not so attractive to entrepreneurs because any other place could provide same, or even better rewards. Policies about entrepreneurship are much more complex than some foreign countries."*

Many agents come to ZGC mainly for the commercial opportunities, while policies and subsidies are supportive to their willingness to join in. Opportunities comes from the process of this system in which value can be captured and created by any other participants (Thomas and Autio, 2012). Since the resources and capabilities of individuals are limited, many agents join in the ecosystem to seek the partners to cooperate in order to capture and create values. Thus, it is a process of value co-creation. For instance, some law service providers capture the value of law service in entrepreneurship process, and they cooperate with other service providers such as acceleration centers and collocation places to create value through solving law problem of entrepreneurs. The value co-creation also occurs at the individual level, which is attractive to the digital entrepreneurs. Many entrepreneurs come to ZGC for information exchange and contestation of innovation ideas. During the process of exchanging and contestation, the ideas have been enhance and even become more valuable for combination of other innovation ideas.

The value co-creation provides with the reward to the agents who pay effort for it. This reward is distributed through the mechanism of pay-by-effort, which is like the mechanism of the commercial market. Thus, this distribution process is fair and free-riding problem which is the main concern of the open community (Puranam *et al.*, 2014) that doesn't exist. At least in the ZGC case, no evidence is found that free-riding has been paid attention to fix it. As for the problem of stealing innovation ideas, since the resource-based views are widely accepted by people, entrepreneurs, never worry about that because they believe that they have unique resources to achieve their ideas, while others cannot do as well as them. As one entrepreneur explained, *"I never worry about the problem of idea copying, because I have unique resources to achieve my idea which others cannot copy. In contrast, I will be glad if my idea is copied by others. It means that my idea is valuable and worthy to be achieved."*

Therefore, reward distribution is achieved through *value co-creation*.

The other factor that enhances the reward distribution is supportive culture. Culture provides repertoire of shaping actions of people, just like "tool kit" in which habits, skills, and styles construct the strategies of action (Swidler, 1986), and culture also can enhance other attributes of ecosystem (Spigel, 2015). In the ZGC case, we find that culture supports and normalizes the entrepreneurial activities, and ensures the fair distribution of rewards.

The supporting and normalization of the entrepreneurial activities are the great motivational factors for entrepreneurs to join in because this culture supports risk taking and provides entrepreneurs and other agents with social prestige, which enhances their legitimacy in the society. One entrepreneur who is a stranger to Beijing ZGC, said, "in my hometown, people consider entrepreneurship as a bad job. But the situation is totally different in ZGC, because it is the hometown of entrepreneurship."

Culture also ensures the fair distribution of rewards through establishing social norms (Shah, 2006). Social norms both encourage value co-creation and protect members from cheating or free-riding. As we discussed in the value co-creation part, there is a risk of cheating and free-riding, in which the mechanism of the commercial market may not be helpful. Under this situation, social norms provide a way to constrain the occurrence of cheating and free-riding (Puranam *et al.*, 2014). In ZGC case, people consider themselves as generations of internet, in which sharing is pride and cheating or free-riding is seriously dishonorable. This social norm protects them and also encourages people share their ideas and achieve value co-creation and digital innovations.

Therefore, reward distribution is achieved through *entrepreneurial culture.*

Information flow

Information flow is accomplished through (1) physical collocation plus virtual tools supporting and (2) intensive conferences.

Information flow is common in the physical collocation and grouping, and it is also the basic way of coordination (Puranam *et al.*, 2014). In ZGC case, physical collocation and grouping are accomplished through geographical proximity, resource similarity, and live activities. Members of ZGC were all located in the same street. This geographical proximity allowed them to exchange information and collocation conveniently. For example, the company A provides promotion services, and its neighbor, company B provides accelerating services. To provide more complete service, they established a deep coordination.

Virtual support infrastructure and tools include group chatting software, website platforms, applications of mobile phone, and so on. With the rapid development of the mobile network in China, it is very convenient to communicate through a smart phone. In the ZGC case, an Instant Messaging application named WeChat was widely used. It supported group chatting so that the information could flow broadly and quickly. Some service providers established website platforms to connect entrepreneurs, service providers, and investors. For example, one service provider in ZGC established a website platform, on which entrepreneurs can upload their business plans. The officers of this website then will give expert feedback about the business plan and also introduce some investors to entrepreneurs. The virtual support infrastructure and tools facilitate the flow of information, and also enable coordination to occur without the limitation of geography.

Therefore, information flow is achieved through *physical collocation plus virtual tools supporting.*

Besides the common physical collocation and virtual tool supporting, the incentive activities or conferences play a significant role in information flow. Conference provides venues for interaction of actors, exchanging of information and contestation of different opinions (Garud, 2008). In the ZGC case, for variable participants within DEE and existence of the heterogeneous field, intensive conferences connect each other and ensure the efforts from different participants can be integrated.

According to the official website of ZGC DEE, established in June 2014, more than 2,000 conferences are held in the ZGC. In the weekly notice board of ZGC, about four big conferences and several small collective activities are held in average, such as workshops, seminars, and road shows. The intensive conferences bring a wide information flow that enable the deep coordination. For example, in an elder-caring technology seminar, much of the frontier information in this field was uncovered, and the participants could know how they supported the development of this field.

Therefore, information flow is achieved through *intensive conferences*.

Discussion

This chapter is a response to the call of researches on digital entrepreneurship (Shen *et al.*, 2015) and entrepreneurship ecosystem (Autio *et al.*, 2015). Using case study approaches, this chapter found a bundle of solutions to organize DEEs through the case of ZGC (findings are summarized in Figure 1).

The solutions of these four organizing problems (task division, task allocation, reward distribution, and information flow) cannot be separated (Puranam *et al.*, 2014). When the solution of one problem is decided, it could influence others and others' solutions must fit it. For example, self-selection — a common solution to task allocation in new forms — needs a low-centralized task division and tasks should be visible so that members can select them by themselves. Moreover, the reward distribution and information must fit the pattern of self-selection. Each part of the problem has many different solutions, but not every solution suits each other. In this sense, when designing a DEE, it is critical to understand what kinds of solutions are suitable. Our findings provide one kind of bundles of

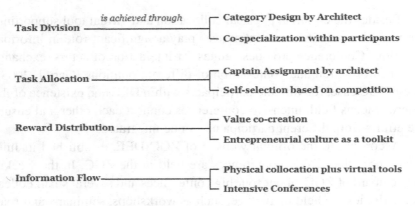

Figure 1.   DEE as a New Form of Organizing

solutions in the context of ZGC. It is not a general solution, but it provides some implications and guidance to designing and constructing DEE.

The theoretical framework of forms of organizing provides a structure to analyze the DEE as the four problems are operational for analyzing. Our findings correspond to the four problems which are divided from the two universal problems of organizing (the division of labor and the integration of effort). However, these findings do not achieve the two universal problems directly. Hence we need to integrate these findings to correspond the problems of the division of labor and the integration of effort. After discussing, we find that the dynamic balance of centralization is important for the division of labor, and the supportive elements are critical to the integration of effort.

The division of labor

For ecosystem, low centralization is the key feature because of its openness and self-organizing nature. However, centralization is not excluded from the ecosystem (Gulati *et al.*, 2012). Somewhat centralization is necessary for establishing the ecosystem. At the early stage of ZGC, task division is designed and task allocation is assigned, which is a high-centralized process. These high-centralized movements enhance the control of agents in the ecosystem. Through the category design, irrelevant members are excluded. The assignment ensures the task was allocated to the agent with basic capabilities, in which members without enough capabilities are excluded. Meanwhile, the centralization ensures this ecosystem moves forward to its goal, instead of random walking. The categories are designed based on the system-level goal, which constrains the varieties of works that ZGC provides. The assignment ensures the members have ability to manage the categories well and support to achieve the system-level goal.

However, the ecosystem is too complex to be designed well, and with numerous resources, the process of assignment can be very costly. Thus, contributions from button up complement the weakness of high-centralized processes and complete the division of labor (Puranam *et al.*, 2014; Thomas and Autio, 2012) such as subtasks division through co-specialization and task allocation through self-selection.

In the next stage of ZGC, low centralization dominates the division of labor, as the beginning is to control members to achieve the system-level goals and exclude irrelevant members. While members are on the road to move forward to the system-level goal, complementariness of the task division and efficiency of the task allocation become the main request. Therefore, low centralization dominates at this stage. But that does not mean the disappearance of centralization at the second stage. When the ecosystem goes wrong, for example, the reward distribution becomes unfair, the architect can fix it through the high-centralized process like draining value jobs to destroy the members who own the rewards unfairly (Spigel, 2015).

Therefore, the division of labor in the ZGC case is a dynamic balance of centralization: in the early stage, the high-centralized process domains for the controlling and in the next stage, the low-centralized process domains for the complementariness of division of labor.

The integration of effort

As for the integration of effort, the connection among agents within DEE is important. The common methods they achieve are found in the ZGC case such as value co-creation and physical and virtual collocation (Gulati *et al.*, 2012; Puranam *et al.*, 2014). These methods achieve the connections that are visible, while some small or hidden connections are invisible and are hard to capture. These connections are like the routine details or hidden rules in the organization which are based on the formal authority and hierarchy. In DEEs, they are more detailed and complex. We argue that supportive elements such as supportive culture and intensive conference enhance these connections and therefore achieve the integration of effort.

Culture influences the actions of people (Swidler, 1986) and is also necessary for the DEE (Spigel, 2015). The effect of entrepreneurial culture shapes the actions of people within DEE, and these people sharing the same culture are connected together to enforce the integration of effort. Agents in the DEE may not share the system-level goal, but they share the same culture, which is critical to shape the connection among these agents. Meanwhile, intensive conferences link the numerous individuals and activities that are hard to capture and have positive effects on the emergence of innovations in certain fields (Garud, 2008). Value co-creation and physical plus virtual collocation construct the main connection among agents, while supportive culture and intensive conferences achieve the detailed connection so that the integration of effort is accomplished. Therefore, the supportive elements of culture and conferences are necessary for the integration of effort.

Contribution and implication

This chapter has several theoretical contributions. First, our study contributes to the digital innovation study by extending the scope of digital innovation to the ecosystem level. Most researches on digital innovation focus on individual, organizational, and industrial levels (Bharadwaj *et al.*, 2013; Sambamurthy *et al.*, 2003; Yoo *et al.*, 2010), little is known about the ecosystem for digital innovations. Even some researches focus on digital innovation at the ecosystem level, their analysis units are still individuals or organizations under the ecosystem context, instead of the entire ecosystems (Shen *et al.*, 2015). Therefore, our chapter responds to this research gap by considering the DEE as a new form of organizing, which provides us with an operational analysis framework and also enables us to understand DEE as a whole.

Second, our chapter complements the design study of organization by revealing the new form of organizing of DEE. In organizational design study, the collaboration among legally autonomous actors challenges the traditional thinking about organizational design because these actors collaborate effectively without traditional organizing elements such as formal authority and incentives (Gulati *et al.*, 2012). In order to overcome the challenge, this kind of collaboration is considered as a new form of organizing (Gulati *et al.*, 2012; Puranam *et al.*, 2014), which is adopted in our chapter as the theoretical framework. One worthy research question, which is answered by our findings, is exploring how the designers of new form of organizing specify a division of labor (Gulati *et al.*, 2012, p. 580).

Third, our chapter also contributes to the entrepreneurship literature for unveiling the organizing process of an entrepreneurial ecosystem. DEE is not only an ecosystem generating digital innovations, but also an ecosystem support entrepreneurship based on digital innovations. Because limited researches focus on entrepreneurial ecosystem, *Strategic Entrepreneurship Journal* (SEJ, a top journal in entrepreneurship field) called for a paper on entrepreneurial ecosystem (Autio *et al.*, 2015). Thus, our chapter also responds to this research call by analyzing the DEE.

Our findings also have practical implications. As the establishment of DEEs is hot in practice, this chapter may give some implications to the architects and policy makers. The theoretical framework of forms of organizing (task division, task allocation, reward distribution, and information flow) also provides a powerful instrument to both researchers and practitioners to better understand the forms of DEE's organizing. As to members in DEE, our findings enable them to know better about DEE and to have a better involvement in DEE. This is helpful to reduce the failures of entrepreneurship.

Limitation and future research

This chapter has some limitations. First, although we try to make our findings as inclusive as possible, we must acknowledge that it is hard to completely identify all the possible activities which compose the new forms of organizing within DEE. For the huge amount of agents and activities existing within DEE, it is hard to identify each of them. Thus, we try to capture the core activities that are mainly effective for the organizing process. Moreover, our single-case study of ZGC also cause this limitation considering that different DEEs have different contexts. Therefore, future researches can focus on multiple cases of DEE under different contexts, or applying the framework of forms of organizing to analyze other DEEs.

Second, the environment of ZGC as a DEE is relatively special because China's government and state-owned enterprises play an important role in design and development of ZGC. However, in other regions, such as Silicon Valley and India, the involvement of government in DEE's creation and expansion is much less than China's condition (Saxenian, 2004). This difference may influence the practice of organizing forms of DEE, and some new organizing forms may be identified under different contexts. Because the best practice of DEE does not exist until now, different designers have their own methods of exploring the forms of organizing. Thus, future researches can focus on DEEs in other regions which are quite different from China, or focus on the comparison of DEEs under different environments.

Conclusion

Collective collaboration gives positive effect on digital innovations for the combination of heterogeneous resources. This highlights the importance of DEE for digital innovations because DEE contains variable resources and provides a platform for boundary-spanning practices. However, the understanding of DEE is still limited (Spigel, 2015). From our observations, we argue that DEE is not only a combination of resources (Spigel, 2015), but also a new form of organizing (Gulati *et al.*, 2012; Puranam *et al.*, 2014). In order to achieve the system-level goal, DEE has to organize resources efficiently and effectively.

Through this case study, we found eight activities which compose the organizing form of DEE. These activities give us some insights that balance of centralization is important to control and complement the division of labor; the supportive elements such as culture and conference are necessary for the integration of efforts. Our findings and insights deepen the understanding of DEE and give some implications for the practice of DEE.

Acknowledgments

This research is supported by the National Natural Science Foundation of China (71402187).

References

Adner, R., and Kapoor, R. 2010. "Value Creation in Innovation Ecosystems: How the Structure of Technological Interdependence affects Firm Performance in New Technology Generations," *Strategic Management Journal*, 31(3), 306–333.

Autio, E., Nambisan, S., Wright, M., and Thomas, L. D. 2015. "Call for Papers for a Special Issue: Entrepreneurial Ecosystems," *Strategic Entrepreneurship Journal*. Available at: http://onlinelibrary.wiley.com/store/10.1002/(ISSN)1932-443X/asset/homepages/SEJ-Entrepreneurial_Ecosystems.pdf?v=1&s=4548d7b 62c28292b826ef7d74eae7bfcd396f34a&systemMessage=Please+be+advised+t hat+we+experienced+an+unexpected+issue+that+occurred+on+Saturday+and+ Sunday+January+20th+and+21st+that+caused+the+site+to+be+down+for+an+ extended+period+of+time+and+affected+the+ability+of+users+to+access+cont ent+on+Wiley+Online+Library.+This+issue+has+now+been+fully+resolved.+ +We+apologize+for+any+inconvenience+this+may+have+caused+and+are+w orking+to+ensure+that+we+can+alert+you+immediately+of+any+unplanned+ periods+of+downtime+or+disruption+in+the+future.&isAguDoi=false

Baldwin, C. Y., and Clark, K. B. 2006. "The Architecture of Participation: Does Code Architecture Mitigate Free Riding in the Open Source Development Model?" *Management Science*, 52(7), 1116–1127.

Bessant, J., and Tidd, J. 2007. *"Innovation and Entrepreneurship,"* John Wiley & Sons, Hoboken, New Jersey.

Bharadwaj, A., El Sawy, O. A., Pavlou, P. A., and Venkatraman, N. 2013. "Digital Business Strategy: Toward a Next Generation Of Insights," *Mis Quarterly*, 37(2), 471–482.

Corbin, J., and Strauss, A. 1990. *"Basics of Qualitative Research: Grounded Theory Procedures and Techniques,"* Sage Publications, Michigan.

Delgado, M., Porter, M. E., and Stern, S. 2010. "Clusters and entrepreneurship," *Journal of Economic Geography*, 10(4), lbq010.

Eisenhardt, K. M. 1989. "Building Theories from Case Study Research," *Academy of Management Review*, 14(4), 532–550.

Garud, R. 2008. "Conferences as Venues for the Configuration of Emerging Organizational Fields: The Case of Cochlear Implants," *Journal of Management Studies*, 45(6), 1061–1088.

Gulati, R., Puranam, P., and Tushman, M. 2012. "Meta-organization Design: Rethinking Design in Interorganizational and Community Contexts," *Strategic Management Journal*, 33(6), 571–586.

Hackman, J. R., and Oldham, G. R. 1976. "Motivation Through the Design of Work: Test of a Theory," *Organizational Behavior and Human Performance*, 16(2), 250–279.

Herrmann, B. L., Gauthier, J. F., Holtschke, D., Berman, R., and Marmer, M. 2015. "The Global Startup Ecosystem Ranking 2015," *Technical Reports*.

Klein, H. K., and Myers, M. D. 1999. "A Set of Principles for Conducting and Evaluating Interpretive Field Studies in Information Systems," *MIS Quarterly*, 23(1), 67–93.

Lee, J., and Berente, N. 2011. "Digital Innovation and the Division of Innovative Labor: Digital Controls in the Automotive Industry," *Organization Science*, 23(5), 1428–1447.

Lindgren, R., Andersson, M., and Henfridsson, O. 2008. "Multi-contextuality in Boundary-Spanning Practices," *Information Systems Journal*, 18(6), 641–661.

MacCormack, A., Rusnak, J., and Baldwin, C. Y. 2006. "Exploring the Structure of Complex Software Designs: An Empirical Study of Open Source and Proprietary Code," *Management Science*, 52(7), 1015–1030.

McKinsey Global Institution 2015. "China's Innovation Imperative | McKinsey & Company," Retrieved March 28, 2016. http://www.mckinsey.com/business-functions/strategy-and-corporate-finance/our-insights/chinas-innovation-imperative.

Moore, J. F. 1993. "Predators and Prey: A New Ecology of Competition," *Harvard Business Review*, 71(3), 75–83.

Nambisan, S., and Sawhney, M. 2011. "Orchestration Processes in Network-Centric Innovation: Evidence from the Field," *The Academy of Management Perspectives*, 25(3), 40–57.

Peltoniemi, M., and Vuori, E. 2004. "Business Ecosystem as the New Approach to Complex Adaptive Business Environments," in *Proceedings of eBusiness Research Forum*, Citeseer, pp. 267–281.

Prendergast, C. 1999. "The Provision of Incentives in Firms," *Journal of Economic Literature*, 37(1), 7–63.

Puranam, P., Alexy, O., and Reitzig, M. 2014. "What's 'New' About New Forms of Organizing?" *Academy of Management Review*, 39(2), 162–180.

Sambamurthy, V., Bharadwaj, A., and Grover, V. 2003. "Shaping Agility through Digital Options: Reconceptualizing the Role of Information Technology in Contemporary Firms," *MIS Quarterly*, 27(2), 237–263.

Saxenian, A. 2004. "The Silicon Valley Connection: Transnational Networks and Regional Development in Taiwan, China and India," in *India in the Global Software Industry*, A. P. D'Costa and E. Sridharan (eds.), Palgrave Macmillan, UK, pp. 164–192. http://link.springer.com/chapter/10.1057/9781403943842_7.

Schilling, M. A., and Phelps, C. C. 2007. "Interfirm Collaboration Networks: The Impact of Large-Scale Network Structure on Firm Innovation," *Management Science*, 53(7), 1113–1126.

Selander, L., Henfridsson, O., and Svahn, F. 2010. "Transforming Ecosystem Relationships in Digital Innovation." in *ICIS*, Saint Louis, p. 138. Available at: http://aisel.aisnet.org/icis2010_submissions/138/.

Shah, S. K. 2006. "Motivation, Governance, and the Viability of Hybrid Forms in Open Source Software Development," *Management Science*, 52(7), 1000–1014.

Shane, S., and Venkataraman, S. 2000. "The Promise of Entrepreneurship as a Field of Research," *Academy of Management Review*, 25(1), 217–226.

Shen, K., Lindsay, V., and Xu, Y. (Calvin) 2015. "Information Systems Journal Special Issue on: Digital Entrepreneurship," *Information Systems Journal*. Available at: http://onlinelibrary.wiley.com/store/10.1111/(ISSN)1365-2575/ asset/homepages/ISJ_SI_Digital_Entrepreneurship.pdf?v=1&s=696d716f21 e6137e1fbe32f3b0fd4afee81c9618&systemMessage=Please+be+advised+t hat+we+experienced+an+unexpected+issue+that+occurred+on+Saturday+a nd+Sunday+January+20th+and+21st+that+caused+the+site+to+be+down+f or+an+extended+period+of+time+and+affected+the+ability+of+users+to+a ccess+content+on+Wiley+Online+Library.+This+issue+has+now+been+ful ly+resolved.++We+apologize+for+any+inconvenience+this+may+have+ca used+and+are+working+to+ensure+that+we+can+alert+you+immediately+ of+any+unplanned+periods+of+downtime+or+disruption+in+the+future.&i sAguDoi=false

Spigel, B. 2015. "The Relational Organization of Entrepreneurial Ecosystems," *Entrepreneurship Theory and Practice*, 41(1), 49–72.

Swidler, A. 1986. "Culture in Action: Symbols and Strategies," *American Sociological Review*, 51(2), 273–286.

Thomas, L., and Autio, E. 2012. "Modeling the Ecosystem: A Meta-synthesis of Ecosystem and Related Literatures," *DRUID Society*. Available at: http:// conference.druid.dk/acc_papers/3j47kk0b5qlck1ghyor6f8osorh8.pdf.

Yip, G. 2015. "The 'Three Phases' Of Chinese Innovation," *Forbes*, http://www. forbes.com/sites/ceibs/2015/03/23/the-three-phases-of-chinese-innovation/. Last accessed: September 15, 2017.

Yoo, Y., Henfridsson, O., and Lyytinen, K. 2010. "Research Commentary — The New Organizing Logic of Digital Innovation: An Agenda for Information Systems Research," *Information Systems Research*, 21(4), 724–735.

Zahra, S. A., Wright, M., and Abdelgawad, S. G. 2014. "Contextualization and the Advancement of Entrepreneurship Research," *International Small Business Journal*, 32(5), 479–500.

Appendix A

Table A.1: List of Interviewees

Categories (Number of Interviewees)	Examples
Entrepreneurs ($N = 16$)	• Founder of an entrepreneurial company of Internet education, former employee employee of Midea (a large white appliance company in China) • College students who are preparing to set up their own company • Mr. Chen, founder of an entrepreneurial company in Internet medical care, owning a successfully IT company which is still running
Government/ State-owned Enterprise ($N = 8$)	• Senior Services Informatics Development Committee (SSIDC), a facility of China Association of Social Welfare. It is founded to improve the innovation and development of information senior care • Haizhi Kechuang (HZKC), an institutional skate holding company that designed the ZGC innovation street and maintain it functional • ZAC, a government agent that guides the development and construction of ZGC
Accelerator Centers ($N = 10$)	• Asia America Multi-Technology Association (AAMA), an association focusing on accelerating technical start-ups. AAMA established its angel fund in 2012 and set up an accelerator and coffee shop in 2014 in ZGC • Legend Star, providing entrepreneurial services such as mentor guiding, accelerating, and angel investment • 3W coffee shop, a company that services internet entrepreneurship and it has its own coffee shop, accelerator, training program, and angel fund
Third-party Service Provider ($N = 7$)	• Angel Service, a web platform connecting entrepreneurs and investors. It also provides training service to help entrepreneurs perform better in the meeting of investors • Law Service, a company providing law services for start-ups, such as company register, contract drafting, patent appliance, and so on • E-Capital, providing financial advice services for companies
Investors ($N = 10$)	• YCT, a venture capital investment company that focuses on catering, cultural and technical industry • Mr. Guo, an angel investor after successfully setting up XN Media • Zhejiang PD Investment Company, a company located in Zhejiang Province

Total Number of Interviewees $N = 51$

Appendix B

Table B.1:   Archival Data

Category	Examples
Government/ Official information	<ul><li>Official Website of ZGC Innovation Way. "Introduction." http://www.z-.com/index.php?app=web&m=Article&a=detail&id=16.</li><li>Official Website of Beijing Government (12 October 2015). "Advanced Innovation Way" 'Expending 7.2 kilometers', Retrieved 15 January 2016. http://www.beijing.gov.cn/tzbj/tzxx/kfqdt/t1405612.htm.</li><li>Ministry of Science and Technology of the People's Republic of China (2014, 18 June). "The opening of ZGC Innovation Way", Retrieved 15 January 2016. http://www.most.gov.cn/kjbgz/201406/t20140617_113821.htm.</li></ul>
News/ Reporting	<ul><li>*China Daily* (13 June 2014). "Beijing Zhongguancun opens innovation street", Retrieved 15 January 2016. http://www.chinadaily.com.cn/beijing/2014-06/13/content_17584416.htm.</li><li>Xinhua Net (20 March 2015). "Beijing's Zhongguancun Innovation Street Services for Startups", Retrieved 15 January 2016. http://news.xinhuanet.com/english/photo/2015-03/20/c_134082125.htm.</li><li>People.cn (7 May 2015). "Premier of China Mr. Li is present in ZGC Innovation Way: Something Details You Don't Know", Retrieved 15 January 2016. http://politics.people.com.cn/n/2015/0507/c1024-26965741.html.</li></ul>
Videos	<ul><li>CCTV.com (24 May 2015). "Dialogue: the sequel of ZGC Innovation Way", Retrieved 15 January 2016. http://jingji.cntv.cn/2015/05/24/VIDE1432481428440900.shtml.</li><li>Guangming TV (19 October 2015). "The disappearance of ZGC! Upgrading from Electronic Market to Innovation and Entrepreneurship Street", Retrieved 15 January 2016. http://v.gmw.cn/2015-10/19/content_17376721.htm.</li><li>CCTV.com (7 May 2015). "Premier of China Mr. Li is present in Chinese Academy of Sciences and ZGC Innovation Way", Retrieved 15 January 2016. http://news.cntv.cn/2015/05/07/VIDE1430997481826462.shtml.</li></ul>

Chapter 2

Mechanism of Balancing the Tension between Consistency and Relevance of Brand Ambidexterity by Digital Enablement — A Case Study of HUANYI International Travel Agency

Chunqing Li

School of Economics and Management
Xi'an Technological University, Xuefuzhonglu 2,
Xi'an, Shaanxi Province, 710021, China
lichunqing@xatu.edu.cn

Songling Li

Shaanxi YI An Kong Network Technology Co. Ltd.
Yanxianglu 99, Xi'an, Shaanxi Province, 710000, China
muzi198809@sina.com

Abstract

According to Taoist Yin-Yang thinking, we enrich the connotation of brand ambidexterity (Beverland *et al.*, 2015) and illustrate the mechanism on how digital technology can promote and enable the integration of brand consistency and relevance. Based on an in-depth case study of the firm named HUANYI in China, we identify that digital enablement can trigger brand ambidexterity from outward and inward during a three-stage process: the outward logic of digital enablement is "consistency is in relevance", which is to achieve customer identification normalized and visualized through interaction of brand identity and digital enablement; the inward logic is "relevance is in consistency", which is to arouse employees' belongingness in the same way as outward. We conclude with suggestions on how to make digital technology useful for brand ambidexterity in theoretical and practical contributions, the limitations and implications for future research are also mentioned.

Keywords: Brand ambidexterity, Taoist Yin-Yang thinking, Digital enablement, Brand identity, Case study.

Introduction

Strong brands deliver many valuable outcomes for firms, including significant price premiums, loyal customers, sales, employees' belonging-ness, and ultimately higher firm valuation (Beverland *et al.*, 2015; Fischer *et al.*, 2010; Helm *et al.*, 2016; Madden *et al.*, 2006). The emphasis of both academia and industry in digital technology-related fields has shifted to understanding the nature and implications of "digital enablement", which refers to the consumerizational and transformational effects of digital technology in driving business and social innovation (Maynard *et al.*, 2012; Leong *et al.*, 2016; Leong *et al.*, 2015).

Once a brand is developed, managers must defend, preserve, and increase the brand's equity against a backdrop of a changing market environment (Van Rekom *et al.*, 2006). To do so, brand managers must maintain consistency (in both image and marketing support), take a long-term view, and carefully leverage existing brand equity (Delgado-Ballester *et al.*, 2012; Keller *et al.*, 2002; Park *et al.*, 1986). Yet, at the same time, they must also maintain brand relevance, which may require change and, importantly, innovation (Aaker, 2012; Beverland *et al.*, 2015; Holt and Cameron, 2010; Kapferer, 2014), especially in the era of digital innova-tion as a fundamental and powerful concept in the information systems curriculum (Fichman *et al.*, 2014). Integrating the competing objectives of consistency and relevance is not easy. On one hand, brand managers must establish a clear frame of reference for the brand and reinforce the brand's image over time; on the other, they must innovate to adapt to market changes (Beverland *et al.*, 2010; 2015).

Taking a close look at current enterprises' brand management, we note that with the help of digital technology, a local travel agency named HUANYI with business-to-business (B2B) markets in China is able to balance the tension between consistency and relevance of brand ambidexterity and gets good performance in the market. It provided the local-guiding service in Italy for 60% of the Chinese tourists to the 2015 Milan Expo. In this chapter, we present one case of a local travel agency in China to address the research question: how does digital technology promote and enable the integration of brand consistency and relevance?

Theoretical background

Taoist Yin–Yang thinking

Taoist Yin-Yang's thinking involves a basic understanding that Yin and Yang are two patterns (two interactive forces), which coexist and interact with one another (Chen *et al.*, 2009). The founder of Taoism Lao Tzu said: "all things are shoulder Yin and hug Yang", "Yin is in Yang and Yang is in Yin" (Lao, 2006), the valuable book of Chinese medical science Huangdi Neijing also said: "Yin cannot grow alone, either single Yang" (Huang, 2010). Taoist Yin-Yang's thinking is also called the philosophy of Taoism (Tao), and it is the core thinking system in the Chinese civilization (Bai and Roberts, 2011). It exerts the most profound influence over Chinese culture that no other philosophy does in the same way (Bai, 2008). Taoism as a philosophy emphasizes a holistic study of the universe and mankind, which is characterized by both a macro and a micro approach, and provides dialectic investigation on all the subjects covered (Feng, 2004; Zhang, 1992). Taoist Yin-Yang's thinking has four meanings: first, unity of opposites: Yin and Yang are things of two properties, it is both on behalf of the contradictory and unified; second, interdependency: that is, "Yang is in Yin" , "Yin is in Yang", between them, there exists a mutual growth, interdependent relationship, in other words, any side Yin or Yang, all cannot leave the other and exist alone; third, growth and decline: that is the ebb and flow of Yin and Yang refers to the two sides of Yin and Yang on the basis of opposing each other's root which are perpetually changing and continuously emerging from the phenomenon of "Yin decline and Yang growth" and "Yang decline and Yin growth", this is the process of movement and development for everything; last, conversion/transformation: that is the unity of Yin and Yang, under certain conditions, when it develops to a certain stage, the two sides can respectively transform to its opposite, Yin can be converted into Yang, Yang can be converted into Yin, called "transformation" of Yin and Yang. It is very important to explore the use of Taoist Yin-Yang thinking in brand management.

The paradox of managing brand

Brand ambidexterity refers to a marketing capability (Day, 1994) whereby a brand is strategically managed to create value through the pursuit of both consistency and relevance (Beverland *et al.*, 2015). This concept, based upon organizational ambidexterity (March, 1991), is similar to what is argued by ambidexterity researchers (Birkinshaw and Gupta, 2013; Cao *et al.*, 2009). According to Beverland *et al.* (2015), brand consistency refers to the standardization and preservation of a defined brand image and associated meanings over time and place, for example, through names, symbols, and positioning themes (Bengtsson *et al.*, 2010). Therefore, although brand consistency is important, so is relevance, the latter refers to the perception "that the brand has something that is personally relevant or appropriate to the consumer" (Rosenbaum-Elliott *et al.*, 2011). According to Aaker (2012), relevance exists when a product or service category or subcategory emerges; yet there is a perceived need or desire on the part of a group of customers for that category; and the focal brand is in the consideration set of desirous customers. So we can conclude the meaning of brand ambidexterity is constructed by two paradoxical elements of consistency and relevance, and they coexist. But according to Taoist Yin-Yang thinking, for the brand ambidexterity, it is not enough to take consistency and relevance as paradoxes and coexist, there is a richer relationship and connotation between consistency and relevance, we will explain it in the mechanism model in detail.

Digital enablement

Digital enablement is developed on the basis of the empowerment theory (Maynard *et al.*, 2012; Leong *et al.*, 2015; Leong *et al.*, 2016). The main idea of empowerment is that its initiatives enhance employee performance, well-being, and positive attitudes (Hempel *et al.*, 2012; Lewin, 1947; Kanter's, 1977; Spreitzer, 2008; Wagner, 1994). As a result of these suggested benefits, approximately 70% of organizations have adopted some forms of empowerment (Lawler *et al.*, 2001). However, despite this extensive foundational literature, history, and use within organizations, many questions still surround the business management with enablement (Maynard *et al.*, 2012)., especially how to use the powerful digital technology to manage the brand.

Methodology

The case study methodology is adopted because it is appropriate for such exploratory research (Pan and Tan, 2011; Siggelkow, 2007). Our data are collected from interviews and archival data. The average interview session took 1.5 hours, and the interviews adhered to a protocol that evolved during the research project (Strauss and Corbin, 1998). All interviews were taped and transcribed for detailed analysis (Walsham, 2006). Supplementary data were collected from public sources including books, newspaper articles and the official website of HUANYI to corroborate primary data that were collected.

Digital enablement in brand developing

HUANYI International Travel Agency, established in 2009 in Rome, is engaged in providing customized local service in Italy for Chinese high-end visitors. Before establishment, it operated under the brand of Italy Mistral Travel during 1998–2009.

In 2009, when Italy Mistral Travel exited from the Chinese market, Ms. Huan Zhang, the chief representative of Mistral Travel in China and her team decided to launch a new brand, "HUANYI" for their local service, which was clearly positioned as a "Single-source group tour local service provider." This case will be described in three phases, i.e. the birth, growth, and update of the brand, respectively. In each phase, HUANYI made different efforts in the digital enablement to balance its brand ambidexterity as shown in Table 1.

Birth (2009–2012)

With the concept of "single-source group tour" developed, HUANYI as a brand was created officially. Around the brand identity, digitization and deployment were made. Ms. Zhang, the founder of HUANYI, said that "since 2009, the whole management realized that it was essential to leverage Internet as a 24*7 marketing tool." HUANYI was named to focus on "single-source group tour." Digitization helps HUANYI present and deliver the key messages of the brand to the target audience to allow them to access and understand the brand in 24*7 manner. Due to the unique nature of the travel industry, the information of customers may be held by employees, which creates a serious situation of islands of information with disordered information management. Businesses may experience material damage due to the churn of employees. It was one of the reasons that HUANYI introduced the enterprise resource planning system.

Ms. Wang, the head of Marketing, said: "We collect all the information about the customer, including the details of each promotion activity entered into the ERP system to provide proper customer management. This helps prevent customer information loss due to the churn of employees or other situation." Using this system eliminates islands of information, streamlines and standardizes business processes, which makes communication transparent, and the voice of brand penetrates throughout every aspect of the digitization, leading the employees to a new code of conduct enabled by digitization enablement.

Logistics head, Ms. Xi said: "I have gone through the time without and with the ERP system. During the time without the system, we basically relied on verbal communication between the seats, messages, and e-mail, etc., One thing needed to communicate for several times with different people. This has been changed since the introduction of the ERP system. The information is entered for once, and can be accessed from any

Table 1. Digital Enablement in Developing Ambidexterity for Brand Development

Digital Enablement	How Digitization Acts on the Role of Critical Actors	Penetration and Implication of Digitization on the Key Factors Driving the Growth of the Brand
Stage of Brand Development: Birth		
Digital enablement allows transparency of communication	Digitization allows internal data management transparency with adjustment of ERP	A new work habit is shaped through the use of digitization
Critical actor: Employees		• Employees can adjust and discipline their behaviors through learning and using the EPR system, which helps enhance the consistency of brand promise internally
		• The voice of brand penetrates into every single step of digitization and leads the employees to shape new rules of behavior
Fast penetration of Digital enablement	Digitization allows the employees to have a consistent recognition on the brand in a fast manner	Fast penetration of digitization into employee's mentality
Critical actor: Employees		• Employees passing through the brand identity personally
		• The voice of brand is digitalized through employees, and in turn, promoting employee's awareness of brand consistency

(Continued)

Table 1. (*Continued*)

Digital Enablement	How Digitization Acts on the Role of Critical Actors	Penetration and Implication of Digitization on the Key Factors Driving the Growth of the Brand
Digital enablement expands Communication channels with prolonged brand communication effectiveness. Critical actor: customers	In addition to traditional communication channels like tradeshows, magazines, etc., digitization helps customers become aware of the brand identity any time anywhere, which enhances knowledge of the brand	The use of Digital channels enables fast communication of the brand voice • Customers can search and understand the brand promise online without the limitation of time and geography • Digitization diversifies the channels to be used for the enhanced communication of brand identity
Stage of Brand Development: Growth Digital enablement helps normalize the development of brand Critical actor: employees	Digital enablement enables an ongoing improvement process through awareness and modeling	The use of digital channels may change the behaviors of the employees • Digitization process may continuously adjust and discipline employee's behavior in alignment with the brand identity • The ongoing improvement enabled by digitization drives the evolution of the brand and shortens the time of the employees to realize the brand promise

The concept of "usefulness" is enriched by Digital enablement

Critical actor: customers

Digitization enables diversified modes to communicate the relevance of the brand and customers

The use of digital channels enables diversified and rich presentation of brand concept

- By leveraging digital channels, business may let customers be aware of the dynamics of the brand through the creation of useful content
- Customers may quickly capture and actively disseminate useful information of the brand

Stage of Brand Development: Self-update

Digital enablement changes the competition landscape

Critical actor: employees

Digitization breaks the entire market landscape, and change the rules of conduct of the employees in the market

Digitization reshapes the mentality of the employees

- While competitors are uncertain, employees may overthrow the operation not valid in the past as soon as possible once they hold the core of the brand
- Digitization enables every employee to have more autonomy in their self-development process

Digital enablement blurs the boundaries of customers

Critical actor: customers

Free links, and irregular collision eliminates the traditional boundaries of the customer

Digitization allows free links to the customers

- During the process, customer demand can be created and guided with resource integration
- Digitization allows one to combine different segments of consumer

position, from the finance and cashier to Reservation. All the details can be viewed on the system. This helps improve both the efficiency and transparency. Quite effective." Therefore, the enabled communication transparency allows employees to learn and use the ERP system to regulate their behavior. They consciously practice and realize the promise delivered by the brand by refining the service processes, improving service quality, and reducing service failures, etc.

Staff attitude to brand identity will have a crucial impact on customer perception, and digitization reveals the inner recognition of the employees through efficient and standard service process. These are the personal behaviors of employees that deliver the brand identity. The explicit content and behavior are relevant with customer acceptance, which may have a direct impact on brand asset.

Growth (2013–2014)

At this stage, although HUANYI brand had been recognized in the industry, and business had also been greatly improved. But with the development of Internet economy, the market became more transparent, and businesses began to streamline the intermediate links. HUANYI first started streamlining the offline service details without compromising the quality, which was in line with the message of "local service provider providing controllable and high quality services for single-source group tour" delivered by HUANYI in the development process. For example, HUANYI first broke the driver and tour guide combined service model.

Ms. Zhang, HUANYI founder, said, 'We proposed to provide controllable and high-quality local service for single-source group tour, and the website immediately was updated accordingly.' HUANYI' COO, Ms. Zhang said, "The website is a window for communicating our business concept and for interaction as well. We posted the comments from customers on our concept of single-source group tour and our service, and our staff may also share their own experiences and the concerns of customers. For example, 'The mode with separate driver and tour guide is safer for corporate group tour,' commented by our customer. Other posts include the article 'where comes the Vitality of single-source group tour' published on 'Travel Agency' on March, 2013, comment from 'Sino-Italy

Foundation': Thank the contribution of HUANYI and Italian Airline to Italy, and the Cover story from 'Travel Agency': HUANYI cares more on service quality than quantity etc." Corporate brand development was shaped by digitization. During this process, staff can fast access customer feedback, and enhance the connotation of the brand. The evolution of the brand requires digital transformation, which led to the second revision of the website to match the brand identity.

HUANYI founder Ms. Zhang noted "with ERP systems, we get the information, including how many customers we have, their characteristics etc. and can also provide proper management of offshore resources, such as what groups the oversea guides served, what kind of groups that he or she is good at. The combined management of customer and the oversea guides allow us to have insight on our weakness through data analysis." This can explain how digitization enablement penetrates into and regulates the behaviors of employees. At the same time, the digitization fast feedback shortens the time that the employees spend in brand recognition, and allows them to timely adjust their behaviors accordingly. Moreover, the digitization fast feedback will continue to promote the self-development of the brand, and shorten the time that employees realize the brand promise.

Digital enablement has changed the way people receive information, also changed the content and mode that businesses transfer. In 2014, Ms. Zhang was interviewed at CCTV "charm of Milan" program as the discovery messenger and illustrated an in-depth Milan from food, art, fashion, and design etc. This was the first show of HUANYI in the public by leveraging a powerful digital platform. HUANYI website manager Mr. Wang said, "we continuously change the presentation of information with the purpose to deliver useful information to customers. In the past, we just display the information to let the customer know what we offered without active communication. Now, we try to let people follow and communicate us actively." Usefulness of the digitization is reflected in the brand. The business creates useful digital content to customers to attract the customers to actively follow the dynamics of the brand. At the same time, customers can quickly capture the corporate brand voice. In this process, the business gradually changes the way to deliver the brand message to customers, and employees have an increasingly digital consciousness.

In this way, the employee's brand awareness and customer needs are combined, which are injected with digital consciousness or thinking to convey to their customers, and attract them to follow the dynamics of the brand.

Update (2015–2016)

With the development of digital life, Online Travel Agent (OTA) became the first choice of customers, and began to gradually erode the traditional market. OTA has changed the game rule of the market, and makes HUANYI have a deep sense of crisis. To enhance the relevance of HUANYI and the tourists, and eventually make HUANYI the sole option for tourists in Italy, the ultimate goal of HUANYI became: HUANYI = tourist choice in Italy. Meanwhile, HUANYI began to realize that showcasing of HUANYI brand identity on corporate website only had been unable to get an echo from the market. HUANYI founder Ms. Zhang said, "as people like to read stories instead of corporate information, we began to release stories on our WeChat platform." Digitization broke the traditional competition landscape, and changed the rules of the employees' conduct. Employees started to have the initial digital consciousness with rapid feedback according to data by overthrowing the previous less efficient operations. During the collaboration, each staff also has more autonomy over their work thanks to the digital consciousness.

Being totally digitized is not enough, which only creates digital awareness of the employees internally. It is a big program that requires an organic linkage of the website, WeChat channel and other major digital platforms. Logistics manager Ms. Xi said, "change the way to present the information on the website is a turning point for us. In the past, we used it as a place for image presentation, now we focus more on functionality and customer acceptance. For example, customers can add their favorite products even place orders." Such action blurs the boundaries of customers, HUANYI and OTAs are partners but also competitors, which is not the relationship with traditional travel agencies and distribution channels. The free links and irregular collision eliminates the traditional boundaries of the customer, which also helps HUANYI take advantages of digital awareness in the market to guide the consumption of online consumers through continuous integration of offline resources. HUANYI creates and guides the demands of customers during the free link with customers to realize the combination of employee's practice of brand promise and the relevance with customers.

Data structure and mechanism model

The Chapter creates a data structure in line with the case, and develops an effective mechanism model of digital enablement on brand ambidexterity according to the logic of the data structure diagram.

Data structure

This part first provides the empirical observations on the performance of the company, and then identifies the theories behind them, and ultimately builds a theory accordingly. The data structure is plotted in Figure1 after analysis. As shown in Figure 1., different empirical observations can lead

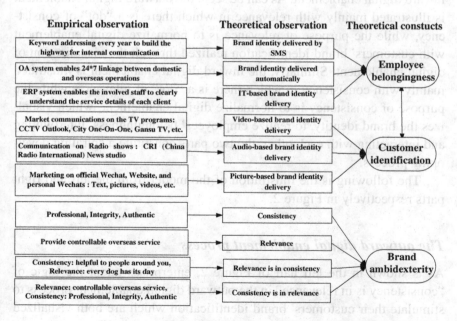

Figure 1. Data Structure

to relevant theoretical observations and theory building. Through the empirical observations, we can conclude the change of the brand identity during the digitalization, and the corresponding key concepts: employee ownership, customer acceptance, and brand ambidexterity.

Mechanism model

During its development, HUANYI managed to balance its brand ambidexterity of consistency and relevance through both inward and outward digital enablement. The main purpose of this research is to explore the mechanism on how digital enablement balances a brand's dual capacities to open the "Black Box" through the digital enablement process of the brand identity.

The mechanism model is shown in Figure 2., a typical Taoist Yin–Yang thinking diagram divided into two intertwining parts. The left part, a white fish with a black dot in the head, represents outward digital enablement, while the right part, a black fish with a white dot, represents inward digital enablement. As can be seen, the outward digital enablement is illustrated mainly with relevance in which there is a "dot" of consistency, while the purpose of relevance is to normalize digital enablement with customers' brand identification realized through the visualization of digital enablement. Similarly, the inward digital enablement is illustrated mainly with consistency in which there is a "dot" of relevance, while the purpose of consistency is to normalize digital enablement, which visualizes the brand identity, to realize employees' belongingness. Intertwining and interacting with each other, the two parts constitute a spiraling developing process.

The following is the illustration of the model from the left and right parts respectively in Figure 2.

The outward digital enablement process

As is shown in the left half of Figure 2, enterprises adopt the logic of "consistency is in relevance" in the outward digital enablement process to stimulate their customers' brand identification which are both visualized

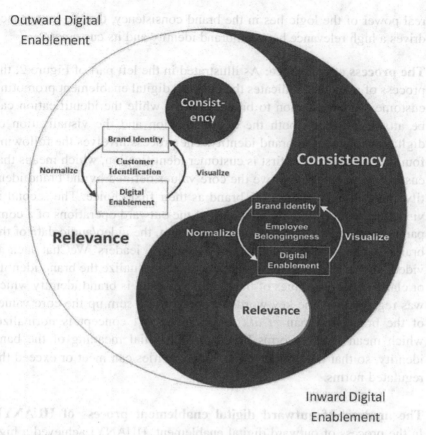

Figure 2. Mechanism Model of Balancing the Tension between Brand Ambidexterity by Digital Enablement

and normalized through digital enablement. The illustration and analysis of the process are as follows:

The logic of "consistency is in relevance": The logic of "consistency is in relevance" means that an enterprise can not only keep a high relevance between its brand and customers by stimulating the latter's or employees' interest, but also maintain a consistent core value conveyed to its customers or employees, namely, keeping the consistence of the brand identity, which can raise the customers' identification to the brand identity. The real power of the logic lies in the brand consistency, that is, consistency drives a high relevance between brand identity and its customers.

The process of relevance: As illustrated in the left part of Figure 2, the process of relevance indicates the outward digital enablement promoting customers' identification to brand identity, while the identification can be attained through both the nominalization and the visualization of digital enablement to brand identity. The process involves the following four key concepts. The first is customer identification, which means that customers sincerely approve the core values defined by the brand identity and willingly choose the brand as their first choice. The second is visualize, namely, the digitalization of the outward operations of a company; it may be the WeChat, official account, the video/audio data of the brand, or the personal accounts of a company leaders' WeChat such as video, audio, graphics, texts, etc., which can visualize the brand identity or clarify the core values of the brand. The third is brand identity which was regarded as "the key words or phrases that sum up the core values of the brand(Coleman *et al.*, 2011)." The last concept is normalize, which means to set norms based on the initial meaning of the band identity, so that the digitalized acts or activities can meet or exceed the regulated norms.

The analysis of outward digital enablement process of HUANYI: In the process of outward digital enablement, HUANYI achieved a high relevance between its tourism brand and the direct customers (travel agents) as well as indirect customers (terminal tourists) through various means of digital information communicating, such as CCTV outlook, city to city TV programs between China and Italy, studio of China radio international, constant revision of the company's homepage, building up the WeChat platform, and the company leaders' personal WeChat Moments, in addition to the collaboration with other digital platforms (Italian National Tourist Board, Embassy of Italy in Beijing). Meanwhile, the company visualizes the relevance of its brand to its customers through texts, images, audio/video and other digital means, ultimately motivating the customers' identification with the brand identify of HUANYI.

The inward digital enablement process

As shown in the right half of Figure 2, enterprises adopt the logic of "relevance is in consistency" in the inward digital enablement process to stimulate their employees' belongingness to brand identity which are both visualized and normalized through digital enablement. The illustration and analysis of the process are as follows:

The logic of "relevance is in consistency": The logic of "relevance is in consistency" means that an enterprise needs not only to convey the consistent core values to the employees or customers during brand development, but also maintain a high relevance to the needs of its customers or employees, when the outward situations change over time, that is, arousing customers' identification or employees' belongingness by stimulating their interest, concern, and passion to the brand. Thus, the real power of this logic lies in the brand relevance, that is, the fundamental driving force is kept relevant with the need of the customers' or employees.'

The process of consistence: As illustrated in the right part of Figure 2., the process of consistency indicates the inward digital enablement promoting employee' belongingness to brand identity, while the belonging can be attained through both the nominalization and visualization of digital enablement via brand identity. This process also involves the following four key concepts. The first is employees' belongingness which means they heartily approve and willingly devote to the core values defined by the brand identity which is capable of manipulation. The second is visualization, that is, the digitalization of inward brand operation which might be the Office Automation System, the ERP System, or the inward communication channels, such as can be video/audio, graphics, or texts, etc., which can visualize the brand identity, in other words, simplify or clarify the abstract brand core values (i.e., brand identity). The third and the fourth concepts of "brand identity" and "normalize" are the same as the process of relevance's definition.

The analysis of HUANYI inward digital enablement process: Ms. Huan Zhang, the leader of HUANYI, in order to make the brand identity feasible, solidifies it in simple slogans from "Take care of everybody around you heart and soul, know more about Italy" to "Be a useful person to those around you, know more about Italy." In addition, she proposes "a keyword of the year", and sends it to each employee as a Chinese New Year's short message to present the core values in a simple and clear way; hence, the employees can normalize the brand identity to digital enablement feasibly. HUANYI visualizes its brand identity in the process of digital enablement via various means of SMS, WeChat, website design, Office Automation System, ERP, etc. in the digital enablement process, so as to arouse the employees' belonging through the interaction of brand identity and digital enablement.

Implications and conclusions

Involving the concept of brand ambidexterity, the theoretical framework elaborating how digital technology can promote and enable the integration of brand consistency and relevance offers two contributions.

First, this chapter enriches the connotation of brand ambidexterity (Beverland *et al.*, 2015). Previous scholars have put forward brand ambidexterity are constructed by two paradoxical elements of consistency and relevance, and they coexist. However, based on the observation of phenomena and Taoist Yin–Yang thinking (Bai and Roberts, 2011), we found that the two elements, consistency and relevance, not only are paradoxes and coexist, but also interact with each other, and have the other three meanings we mentioned in the theoretical background: interdependency, growth and decline, conversion.

Second, we identify that digital enablement can trigger brand ambidexterity from outwardly and inwardly during a three-stage brand development process. This is different from the findings of Beverland *et al.* (2015)'s design thinking due to three reasons: on one hand, the context of this chapter is the service industry, but Beverland *et al.* (2015) is goods industry; next, the internal relationship between digital enablement and brand ambidexterity can also show this phenomenon; last, the case phenomenon also supports this view.

Third, we show the mechanism of the digital enablement in balancing the tension of brand ambidexterity from different logic, ways and purposes. The outward logic of digital enablement is "consistency is in relevance", the purpose of which is to achieve customer identification by brand identity normalizing digital enablement, in turn digital enablement visualizes brand identity. The inward logic of digital enablement is "relevance is in consistency", the purpose of which is to arouse employees' belongingness the same way as outward digital enablement. More importantly, our study opens the "black box" of how digital enablement balances the tension of brand ambidexterity and offers a novel perspective of using digital enablement to enhance recognition of the inward staff and outward customers to the brand identity, thus enriching the theories of brand management and digital enablement.

In terms of practical implications, this chapter provides insightful and detailed practical actions that organizations may use digital enhance recognition of the inward staff and outward customers to the brand identity. These actions involve adopting digital enablement under the background of informationalization and digitalization, in which paradoxical challenges universally exist. The digital enablement commonly observed in practice in this study sheds light on the necessary considerations for organizations in constructing brand ambidexterity to establish strong recognition of the inward staff and outward customers to the brand identity. Moreover, this chapter analyzes the characteristics and process of the digital enablement in balancing the tension of brand ambidexterity, which is helpful to provide inspiration for future practitioners. Especially when encountering difficulties, practitioners could use the process model as a sign, so that they may find the key to adjust the enterprise brand strategy and tap their own potential, adapting to the existing challenges.

Limitations and implications for future research

One limitation of this study is using the single case study, though this method has typicality and rationality (Lee, 2003), still it remains controversial in terms of generality and outward validity (Walsham, 2006). This chapter only uses the case of HUANYI, a sample enterprise from the tourism industry, while for the non-service industry and the monopoly nature of the market enterprises, the conclusion of the study should be confirmed. Secondly, to achieve adequate academic support, there should be further researches on digital enablement. Finally, we consider questions for future researches. In future research, we will collect and analyze examples from other types of industries and markets, to improve and complement the research conclusion systematically to reveal the mechanism of the digital enablement in balancing the tension of brand ambidexterity.

Acknowledgments

This study is supported by the Natural Science Foundation of China (71172133), Academic Discipline Project with Characteristics of Philosophical and Social Sciences of universities in Shaanxi province, Humanities and Social Science Youth Talents support program of universities in Shaanxi province and Scientific Innovation Team Program of Xi'an Technological University.

References

Aaker, D. A. 2012. "Win the Brand Relevance Battle and Then Build Competitor Barriers," *California Management Review,* 54(2), 43–57.

Bai, X. 2008. "The Thinking System of Taoism and Leadership Studies," *Theoretical Investigation,* 1(1), 142–146.

Bai, X., and Roberts W. 2011. "Taoism and its model of traits of successful leaders," *Journal of Management Development,* 30(7/8), 724–739.

Bengtsson, A., Bardhi, F., and Venkatraman, M. 2010. "How global Brands Travel with Consumers," *International Marketing Review,* 27(5), 519–540.

Beverland, M. B., Napoli, J., and Farrelly, F. J. 2010. "Towards a Typology of Brand Position and Innovation Effort," *Journal of Product Innovation Management,* 27(1), 33–48.

Beverland, M. B., Sarah, J. S. W., and Pietro, M. 2015. "Reconciling the Tension between Consistency and Relevance: Design Philosophy as a Mechanism for Brand Ambidexterity," *Journal of the Academy of Marketing Science,* 43(5), 589–609.

Birkinshaw, J., and Gupta, K. 2013. "Clarifying the Distinctive Contribution of Ambidexterity to the Field of Organization Studies," *Academy of Management Perspectives,* 27(4), 287–298.

Cao, Q., Gedajlovic, E., and Zhang, H. 2009. "Unpacking Organizational Ambidexterity: Dimensions, Contingencies, and Synergistic Effects," *Organization Science,* 20(4), 781–796.

Chen, H. J., Tsai, Y. H., Chang, S. H., and Lin, K. H. 2009. "Bridging the Systematic Thinking Gap between East and West: An Insight into the Yin–Yang-based System Theory," *Systemic Practice and Action Research,* 23(2), 173–189.

Coleman, D., de Chernatony, L., and Chrisodoulides, G. 2011. "B2B Service Brand Identity: Scale Development and Validation," *Industrial Marketing Management,* 40(7), 1063–1071.

Day, G. 1994. "The Capabilities of Market-Driven Organizations," *Journal of Marketing,* 58(4), 37–52.

Delgado-Ballester, E., Navarro, A., and Sicilia, M. 2012. "Revitalising Brands through Communication Messages: The Role of Brand Familiarity," *European Journal of Marketing,* 46(1/2), 31–51.

Feng, Y. L. 2004. *"The New Edition of Chinese Philosophy,"* The People's Press, Beijing.

Fichman, R. G., Dos Santos, B. L., and Zheng, Z. Q. E. 2014. "Digital Innovation as a Fundamental and Powerful Concept in the Information Systems Curriculum," *MIS Quarterly,* 38(2), 329–353.

Fischer, M., Völckner, F., and Sattler, H. 2010. "How Important are Brands? A Cross-category, Cross-country Study," *Journal of Marketing Research,* 47(5), 823–839.

Helm, S. V., Renk U., and Mishra A. 2016. "Exploring the Impact of Employees' Self-concept, Brand Identification and Brand Pride on Brand Citizenship Behaviors", *European Journal of Marketing,* 50(1/2), 58–77.

Hempel, P. S., Zhang, Z., and Han, Y. 2012. "Team Enablement and the Organizational Context: Decentralization and the Contrasting Effects of Formalization." *Journal of Management,* 38(2), 475–501.

Holt, D., and Cameron, D. 2010. *"Cultural strategy: Using Innovative Ideologies to Build Breakthrough Brands."* Oxford University Press, Oxford.

Kanter, R. M. 1977. *"Men and Women of the Corporation."* Basic Books, New York.

Kapferer, J. N. 2014. "Brands and Innovation." In *The Definitive Book of Branding,* K. Kompella (ed.), Sage, London, pp. 149–170.

Keller, K. L., Sternthal, B., and Tybout, A. 2002. "Three Questions You Need to ask about your Brand," *Harvard Business Review,* 80(9), 79–86.

Lao Tzu. 2006. *"Tao Te Ching."* Chen Zhong's Version, Culture and History Press of Jilin, Changchun.

Huang Di. 2010. *"Huangdi Neijing Yao Chunpeng's Version",* Zhonghua Book Company, Shanghai.

Lawler, E. E., Mohrman, S. A., and Benson, G. 2001. *"Organizing for High Performance: Employee Involvement, TQM, Reengineering, and Knowledge Management in the Fortune 1000."* Jossey-Bass, San Francisco.

Leong, C., Pan, S. L., Newell, S., and Cui, L.L. 2016. "The Emergence of Self-Organizing E-commerce Ecosystem in Remote Villages of China: A Tale of Digital enablement for Rural Development," *MIS Quarterly*, 40(2), 475–484.

Leong, C., Pan, S.L., Ractham, P., and Kaewkitipong, L. 2015. "ICT-Enabled Community Enablement in Crisis Response: Social Media in Thailand Flooding 2011," *Journal of the Association for Information Systems*, 16(3), 1–39.

Lewin, K. 1947. "Group Decision and Social Change." In *Readings in Social Psychology* by Theodore M. Neweomb and Eugene L. Hartley, Co-Chairmen of Editorial Committee, Henry Holt and Co., pp. 340–344.

Lee A. S., and Baskerville, R. L. 2003. "Generalizing Generalizability in Information Systems Research Information," *Systems Research*, 14(3), 221–243.

Maynard, M. T., Gilson, L. L., and Mathieu, J. E. 2012. "Enablement-Fad or Fab? A Multilevel Review of the Past Two Decades of Research," *Journal of Management*, 38(4), 1231–1281.

Madden, T. J., Fehle, F., and Fournier, S. 2006. "Brands matter: An Empirical Demonstration of the Creation of Shareholder Value Through Branding," *Journal of the Academy of Marketing Science*, 34(2), 224–235.

March, J. G.1991. "Exploration and Exploitation in Organizational Learning," *Organization Science*, 2(1), 71–87.

Park, C. W., Jaworski, B. J., and MacInnis, D. J. 1986. "Strategic Brand Concept-image Management," *Journal of Marketing*, 50(4), 621–635.

Pan, S. L., and Tan, B. 2011. "Demystifying Case Research: A Structured–Pragmatic–Situational (SPS) Approach to Conducting Case Studies," *Information & Organization*, 21(3), 161–176.

Rosenbaum-Elliott, R., Percy, L., and Pervan, S. 2011. *"Strategic Brand Management"*, Oxford University Press, Oxford.

Spreitzer, G. M. 2008. "Taking Stock: A Review of more than Twenty Years of Research on Enablement at Work." In *Handbook of Organizational Behavior*, C. Cooper and J. Barling (eds.), Thousand Oaks, CA, Sage, pp. 54–73.

Strauss A. L., and Corbin J., 1998. "Basics of Qualitative Research: Techniques and Procedures for Developing Grounded Theory." Thousand Oaks, CA, Sage.

Siggelkow, N. 2007. "Persuasion with Case Studies," *Academy of Management Journal*, 50(1), 20–24.

Van Rekom, J., Jacobs, G., and Verlegh, P. W. J. 2006. "Measuring and Managing the Essence of a Brand Personality," *Marketing Letters,* 17(3), 181–192.

Wagner, J. A., III. 1994. "Participation's Effects on Performance and Satisfaction: A Reconsideration of Research Evidence," *Academy of Management Review,* 19(2), 312–330.

Walsham, G. 2006. "Doing Interpretive Research," *European Journal of Information Systems,* 15(3), 320–330.

Zhang, K. Z. 1992. *"The History of Chinese Thinking."* The Water Buffalo Publisher, Taipei.

Appendix

Methodology

This study examines a phenomenon with regard to the brand development of digitization. In this regard, a qualitative, case study research methodology is adopted because it is appropriate for such exploratory research (Pan and Tan, 2011; Siggelkow, 2007) and allows us to unearth the answer to our "how" question in a context-rich environment (Pan and Tan, 2011; Walsham, 1995). Our study is exploratory in that it focuses on theory building, which is based on elements from prior theory that might be of "great help in focusing research efforts at the outset of the project" (Pare, 2004). The average interview session took 1.5 hours, and the interviews adhered to a protocol that evolved during the research project (Strauss and Corbin, 1998). All interviews were taped and transcribed for detailed analysis (Walsham, 2006). Supplementary data were collected from public sources including books, newspaper articles, and the official website of HUANYI to corroborate primary data that were collected.

Data collection

Our data were collected from two primary sources: interviews and archival data. The research data were primarily collected from the following three sources: (1) semi-structured interviews conducted on October 2015; (2) internal archival materials, and (3) public sources, including books, video, news, and publications about HUANYI. The purpose of collecting data from multiple sources was to establish a unique perspective that incorporated the points of view of both organizational insiders and outsiders (Evered and Louis, 1981) and to triangulate themes and conclusions (Miles and Huberman, 1984).

We observed HUANYI for 6 years in a row (2011–2016), 10 research assistants were asked for initial data collection from multiple sources, which were summarized in a document numbering more than 100 thousand words and insights on its brand development, digitalization construction, service process, and new product design were found during those years.

Through our gatekeeper at HUANYI whose title is CEO of this company, we were provided with internal company documents, including partial meeting minutes. A number of semi-formal interviews were conducted via e-mail and telephone before we arrived at the company's organizational headquarters. The purpose of these interviews was to verify gathered secondary data and to establish an accurate overview of HUANYI. We also made official research visits to the organizational headquarters of HYUANYI and collected primary data. During our visit to HYUANYI, extensive interviews and analyses were conducted. For this research, five informants, who were primarily from IT industry, marketing, and operational departments participated in our interview sessions. To minimize issues related to validity and reliability of data, the interview questions were open-ended and focused on the history of the company brand development (see Figure A.1) with three stages: birth (see Table A.1), growth (see Table A.2) and update (see Table A.3). The underlying intention of this methodology was to provide an open environment for the interviewees by probing for answers to broad questions that pertained to our research topics.

Data analysis

Data analysis began during the data collection (Eisenhardt, 1989; Pan and Tan, 2011). The brand ambidexterity and empowerment literature sensitized us to the related information regarding the consistency and relevance — which correspond to different aspects of a challenge in brand development. We summarized in tabular form the relevant information on the actions taken by the critical actors with respect to the development of brand and changes that have occurred over time. Using the summary table as the primary corpus of data, we proceeded to identify the critical actors across three stages of brand development: birth, growth, and update. Subsequently, we ask specific guiding questions in deriving our findings: how digitization elevates the employee in the brand development, or how digitization makes the employee implant brand identity in the customers mind, Critical actors in the brand development, and what behaviors have been changed as a result of digitization use. In doing so, we derive tentative concepts that could provide an encompassing explanation to affordances of digitization in the brand development. We attempted to search for and explicate the new "regularities in social life" (Babbie, 2007, p. 11) from an emerging phenomenon along the lines of enquiry offered by sensitizing concepts.

Next, in order to examine and identify the "underlying coherence" through our interpretation, we juxtaposed tentative explanations for each stage, in preparation for further "abstraction" of tentative concepts that might explain overall actors of the brand, and enablement by digitization. The integrated analysis allowed us to derive concepts that were closely related to the context of brand ambidexterity. An example of abstraction was digitization changed the competition, which changes the employee behavior rules. As we proceeded, each cycle of abstraction and visitation of the empirical data improved the clarity of explanations as a better understanding of the data and the theory was developed in this inductive reasoning process. The cycle was reiterated until all of the tentative explanations were accounted for, and a temporal internal agreement was achieved.

With the emergence of our findings, we consistently ensured the alignment between data, theory, and findings until the findings were finalized. To ensure the convergence of interpretations by interviewees, the rule of triangulation was applied: multiple data sources (interviews, focus groups, and archival data; see Table A.4) were used to filter "false preconceptions" of interviewees and researchers; this ensured consistency of data. Throughout the data collection and analysis, we applied Klein and Myers's (1999) principles to conduct interpretive work.

In each phase, HUANYI made different efforts in the digital enablement to balance its brand ambidexterity as shown below:

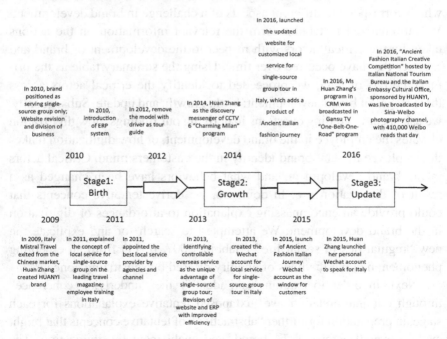

Figure A.1: Milestones along the Digitalization of HUANYI

Table A.1: Summary of Interview of the Executive Team of HUANYI on The Digital Enablement during the Creation of the Brand

Interviewees	Summary of Interview
Assistant of CEO Ms. Zhang	Since 2009, we created the brand of HUANYI to focus on the local service for single-source group tour in Italy instead of the combined group tour. The message of the brand was posted on our website for effective communication to the public
Assistant of CEO, Ms. Zhang	Starting in 2010, we have invested more than 1 million RMB to build a custom-fit online ERP system, which helps transform our entire operation process with more collaborative teamwork and improved productivity
Assistant of CEO, Ms. Zhang	Every New Year's day, I would send a theme to each employee by SMS and organized them to discuss for clarification. For instance, I sent "branding" as the theme for 2009. During the whole year, we had mobilized the employees to give a brand name, HUANYI, for our business. HUANYI is the combination of the world and Italy. The key word for 2010 was "positioning", which indicated that 2010 was the year to position our business after the birth of the brand as the customized local service provider in Italy for single-source group tour organized by Chinese travel agencies. The keyword for 2012 was "helpful." One of the characters of HUANYI's corporate culture is "take care of the people around you." However to realize the promise requires everybody to be capable and useful. More knowledge about Italy would help our employees better understand the inner desire of the customers, which will make them more helpful
Assistant of CEO, Ms. Zhang	The keyword for 2011 was "Essence." HUANYI believed that the core of service is honesty and integrity, and the purpose of service is to create good experience
Vice president, Mr. Li	We provide a clean office environment for the employees, serving them with coffee from Italy, disinfecting the drink ware every day and the meeting room every week. The company shows its care to the staff by offering bonus for their marriage, compensation for family funeral, taking care of pregnant employees, and writing reports to employees' parents and remitting money as well. Each year, we give employees the opportunity to learn and investigate in Italy to improve their knowledge. We claim that we know Italy better!

(*Continued*)

Table A.1: *(Continued)*

Interviewees	Summary of Interview
Logistics manager, Ms. Xi	I have gone through the time without and with the ERP system. During the time without the system, we basically relied on verbal communication between the seats, messages, e-mail, etc., one thing needed to communicate several times with different people. This has been changed since the introduction of the ERP system. The information is entered for once, and can be accessed from any position, from the finance and cashier to Reservation. All the details can be viewed on the system. This helps improve both the efficiency and transparency. Quite effective
The head of marketing, Ms. Wang	We collect all the information about the customer, including the details of each promotion activity entered into the ERP system to provide proper customer management. This helps prevent customer information loss due to the churn of employees or other situation

Table A.2: Summary of Interview to the Executive Team of HUANYI During the Growth of the Brand

Interviewees	Summary of Interview
Assistant of CEO, Ms. Zhang	Digitalization empowers HUANYI with wings, but our root is Italy, where we have our service team, facilities, tour guides, and service staff. Being digital makes us better
Assistant of CEO, Ms. Zhang	The website is a window for communicating our business concept and for interaction as well. We posted the comments from customers on our concept of single-source group tour and our service, and our staff may also share their own experiences and the concerns of customers. For example, "The mode with separate driver and tour guide is safer for corporate group tour," commented by our customer. Other posts include the article "Where comes the Vitality of single-source group tour" published on "Travel Agency" on March, 2013, comment from "Sino-Italy Foundation": Thank the contribution of HUANYI and Italian Airline to Italy, and the Cover story from "Travel Agency": HUANYI cares more on service quality than quantity, etc.

(Continued)

Table A.2: *(Continued)*

Interviewees	Summary of Interview
Assistant of CEO, Ms. Zhang	In 2013, HUANYI was more lightly operated by dismiss's some time-wasting and useless staff and making work and life more orderly to save time and improve efficiency
Operation director, Ms. Zhang	HUANYI built the website by emphasizing the more controllable overseas service with single-source group tour. The homepage would impress customers once then entering our website with the banner slogan — more controllable overseas service with single-source group tour. The whole website and the columns are organized around the theme
Logistics manager, Ms. Xi	For the company, it is regulated as all the information of customer and team are entered into the system, and collected and stored by the front office. Meanwhile, the system combines the corporate organization and structure, which functions as the joints for the work. No matter which joint you are, it is a team that serves the customers, rather an individual like the situation before, who would open his or her own business by leveraging the customer resource collected
Assistant of CEO, Ms. Zhang	With ERP systems, we get the information, including how many customers we have, their characteristics, etc. and can also provide proper management of offshore resources, such as what groups the oversea guides served, what kind of groups that he or she is good at. The combined management of customer and the oversea guides allow us to have insight on our weakness through data analysis
Website manager, Robin	Our website and WeChat channel deliver the content around useful stories and information instead of corporate information. We have changed our website presentation to emphasize more on story-based useful information, which is more acceptable for customers
Marketing manager, Mr. Wang	We continuously change the presentation of information with the purpose to deliver useful information to customers. In the past, we just display the information to let the customer know what we offered without active communication. Now, we try to let people follow and communicate us actively

Table A.3:   Summary of Interview on HUANYI during the Update of the Brand

Interviewees	Summary of Interview
Assistant of CEO, Ms. Zhang	Our official WeChat account for the ancient fashion Italian tour now is certainly difficult to maintain. So I wanted to use my own personal self-media account to break the bottleneck. This brought us more business as I delivered the content in my friends circle, Italian Embassy, even the Italian Ambassador have my WeChat account, giving me a thumbs up
Assistant of CEO, Ms. Zhang	Starting from 2015, HUANYI brand has been carried by leveraging the boat of "Ancient fashion Italian Journey" from the domestic travel agencies. The climax of the brand communication was the broadcast in Gansu TV "One-Belt-One-Road" program
Assistant of CEO, Ms. Zhang	The communication media for HUANYI brand comprised WeChat, which includes the official account of the Ancient fashion Italian Journey and my own account, our website, and videos
Assistant of CEO, Ms. Zhang	HUANYI has a strategy which is our ultimate goal to become the representative of Italy tour. We need the campaign of Ancient fashion Italian Journey to implement the strategy
Assistant of CEO, Ms. Zhang	In the future, we plan to add more stories on the WeChat platform, because people love to read it
Logistics manager, Ms. Xi	Change the way to present the information on the website is a turning point for us. In the past, we used it as a place for image presentation, now we focus more on functionality and customer acceptance. For example, customers can add their favorite products even place orders
Website manager, Robin	We have worked with 20 areas in Italy to collect and abstract the information of all the 20 areas and communities to develop into an informative, real, and in-depth story
Assistant of CEO, Ms. Zhang	People want to get to know Italy through digitization, they would go to search engines as Baidu and Wikipedia to find a lot of attractions from HUANYI, linking their trip with HUANYI
Assistant of CEO, Ms. Zhang	Using digital technology as WeChat, website, videos, we can communicate HUANYI to our consumers
Assistant of CEO,Ms. Zhang	When I can't find the way to solve the problem, calm down myself, always a moral by word will give me guidance

Table A.4: Archival Data

Category	Details
News/Magazine Article	Huanqiu Network. (26 July 2015). Idea megagame "Italy of fashion and ancient country" open fervently, Retrieved 26 July 2016. http://china.huanqiu.com/hot/2016-07/9233832.html
	China daily 12 December 2015. More Chinese are setting foot in 'the boot', Retrieved 28 December 2015. http://www.chinadaily.com.cn/kindle/2015-12/14/content_22709820.htm
	Headlines today. "Chengdu Chongqing. Auditorium of Fashion and Ancient Country of Travelling to Italy," Retrieved 20 July 2016. http://toutiao.com/i6298191903573688833/
	Global Times. "Fashion in Left Hand and Ancient Country in Right Hand, Travel in Italy with Concentrated Attention," Retrieved 25 November 2015. http:// www.itatour.net
	Ishenbao. "Experience Report of 'Minority' Who Travels Italy as Relax and Luxurious Methods," Retrieved 4 November 2015. http://www.ishenbao.com/epaper/sjfwdb20151104/201511/t20151104_790338.htm
	China Daily. "Fashion and Ancient Country of Travelling to Italy Become the New Hot of Travel Abroad," Retrieved 16 October 2015. http://news.xinhuanet.com/fortune/2015-10/17/c_128328554.htm
Videos	GSTV. "Direct Connect to One Belt and One Road, the Special Emotion of Italy between Silk Roads," Retrieved 3 June 2016. http://www.iqiyi.com/a_19rrha9akl.html
	CNC. "Fashion and Ancient Country of Travelling to Italy News Conference of HUYI," Retrieved 3 November 2015. http://www.china.com.cn/v/travel/2015-10/16/content_36825212.htm
	CCTV4. "The silk road city, Xi 'an, China–Italy, Rome," Retrieved 19 April 2015. http://tv.cntv.cn/video/C25535/99029ca32e0143869389340687fef569
	CCTV Discovery walks. "A series report of program called the air hostess found," Retrieved 3 June 2014. http://v.ifeng.com/documentary/travel/2014007/035703bf-fafe-4af6-a73a-93392c2e94fb.shtml

Chapter 3

The Characteristics of Sustainable Supply Chain Innovation: A Case Study of YHD, China

De Gao, Zhiduan Xu, Man Gu, Yilong Z Ruan

School of Management, Xiamen University

Abstract

The sustainable innovation in the supply chain has been considered as an effective way to face the challenge of resource shortage and help organizations build the competitive advantage. However, the understanding on the characteristics of sustainable supply chain innovation (SSCI) still remains unclear. This study aims to explore and identify the characteristics of SSCI by examining a case of YHD, the first and major online retail enterprise in China. The findings of this case identify the characteristics of SSCI in seven dimensions. It emphasizes that SSCI can be generated at interfaces among supply chain participants in the network covering various innovation types. This case helps organizations to better manage and allocate resources to support their SSCI. Further, this case also informs us about the two interacted phases of SSCI.

Keywords: Sustainable supply chain innovation, Characteristic, Case study.

Introduction

Innovation has been considered as an effective way to solve the problem of lack of resources, which has become increasingly serious. Sustainable innovation as a result was brought up, with the aim of not only maximizing the economic return but also seeking a balance among economic, environmental, and social performances (Hockerts, 2003). To satisfy the requirements from various stakeholders, the sustainable innovation must consider interaction between the upstream and downstream elements of supply chain (Gualandris and Kalchschmidt, 2014).

Although the concept of sustainable supply chain innovation (SSCI) is relatively new for research, it has garnered considerable attention recently. Extant research has shown that SSCI is an aggregation of interacting activities involving different participants to achieve a common goal. It requires both internal and external capabilities including dynamic capability to adapt to the rapidly changing environments. The collaboration enables participants to create the complementary effect to sustainable targets and deal with the complexity due to the supply chain network, so that SSCI can be defined as an integrated change from incremental to radical changes in product, process, marketing, technology, resource and/or organization, which are associated with all related parties covering all related functions in supply chain and creating value for all stakeholders, and results in balanced performance of economic, social, and environmental dimensions.

Despite the previous research that provides some descriptions of SSCI, the systematic understanding on SSCI is still limited, particularly based on the case study. Therefore, the objective of this chapter is to identify the characteristics of sustainable innovation in supply chain though a case study of YHD in China. Specially, this research follows the case study approach prescribed by Pan and Tan (2011). The findings of this case provide a set of clear identifications of SSCI, which helps organizations to make sense of SSCI and evaluate its sustainable innovations in the supply chain. With an accurate understanding on SSCI, organizations can better allocate the resources to innovation and achieve the sustainable performance which helps form the competitive advantage. By doing so, this study highlights the characteristics of SSCI in seven dimensions.

Case background

China's online retail business started at the end of 20th Century and has been booming since then. In 2015, the online retail transaction amount has reached 3.8 trillion yuan, which will grow up to more than 10 trillion yuan in 2020 according to the prediction by economic experts.

YHD (www.yhd.com) is the first online retail enterprise in China which was founded in 2008 and praised as "Wal-Mart online." YHD is devoted to fulfil the needs of each family by providing one-stop shopping on fast-moving consumer goods (FMCGs). YHD had created a wonder of business as its annual sales rose from 4.17 million yuan in 2008 to nearly 20 billion yuan in 2014. In 2015, YHD had already owned more than 90 million registered users with over 2,000 million daily page views. YHD has established an advanced logistics system in more than 40 cities. As a result, it has been ranked as one of the top three most powerful online retail enterprises.

In recent years, YHD has carried out some sustainable innovative activities in the supply chain in the aspects of the upstream suppliers, the downstream customers, and the operation itself in order to maintain its position in the competitive market.

The innovation with upstream suppliers

Along with upstream suppliers, YHD implemented a "pallet pooling" innovation. Pallet pooling is an advanced logistics model based on the concept of pallet sharing which aims to transfer goods right throughout the supply chain with minimal manual handling of products. The standard pallet is generally owned by a third party provider. As the product flows through the supply chain, pallets are transferred from one participant's account to the next in a truly user pays arrangement. Adopting pallet pooling system in FMCG industry from the manufacturer DC (Suppliers) to retailers (YHD) DC remains difficult because of multi-product categories, various conditions required in transportation, dispersed locations, poor pallet standardization, serious self-protection of participants, and the low interest to participate. Besides this, the way to evaluate its input–output is the key barrier in adoption.

Therefore, YHD collaborated with its core suppliers as well as the pallet polling service provider, LOSCAM, to first successfully apply pallet pooling system in FMCG industry by the following steps.

Firstly, big data were collected to compare the cost among capital investment, repair, depreciation, maintenance, and rent for making decisions regarding purchase or lease of pallets. Secondly, it was noted that leasing pallets was better in coping with seasonal fluctuation of business and avoiding the pallets management and maintenance. Moreover, it was verified that pallet pooling model lowered the quality risks by reducing the product loading and unloading. Particularly, operating by pallet is much more efficient than doing by piece while promoting unsuspecting goods receipt. Finally, considering reduction of truck space due to this method, YHD works with LOSCAM to find out an appropriate prediction model. The prediction model shows that the transportation distance within 150 kilometers is the proper range to adopt pallet pooling system, and the benefits increase with the shortening of distance.

Innovation within YHD itself

The achievement of paperless operation within YHD is another innovation which reflects the improvement in the IT system and process operations. Given the category-based warehouse management, YHD dealt with customer sales order (SO) by decomposing into demand orders (DOs), grouping similar DOs into a batch, picking items by batch, sorting items by DO, and final packing. This preparation process involved printing a large number of documents such as dispatch list, invoice and picking list. It took more than 70 persons in YHD to process hundreds of thousands of orders everyday. There are many wastes of paper, consumable and manpower that accounted for a high proportion of operating costs.

Based on the principles of eliminating waste in the process, YHD developed an intelligent distribution system and a set of handheld terminals, which was the best practice for eliminating wastes in the FMCG industry. The vision of YHD's warehouse management was towards the fully-automatic unmanned operation.

Innovation with downstream customers

While online shopping becomes more and more popular in modern life, it brings an issue of carton waste and results in excessive demand for timber. This issue has aroused widespread concern in China. In 2014, YHD pioneered to propose a carton reuse program which encouraged customers to return YHD's carbons and gain some points as reward. This idea originated from goods inspection service during distribution. It has evolved gradually into a carton reuse process of returning, cleaning, storing, screening, and reusing of the cartons, in which customers, delivery staff, truckers, and warehouse keepers participated. In the meantime, an IT system for carton reuse program was designed and applied to improve the efficiency so as to lessen the burden on the staff.

The characteristics of sustainable supply chain innovation

YHD's innovations are based on the supply chain structure and sustainable orientation which intend to maximize the supply chain profitability and the social well-being while minimizing the environmental impact.

The structure for SSCI

The structure of supply chain is used to include the end users, recyclers, logistics, manufacturers, and third party service platforms. When YHD launched its SSCI activities, many direct and indirect stakeholders were involved. As Mr. Wang H. H., the vice president of operations introduced:

> "Besides YHD's distribution centre, warehouse, IT department and retail stores, there are many external supply chain participants who play a key role when we implement those three innovative activities, such as the end users, the product suppliers like P&G, the third leasing party of pallet like LOSCAM, etc. The supply chain industry association, tax department and social media also keep focus on our innovation while providing us necessary supports."

The target for SSCI

As the mission of YHD is mentioned, YHD is trying to provide service to clients with less money, less labor, and less time. All participants in their supply chain set sustainability as the common goal of their innovations. As Mr. Wang J. H., the director of supply chain planning and strategy department recalled:

> "Although these three innovative activities focus on different stages of supply chain, the common goal they have is to reduce waste. The 'pallet pooling' project considered how to improve supply chain efficiency and reduce the workload of carriers by removing all wastes in transportation. The original purpose of 'paperless operation' project was to utilize the paper, but we found that the maximum of reusing paper was only twice, so paperless system became the choice. The 'carton reuse' project had the similar concept which was the higher reuse rate of carton, the lower waste and cost."

The principles for SSCI

Not all of the innovative activities in the supply chain are launched at the same time, but are sparked by certain core members in the supply chain. Some related parties may adopt a wait-and-see strategy at the beginning of innovation, the others even doubt or resist to the changes as their benefit may be impacted. However, it is expected that when the innovation pilot succeeds, the best practice will be diffused and adopted by followers. In fact, collaboration, coordination, and establishment of the all-win culture become necessary approaches for SSCI. As Mr. He, the project manager of the "pallet pooling" project recalled:

> "When we started to pilot the "pallet pooling" method, we expected the third-party logistics (TPLs) service providers would be pleased, since it could reduce their workload and improve the efficiency. Unfortunately, they were not interested because they signed a contract with lump sum price and the new method could make them lose business. For this reason, we specially designed a green channel for those TPLs using pallet pooling system. Our move encourages TPLs to adopt the new pattern, and they finally enjoy this innovation as they find the total cost decreased."

The process of SSCI

Once a certain supply chain innovation is implemented, the lead innovative organization will usually gain better performance, which may break the original balance of interests. With the diffusion and the adoption of best practice, as a result, the performance of followers will be improved and new benefit balance will be reached accordingly. To maintain or gain the competitive advantage, organizations have to conduct continuous innovations, which form an innovative cycle. This cycle will always repeat itself and the performance will spiral up.

As Mr. Wang J. H. described:

> "These three innovative activities have a common thinking about how to reuse the resources such as the pallet, paper and carton. When an activity is successfully implemented, it will become a lesson for others. Of course, it will also bring pressure to others. The mission of my department is to keep looking for the improvement opportunities in the supply chain. Improvement is endless, and innovation is also never-ending in YHD."

The pattern of SSCI

Innovation is generally broken into two types according to the level of novelty. Researchers have identified 'radical innovation' as a major change in processes or product, while 'incremental innovation' refers to the improvement of existing systems (Bessant, 1992). Innovations can be conceptualized as a sequence of S curves. Each S curve represents a distinct type of base technology with its own stream of incremental innovations. Incremental innovations are considered to move along the same S curve; in contrast, radical innovations are considered as moving from one S curve to another (Roy *et al.*, 2004). The interactions of partners in supply chain generate both incremental and radical innovations. As Mr. Wang J. H. commended:

> "Both radical and incremental innovations exist in YHD. In a sense, the 'pallet pooling' project is more like a radical innovation, but the 'paperless operation' and 'carton reuse' projects are more like incremental innovations. Because YHD is an e-commercial enterprise, we prefer incremental innovation than the radical, for the former matches our

guiding paradigm called 'small step sprints.' When the opportunities are identified and evaluated, we are required to act immediately rather than wait for 100% readiness."

Risk management in SSCI

Each enterprise in the supply chain has to face a rapidly changing environment, particularly, the needs of customers, which is considered as a dynamic environment. The uncertainties in the dynamic environment will doubtless increase the risk of SSCI. The lead innovative organization must foster learning capability to absorb the valuable tangible or intangible resources in the supply chain. In view of this, project management has become a necessary tool to manage the risk in innovation. As Ms. Gu, the manager of warehouse recalled:

> "E-commercial business is developing rapidly. It requires us to adapt our process in a very short time. YHD has a successful project management process. Each innovation project team could seek experienced expert's support from the project management office (PMO) to control the risk. In addition, all projects must be reviewed by a multi-functional management team at each gate which has been set in project planning."

The result of SSCI

Most of the innovations in the supply chain focus on the profit return only. SSCI, however, is a sustainable-oriented innovation in the supply chain which considers the balance among economic, environmental, and social aspects of sustainability. It is a vital evaluating indicator in project selection and final review. As Mr. Wang J. H. introduced:

> "When the innovative proposals are raised, YHD provides all project teams a fair PK competition. Sustainable output is the first indicator evaluated to screen out high potential sustainability-oriented innovations from those that are only economics-oriented. All those three innovative projects achieve the significant and positive performance in reducing the total cost of supply chain operation, fulfilling the social responsibility well and protecting environment by lowering the consumption of wood and energy."

Lessons learned

Generally speaking, this case introduces three of YHD's sustainable innovative activities at different stages of the supply chain. It provides an overview of SSCI's characteristics in seven dimensions, which are summarized in Table 1.

Table 1. Various Characteristics of SSCI

Dimensions	Characteristics of YHD's SSCI	General Characteristics of SSCI
Structure	Internal and external participants in the upstream and downstream of YHD's supply chain	Lead innovative organization centered supply chains, including all related stakeholders
Target	To reduce any wastes in the supply chain operation	To achieve balance among economic, environmental, and social aspects of sustainability
Principles	YHD lead the innovations, while other supply chain participants follow it. Collaboration, coordination and all-win culture are required	Leading & following, collaboration, coordination, and all-win culture are essential principles
Process	Balance–Improve–Rebalance endless cycle processes	Balance–Innovation–Diffusion–Rebalance endless cycle process; Lead innovative activities by turn
Pattern	"Small step sprints" pattern indicates a more incremental than radical pattern	Both incremental and radical patterns exist at the same time
Risk management	Business environments develop rapidly which requires better learning and project management skills to reduce risk	Risk is caused by uncertainties in dynamic environments. Learning and project management skills help
Result	Lower total supply chain operation cost, good social image and lower wood and energy consumption	Significant and positive economic, environmental, and social performances

The general characteristics of SSCI have been clearly identified in Table 1 which helps form a unified understanding of the sustainable innovations in the supply chain for research. Supplemented implications from this case study can be further discussed as follows.

First, this case demonstrates that SSCI successfully occurs at the interface of lead innovative organizations with upstream suppliers, downstream customers and, internal operation. It could imply that SSCI can be generated at other interfaces among various supply chain participants such as different suppliers.

Second, this case shows that SSCI can be related to process, product, technology, IT, and service innovations. It could imply that SSCI covers various types of innovation with similar characteristics.

Third, this case indicates that SSCI can be divided into two consecutive phases, "innovation realization" and "innovation diffusion." These two phases interact with each other. For instance, better realization makes innovation easier to be accepted and adopted by followers. Instead, wider diffusion improves the innovation performance and also enhances the capability to realize further innovation.

Last but not the least, this case informs us that the resistance to change is a common phenomenon in SSCI because each change might affect the interests of organizations in varying degrees. The sustainable development requires that exploiting resources to meet the present needs should not be at the cost of the ability of future generations. Proper communication to look for complementary or multi-win innovations with sustainable goals may be the most effective way.

Conclusion

YHD has already successfully demonstrated a typical SSCI. The findings from this case study highlight seven representative characteristics of SSCI which were not completely discussed in previous research. The findings may provide some practical implications for organizations to better manage their sustainable innovations in the supply chain, such as how to allocate resources to support the innovation and to achieve the sustainable performance, which consequently helps organizations to gain a competitive advantage. Future research may extend the focus to the detailed process of SSCI realization and its diffusion.

Acknowledgments

This research was supported by the Soft Science Research Project in the Science and Technology Program of Fujian, China (No: 2013R0094).

References

Bessant, J. 1992. "Big Bang or Continuous Evolution: Why Incremental Innovation is Gaining Attention in Successful Organisations." *Creativity and innovation management,* 1(2), 59–62.

Gualandris, J., and Kalchschmidt, M. 2014. "Customer Pressure and Innovativeness: Their Role in Sustainable Supply Chain Management." *Journal of Purchasing and Supply Management,* 20(2), 92–103.

Hockerts, K. N. 2003. *"Sustainability Innovations: Ecological and Social Entrepreneurship and the Management of Antagonistic Assets."* Bamberg Difo-Druck GmbH.

Pan, S. L., and Tan, B. 2011. "Demystifying Case Research: A Structured–Pragmatic–Situational (SPS) Approach to Conducting Case Studies. *Information and Organization,* 21(3), 161–176.

Roy, S., Sivakumar, K., and Wilkinson, I. F. 2004. "Innovation Generation in Supply Chain Relationships: A Conceptual Model and Research Propositions." *Journal of the Academy of Marketing Science,* 32(1), 61–79.

Chapter 4

The Role of Social Media in Social Advocacy

Shamshul Bahri

Department of Operations & MIS
Faculty of Business and Accountancy
University of Malaya, 50603 Kuala Lumpur, Malaysia
esbi@um.edu.my

Ali Fauzi

Department of Library & Information Sciences
Faculty of Computer Science& Information Technology
University of Malaya, 50603 Kuala Lumpur, Malaysia
alifauzi@um.edu.my

Abstract

In recent years, the rapid uptake of information and communication technologies (ICTs) in Malaysian civil society has led to the growing participation in the political landscape as a means of addressing community development challenges. In this research-in-progress chapter, we aim to demonstrate the utility of social media technologies in enabling social advocacy. Based on an in-depth case study of the 2014 Soup Kitchen Ban in Kuala Lumpur, this study examines how social media can be used to organize grassroots and communities to push for change, giving rise to technology assisted social advocacy.

Keywords: Social media, Social advocacy, Soup kitchen, Malaysia.

Introduction

Information and Communication Technology (ICT) has always been used to address societal concerns especially by activists and non-governmental organizations (NGOs). Initially, these individuals and groups developed web pages to disseminate their messages to the readers. However, this kind of communication is passive because the message moves uni-directional from the NGOs and activists to the readers but not vice versa. Furthermore, due to technical and costly constraints, having a website can be considered a luxury most of them can ill afford.

Social media has changed the landscape of online activism. Technologies such as Facebook, Twitter, and YouTube have enabled more activists and NGOs to reach their current and prospective members and volunteers. These technologies cost next-to-none and do not require high level of computer expertise to develop. Additionally, social media offers the opportunity for interaction and communication to occur virtually between the activists/NGOs and their prospective members and volunteers. Consequently, the technology has increased the feeling of empowerment (Leong *et al.*, 2015), the ability to mobilize volunteers (Chong *et al.*, 2014), and social advocacy.

Although a number of studies have suggested that social media has enhanced social advocacy, there is a limited number of studies that focus on this concept. It has often been lumped together with empowerment and civic engagement, hence giving the impression that they mean the same when they are not. Empowerment can be considered as the prelude to social advocacy. The community will take action to change the status quo when it feels that it has the ability to do so. However, the transformation from empowerment to advocacy is not automatic. There must be a mechanism that moves the community from simply feeling empowered to taking actions that actually promote change in the society. Social media is one of the tools that can lead to social advocacy. Almost anybody can set up his own social media site and share his opinions with the readers or followers. As a result, it has the ability to gain people's attention and move them towards certain agenda. Unfortunately, the academic community has not investigated the manner in which social media has become the mechanism for social advocacy widely.

This study attempts to overcome this drawback by focusing on social advocacy. Specifically, we intend to explain how social media has the capacity to advance social advocacy. We will use the Kuala Lumpur's soup kitchen ban case as the backdrop of this study. The chapter is structured as follows. After the introduction, the relevant literature will be reviewed. It will be followed by the description of our research method. We will conclude by discussing the potential contribution of the study to the knowledge on social media and social advocacy.

Literature review

Social media studies

The term "social media" is often used interchangeably with social networks, social networking, Enterprise 2.0 and Web 2.0 despite a range of distinctions in the literature (Kaplan and Haenlein, 2010). In this study, we focus on the more popular applications such as Facebook, WhatsApp and to a lesser extent YouTube and Twitter. With their growing popularity, the range of social media applications (also referred to as social media tools) is steadily increasing. It has also been reported that Malaysia has one of the highest number of Facebook users in the world at around 19 million with 15 million classified as active (Leng, 2016). These applications offer various features (such as to share texts, videos and pictures) to their users and facilitate their ability to "socialize" with others.

Social media studies have occurred at two levels: organizational and societal. Studies at organizational level refers to research that have been conducted on the use of the technology by business entities and government departments or agencies. Research in this level often focuses on how the use of social media can enhance organizational performance. For example, Parveen *et al.* (2015) found that business managers in the small and medium enterprises (SMEs) have used social media for various purposes such as promotion, branding, and information search. Consequently, its usage has a positive impact on the financial and non-financial (customer relationship and information accessibility) outcomes (Ainin *et al.*, 2015).

On the other hand, studies at societal level refer to the use of the technology by societies or communities. A number of these studies focus on the use of social media for civic engagement. This area of research looks at how social media is used to engage the community in addressing social issues. One group of people that is extensively using the technology is activists who are reshaping the traditional civic engagement landscape in the digital world (Warren *et al.*, 2014a, 2015). In turn, online civic engagement through social media has increased the trust of the public on the government, police, and justice system (Warren *et al.*, 2014b).

It is evident that social media has advanced from merely engaging with citizens to driver of social movements (Fuentes, 2007). Collectively, individuals can now generate public attention without relying on mainstream media by using social media (Yuce *et al.*, 2014). However, few studies have addressed this perspective. Our chapter has shown that many IS studies focus on verifying the impact of social media on mobilization and activism, but sideline changes to the existing mobilizing agency and the rise of community (e.g., Anduiza *et al.*, 2013; Kumar and Thapa, 2014; Maghrabi and Salam, 2013; McGrath *et al.*, 2011). These studies focus on communication, information dissemination, and consensus mobilization aspects with regards to the use of social media in social movements. For instance, Maghrabi and Salam (2013) have proposed a model to understand the influence of social media on social movements and political change, while Agarwal *et al.* (2012) and Yuce *et al.* (2014) show how issues are propagated and sentiment is diffused in social media networks.

On the other hand, some researchers focus on classifying different types of online actions and information that is posted on social media (e.g., Harlow, 2012; Penney and Dadas, 2014). For instance, Kelly and Etling (2008) cluster bloggers based on their views and topics of interest after analyzing 60,000 blogs using social network and content analysis. There are also a few studies that look into the process or mechanisms of how the use of social media translates into movements (Maghrabi and

Salam, 2013; Valenzuela, 2013). However, these studies have largely assumed that mobilization activities such as social advocacy occur automatically and ignored the mechanism that affects the action. While some researchers have briefly suggested the concept of grassroots mobilization (Mora, 2014; Segerberg and Bennett, 2011), there remains a limited understanding of how ICT enables the community to drive grassroots mobilization (Cardoso *et al.*, 2013), especially social advocacy.

Social advocacy

Social advocacy can be defined as an effort by the society to influence political, economic, and social policies in order to change the status quo. Hence, it is a concept that is closely related to social justice. In a nutshell, social justice means that everyone in a society matters and their voices must be heard and considered. The importance of "getting heard" is especially crucial to those who are at risk of being excluded and people who have particular difficulties in making their views known. This group of people often stay in the fringes of the society. Many of them contribute significantly to the society by working in jobs with meager salaries such as cleaners and rubbish pickers. However, they are largely ignored by society and their ideas on community development are often deemed worthless. This ignored group of people often include the poor, destitute, and homeless (Stachowiak, 2013).

The concept of social advocacy is also closely related to social change. Once people realize the injustice in their society, they will mobilize themselves to overcome the problem. The manner in which one acts to bring about change differs between geographical locations and the tools used. Some communities use a more subtle approach such as petitions to advance their agendas, while others use a more aggressive method such as protesting in front of governmental buildings. Earlier, communities use banners and placards to display the message of change they want to bring forth. Now, many communities are turning to ICTs, especially social media to relay their message to those in power. Despite the difference in approach and tools used, the aim remains the same: to bring social justice to those often neglected by the society (Newman and Yeates, 2008).

Hence, the goals of social advocacy are as follows (Payne, 2006):

- Promoting social change
- Promoting problem solving
- Empowerment and liberation

One useful theory that can be used as a theoretical lens for studying social advocacy is the community organizing theory.

Grassroots or community organizing theory

This theory has a distinct way of looking at how a community could resolve the problems they face. It recognizes that an issue affects individuals and communities differently. As a result, only individuals directly affected by an issue will take action to address the issue. Because the issue often affects a large number of people, the action is often taken by a collective action of the members in that particular community. Organization, meanwhile, plays a different role. Its role is more of a convener or a capacity builder than as a driver. In other words, an organization's role is not to tell its members what to do. Instead, an organization's most important task is to develop the task of its members so that they could address the issues affecting themselves (Biklen, 1983).

The community organizing theory also has a distinct, and some might say a radical, way of viewing power. According to this theory, power is not held exclusively by elites. Instead, it believes that power is changeable and dynamic. Consequently, the grassroots and communities can take the power from the hands of the elites. One of the ways in which power change can be achieved is through mutual action by the grassroots and communities (Alinsky, 1971).

The theory contains some very important assumptions. Power exists when (or because) community members give their cooperation to the organizers. The base of this power can be shifted through actions and events. However, organizers should not take this power lightly. It has to be used to overcome the problem(s) faced by the people, not the wishes of the leaders. The aim of the effort, meanwhile, should be to build the capacity of the community affected by the problem. Eventually, it is the community who will rise to the challenge of addressing the problem(s), not the organization. Hence, the focus of the effort is not to change individuals. Instead, the focus should be on changing the relevant institutions and policies (Alinsky, 1971).

These assumptions have some important implications to social advocacy effort. First, advocacy efforts involve a large number of people who are affected by the issue at hand. Social advocacy will not be effective if it involves only a small number of people affected. Second, there is no leading organization. Instead, the role of the organization involved is to facilitate the collective efforts to achieve social change. Third, there are a few promising strategies that the organization and affected community could take to take the social advocacy effort forward. The strategies include capability building, community mobilizing, awareness building, and media advocacy (Stachowiak, 2013).

Research method

Research approach

This study employs the case study research method for several reasons. First, the case study research allowed us to perform an in-depth study of the communities affected by the soup kitchen ban that is often difficult to achieve through the questionnaire. Second, the method enabled us to develop a richer understanding of the role social media played in helping overturn the soup kitchen ban.

Data collection

We collected the study's data mainly through interviews. We chose the interview technique for several reasons. Through the technique, we were able to capture the true impact of the communities organizing themselves in order to effect policy changes from the people where they are located. The technique also enabled us to probe deeper into interesting issues. The interviews took 1 to 1.5 hours each. Some of the interviews were conducted on a one-to-one basis while others were group interviews. In total, 16 informants were interviewed within a period of one week. Table 1 shows the profile of this study's informants.

Table 1. Profile of the Research Informants

Interview No.	Informants' Roles	Organization
1	Co-founder (two person)	Dapur Jalanan
2	Co-founder	The Nasi Lemak Project
3	Journalist	Says.com
4	Founder	
	Senior volunteer	Pertiwi Soup Kitchen
5	Volunteer (four person)	
6	Program Director	
	Operational staff (two person)	Kechara Soup Kitchen
7	Head of Corporate Communication	
	Social Media Administrator	Federal Territories Ministries
	Administrator Assistant	

The informants consist of two groups. The first group is the NGOs that comprise the soup kitchens, while the second group is the governmental departments that are directly responsible for managing the city of Kuala Lumpur. These groups of informants were selected because they affected and were affected by the case in this study. Their actions led to the grassroots movement to challenge the ban on soup kitchens operating in the city center and consequently the lifting of the ban. Including these informants enabled the study to explore the mechanisms that have enabled the society to give a voice to the homeless in the city center who were largely neglected in its development and marginalized by the initial decision to ban soup kitchens.

Background of the case

On July 3rd, 2014, in an attempt to deter homelessness, the Malaysian government enforced an immediate ban on the operation of all soup kitchens within a 2 kilometers radius of Kuala Lumpur's Lot 10, which covers a significant portion of the city center. Under the directive, soup kitchens in area who continued operations were subject to fines as they "encouraged people to remain homeless and jobless" while allegedly promoting littering, scavenging, and the spread of disease in Kuala Lumpur, tarnishing the city's image. The ban triggered the active involvement of community members, catalyzing an overwhelming public backlash through social media channels. The sheer scale of community discontentment led the Federal Territories Ministry to invite affected soup kitchens to a congregation at Kuala Lumpur City Hall to discuss public sentiments, the homelessness situation, future steps, and strategies to repair the government's relationship with the Malaysian public. The ban was formally reversed within the space of four weeks. Soup kitchens are now permitted to continue operations in selected locations, subject to food, health and safety standards. The Federal Territories Ministry is also working towards a collaborative partnership with soup kitchen organizations to establish shelters for the homeless community and support welfare programs.

Potential contributions of the study

This study has the potential to contribute theoretically and practically to the existing knowledge on social media and social advocacy. Theoretically, this study will add to the spectrum of knowledge on social media which is social advocacy. This study will also add to the knowledge on social advocacy by explaining how social media can be exploited to advance social justice among the communities at the fringes of society. Practically, this study will inform activists and NGOs on how they could use ICTs such as social media effectively to advance their agendas.

Acknowledgment

We would like to thank the University of Malaya, in particular, the Equitable Society Research Cluster (Grant No. RPH004-13ICT) for their generous funding that enabled this study to be conducted.

References

Ainin, S., Parveen, F., Moghavvemi, S., and Jaafar, N. I. 2015. "Factors Influencing the Use of Social Media by SMEs and its Performance Outcomes," *Industrial Management & Data Systems,* 115(3), 570–588.

Anduiza, E., Cristancho, C., and Sabucedo, J. M. 2013. "Mobilization through Online Social Networks: The Political Protest of the Indignados in Spain," *Information, Communication & Society,* 17(6), 750–764.

Agarwal, N., Lim, M., and Wigand, R. 2012. "Raising and Rising Voices in Social Media," *Business & Information Systems Engineering,* 4(3), 113–126.

Biklen, D. P. 1983. *"Community Organizing Theory and Practice."* Prentice-Hall, Englewood Cliffs, NJ.

Cardoso, A., Boudreau, M.-C., and Carvalho, J. 2013. "Think Individually, Act Collectively: Studying the Dynamics of a Technologically Enabled Civic Movement," in *International Conference on Information Systems,* Milan.

Chong, T., Leong, C., Pan, S. L., Bahri, S., and Fauzi, A. 2014. "Use of Social Media in Disaster Relief During the Kuantan (Malaysia) Flood," in: *International Conference on Information Systems,* Auckland.

Fuentes, M. A. 2007. "Digital Activism," in *Encyclopedia of Activism and Social Justice,* G.L. Anderson and K.G. Herr (eds.). Thousand Oaks, CA, SAGE Publications, Inc.

Harlow, S. 2012. "Social Media and Social Movements: Facebook and an Online Guatemalan Justice Movement That Moved Offline," *New Media & Society,* 14(2), 225–243.

Kaplan, A. M., and Haenlein, M. 2010. "Users of the World, Unite! The Challenges and Opportunities of Social Media," *Science Direct,* 53, 59–68. https://www.sciencedirect.com/science/article/pii/S0007681309001232.

Kelly, J., and Etling, B. 2008. "Mapping Iran's Online Public: Politics and Culture in the Persian Blogosphere," *Berkman Center for Internet and Society and Internet & Democracy Project,* Harvard Law School.

Kumar, R., and Thapa, D. 2014. "Social Media as a Catalyst for Civil Society Movements in India: A Study in Dehradun City," *New Media & Society,* 17, 1299–1316.

Leng, L. K. 2016. "Malaysians are the Most Active Instagram Users in Asia Pacific," *The Star Online,* https://www.thestar.com.my/tech/tech-news/2016/09/29/malaysians-are-the-most-active-instagram-users-in-apac/.

Leong, C., Pan, S. L., Ractham, P., and Kaewkitipong L. 2015. "ICT-enabled Community Empowerment in Crisis Response: Social Media in Thailand Flooding 2011," *Journal of the Association of Information Systems,* 16, 174–212.

Maghrabi, R. O., and Salam, A. F. 2013. "Social Media and Citizen Social Movement Process for Political Change: The Case of 2011 Egyptian Revolution," in *International Conference on Information Systems,* Milan.

McGrath, K., Elbanna, A., Hercheui, M., Panagiotopoulos, P., and Saad, E. 2011. "Online Social Networking and Citizen Engagement: Debating the Potential and Limitations," in *International Conference on Information Systems*, Shanghai.

Mora, F. A. 2014. "Emergent Digital Activism: The Generational/Technological Connection," *The Journal of Community Informatics*, http://ci-journal.net/index.php/ciej/article/view/1009/1070.

New, J., and Yeates, N. 2008. *"Social Justice: Welfare, Crime and Society."* Open University Press, Maidenhead.

Parveen, F., Jaafar, N. I., and Ainin, S. 2015. "Social Media Usage and Organizational Performance: Reflections of Malaysian Social Media Managers," *Telematics and Informatics*, 32(1), 67–78.

Payne, M. 2006. *"What Is Professional Social Work?"* Policy Press, Bristol.

Penney, J., and Dadas, C. 2014. "(Re)Tweeting in the Service of Protest: Digital Composition and Circulation in the Occupy Wall Street Movement," *New Media & Society*, 16(1), 74–90.

Segerberg, A., and Bennett, W.L. 2011. "Social Media and the Organization of Collective Action: Using Twitter to Explore the Ecologies of Two Climate Change Protests," *The Communication Review*, 14(3), 197–215.

Stachowiak, S. 2013. *Pathways for Change: 10 Theories to Inform Advocacy and Change Policy Efforts.* Available at: http://orsimpact.com/wp-content/uploads/2013/11/Center_Pathways_FINAL.pdf. Last accessed: August 3, 2017.

Valenzuela, S. 2013. "Unpacking the Use of Social Media for Protest Behavior: The Roles of Information, Opinion Expression, and Activism," *American Behavioral Scientist*, 57(7), 920–942.

Warren, A. M., Sulaiman, A., and Jaafar, N. I. 2014a. "Facebook: The Enabler of Online Civic Engagement for Activists," *Computers in Human Behaviour*, 32, 284–289.

Warren, A. M., Sulaiman, A., and Jaafar, N. I. 2014b. "Social Media Effects on Fostering Online Civic Engagement and Building Citizen Trust and Trust in Institutions," *Government Information Quarterly*, 31(2), 291–301.

Warren, A. M., Sulaiman, A., and Jaafar, N. I. 2015. "Understanding Civic Engagement Behaviour on Facebook From a Social Capital Theory Perspective," *Behaviour & Information Technology*, 34(2), 163–175.

Yuce, S. T., Agarwal, N., Wigand, R. T., Lim, M., and Robinson, R. S. 2014. "Bridging Women Rights Networks: Analyzing Interconnected Online Collective Actions," *Journal of Global Information Management*, 22(4), 1–20.

Chapter 5

Digital Performance Management Based on the Perspective of Organizational Control: A Case Study of Advantech

Ning Zhou

School of Economics and Management
Beihang University, China
zning80@buaa.edu.cn

Xiaoting Han

School of Economics and Management
Beihang University, China
hanxiaoting@buaa.edu.cn

Tingting Hu, Yin Zhou, Wenjun Jiang

School of Economics and Management
Beihang University, China

Abstract

This study uses the case of Advantech Co., Ltd., (referred to as "Advantech") and analyzes the characteristics of its performance management system and mechanisms. The case study investigates the mechanisms that influence performance management from *organizational* control

83

perspective, as well as the positive influences of digital performance management to the overall organizational performance on the basis of the information system. This study is expected to enrich the connotation of *organizational* control and performance evaluation, while serving as a practical reference for companies aiming to increase performance management through digitization.

Introduction

Corporate performance management develops with the changing world. The scientific study and practice of performance management is focused on both the corporation's aim on performance evaluation and all the other aspects of its growth goals. Performance management is a major component to strategy planning and implementation in a business; it functions as a fair evaluation system to the corporation, thus protecting its strategy implementation and diffusion, linking its departments, employees with its strategy, allocating resources efficiently and placing the corporation to a favorable position in the competitive domestic and overseas market.

This case study mainly concentrates on performance management, and utilizes the case of Advantech to outline the factors and mechanism of organizational control effecting performance management. The case study also discusses the positive influences of digital performance management to increase overall organizational performance in addition to providing referencing data.

Literature review

In the past 10 years, research topics and methodology in management accounting has been changing towards an increased focus on incentive pay and performance appraisal; while the diversity of research methodology focused on management accounting has been increased. This has resulted in a proliferation of papers published regarding the theory of management accounting application and the expanded theory (Du *et al.*, 2009). As the highlight research field of management accounting, current research focused on performance management has produced well-established theoretical frameworks and covers both theoretical and empirical research including specific methods of performance management practice (Li *et al.*, 2004; Li and Zang, 2011; Xing, 2012), evaluation index design (Liu *et al.*, 2011), integrating different management accounting tools (Tang *et al.*, 2009). Yet, some questions remain to be investigated, and these include how to seamlessly apply performance management to the corporation context, resolve corporation's tangible issues, and improve corporation's performance.

Organizational control is a type of management mode for aligning personal behavior with organizational goals (Ouchi, 1980). The four modes of organizational control are: behavior control, outcome control, clan control, and self-control (Kirsch, 1997) (See Table 1).

Behavior control and outcome control are part of formal control, while clan control and self-control are part of informal control. Formal control refers to organizational control over its members' behavior through clear regulations, system, and policy. In corporations, formal control can help managers control employees' behavior or goal by using formal structures, systems, and regulations. Informal control exerts control over members' behavior through culture, values, and beliefs without any incentives nor implementation tools, and achieving such control requires employee's conscious behavior.

Organizational control is considered as the guarantee of enterprise operation management. It is of theoretical value and practical significance to probe into the improving mechanism and the enhancing efficiency of digitalization for performance management from the perspective of organizational control.

Methodology

This research focuses on the issue of how to improve organizational performance through organizational control and why organizational control can help managers enhance performance. Quantitative methods can barely meet the research purpose in this study, on the contrary a case study can be well applied in answering "how" and "why" questions (Yin, 2009). Therefore, a case study has been adopted. Using Advantech as the case, a model based on the Structured-Pragmatic-Situational (SPS) (Pan and Tan, 2011) has been developed to further ensure consistency in theory, data, and modeling.

Table 1. Features of Four Types of Organizational Control

Control Mode	Definition	Key Features	Prerequisites	Manifestations
Behavior Control	Organization agrees in advance on what conduct is appropriate, and in accordance with whether to take such incentive (Kirsch et al., 2002)	Rules complete the task	Behavior is observable	Work Description (Orlikowski, 1991) Assignments (Henderson and Lee 1992)
Outcome Control	Reward depends on whether a certain result is reached; the processes are not important (Kirsch et al., 2002)	Outcomes and goals on the basis of the results and incentive plan	Measurable results	Expected level of performance (Henderson and Lee 1992) Set target date and budget (Kirsch, 1997) Incentivize based on goal completion (Kirsch et al., 2002)
Clan Control	Organization members have common standards and values. Incentive depends on individual behavior meeting these criteria and values	Values, beliefs; Identify and strengthen acceptable behavior	The results can not be measured	Common ideology within the organization (Kling and Lacono, 1984) Recruitment and training practices (Klein, 1994) Code of Conduct and values (Kirsch et al., 2010)
Self-Control	Organizations guide members to develop their own goals, and implementation though self-monitoring, self-motivation and self-punishment (Klein and Kraft, 1994)	Self-monitoring, self-rewarding, self-punishment	Complex or non-routine tasks; lack of relevant rules or procedures	Self-management (Klein and Kraft, 1994)

Data collection for this case started on June 2015. After over a year of communicating with the Advantech staff, collecting and sorting 100,000+ words manuscripts, researching into secondary resources scholar articles, uncovering the real situation in Advantech's performance management, extracting Advantech's digital performance management model, we seek to find the secret to maintaining a corporation's sustainable development.

Advantech's digital performance management system

Advantech is a global leader in the intelligent systems industry. After 30 years' development, the company has become the market leader in electronic platform services. Performance management system started in the founding period and primarily relied on manual distribution then and did not form a complete set of performance management system. Advantech has thus far successfully developed a complete performance management system, allowing their performance management procedure to be followed in accordance with four stages of performance management process.

Performance plan

Advantech's performance plan comprises the Annual Business Plan (ABP), financial indicators, and non-financial indicators. Advantech set ABP through its information system, allowing all employees and department leaders to understand the competition rate of the set target for each employee, each type of product and each geographic region. By utilizing digital management, Advantech achieved a "top-down and bottom-up" strategic management, taking full control of planning. Through ABP, employees' performance indicators are decomposed by the corporate strategic planning and reflect the business planning (see Figure 1).

Performance appraisal

Advantech's individual performance appraisal comprises two parts: performance indicators and competence. Advantech's information system supports performance appraisal from both self-assessment and evaluation from managers. Self-assessment is an employee's personal opinion to his/

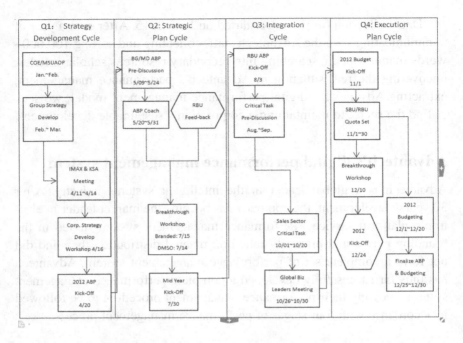

Figure 1. Decomposition of Advantech's Digital Strategic Performance

her work in four areas: KPI, MBO, Quota, and Competence scores. The manager evaluation is the scoring given by the administrative staff. Function supervisor evaluates an employee's competence (work initiative, execution, and learning ability) on a 5-scale rating, incorporating historical assessment data with self-assessment, actual result, and interview when necessary as references.

Performance coaching

Advantech introduced a finance partner in performance coaching, allocating a financial staff to every department to provide information support to the department's management team. Managers of Advantech utilize the information system for communicating, evaluating/reviewing employees' performance, and providing advice for employee development, such as suggesting training courses. Employees utilize the information system to view the performance appraisal result, comment on manager's ratings, and sign their confirmation. The information system provides an effective two-way communication between employees and managers and smoothly resolves issues between them.

Performance feedback

Advantech's performance appraisal results have three levels: overweight, neutral, and underweight. From the learning capability perspective, Advantech's employees can choose training courses to focus on personal ability, self-development, and career management. From career development perspective, Advantech provides suggestions for employees on maintaining existing position, transferring position, promotion, extension of the investigation excusable period, dismissal, or further evaluation.

Organizational management and control mechanisms to improve performance management

Mechanisms of how organizational control effect performance management

Outcome control, behavior control, clan control, and self-control exert influence on organizational performance, which can be reflected from individual performance and organizational performance. First, employees under outcome control and behavior control can execute goals explicitly. Aimed to take outcome and behavior control's incentives, recognizing acts can directly increase organizational performance. Outcome control allows employees to clearly understand performance target, achieve performance indicators, and thus improve individual performance. Behavior control restricts employees' behaviors, aligns employee's ability with corporation's requirements, and thus improves individual's ability and quality. Clan control has an enduring effect on organizational performance through culture infiltration, instills corporate values into employees, and requires employees to conduct business from top to bottom in the formation of "altruism" atmosphere. Self-control helps employees improve individual performance by self-motivation, self-monitoring, and self-punishment. Through constraining their own behaviors, employees achieve set performance indicators and enhance competency Figure 2.

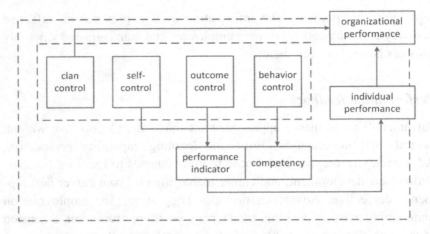

Figure 2. Interactions of Organizational Control and Performance Management

Overall, for informal control, clan control formulates a unified cultural atmosphere to improve organizational performance, while self–control increases individual performance by promoting performance indicators and competency. On the formal control side, outcome control and behavior control increase individual performance by specific employees' performance goals and constraints of behaviors. Specifically, outcome control raises employee's performance indicator, while behavior control raises employee's competency. In the end, individual performance increase cumulates to organizational performance increase, achieving overall organizational performance improvement.

Utility of digital performance management information system

Since inception, Advantech's information system was developed with the idea of a paperless office. The powerful and wide-ranging system helps Advantech to improve work efficiency and reduce operating costs. The information system can help constrain organizational control and is the guarantee basis for the implementation of performance management. Based on a powerful information system, a corporation can allocate targets to every department and every employee by setting ABP to ensure every employee understands the corporate strategy at real time. Employees' performance indicators are decomposed by the corporate strategic planning and reflect the business planning. Employees can check their target complete rate through the system at any time, working harder and achieving better performance. Under this goal, corporations can rely on information systems to understand and control employee's behaviors by implementing incentives and promotion mechanisms to further achieve business goals and enhance organizational performance. Employees can also complete real-time self-supervision through the powerful information system. Overall, the information system allows the corporation to follow set targets and strategies and guarantees organizational control and performance management. Relying on powerful information systems, corporations can be more convenient and targeted to take control measures to enhance organizational performance (see Figure 3).

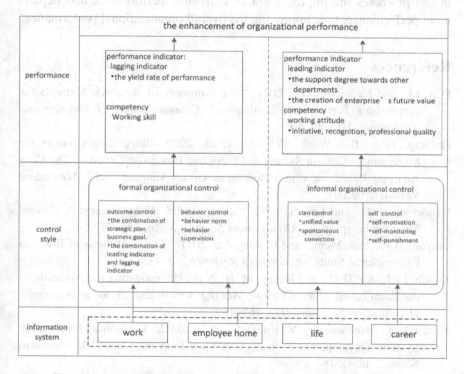

Figure 3: Digital Information System Performance Management Model

Conclusion

This Chapter is an exploratory inductive research which is focusing on Advantech. Its aim is to investigate the impact of organizational control on the business performance management and the role of the information system. Based on performance management and organizational control theories, this case study discussed the role of organizational control on performance management through four factors: outcome control, behavior control, clan control, and self-control. Specifically, clan control, outcome control, and behavior control directly influence organizational performance improvement, while outcome control, behavior control, and self-control can improve individual performance, thus affecting organizational performance. Meanwhile, Digital Information System Performance Management Model can help strategic decomposition and landing, precisely metering work, real-time tracking performance, and performance feedback evaluation. The model promotes the improvement of individual performance and department performance, thus improving the overall organizational performance.

References

Dan, Li., and Fanrong, Zeng. 2011. "The Summary of Research Methods for Enterprise's Performance Evaluation," *Communication of Finance and Accounting,* 1(1), 49–50.

Guliang, Tang., Bin, Wang., Fei, Du., *et al.*, 2009. "Integration Concept for Management Control System in Diversified Enterprise Group — The Case Analysis Based on China Resources Group Vanguard 6S," *Accounting Research,* 02(02).

Henderson, J. C., and Lee, S. 1992. "Managing I/S Design Teams: A Control Theories Perspective," *Management Science,* 38(6), 757–777.

Junyong, Liu., Yan, Meng., and Chuang, Lu. 2011. "The Usefulness of BSC: an Experimental Study," *Accounting Research,* 36–43.

Kirsch, L. J., Ko, D G., and Haney, M. H. 2010. "Investigating the Antecedents of Team-based Clan Control: Adding social capital as a predictor," *Organization Science,* 21(2), 469–489.

Kirsch, L. J., Sambamurthy, V., Ko, D. G., *et al.*, 2002. "Controlling Information Systems Development Projects: The View from the Client," *Management Science,* 48(4), 484–498.

Kirsch, L. S.1997. "Portfolios of Control Modes and IS Project Management," *Information Systems Research*, 8(3), 215–239.

Kling, R., and Iacono S. 1984. "The Control of Information Systems Developments After Implementation," *Communications of the Acm*, 27(12), 1218–1226.

Klein, H. K., and Kraft, P. 1994. "Social Control And Social Contract In Networking: Total Quality Management and the Control of Knowledge Work," *Ifip Transactions A Computer Science & Technology*, 2, 45–53.

Orlikowski, W. J. 1991. "Integrated Information Environment or Matrix of Control? The Contradictory Implications of Information Technology," *Accounting Management & Information Technologies*, 1(91), 9–42.

Ouchi, W. G. 1980. "Markets, Bureaucracies, and Clans," *Administrative Science Quarterly*, 25(1).

Pan, S. L., and Tan, B. 2011. "Demystifying Case Research: A Structured-Pragmatic — Situational (SPS) Approach to Conducting Case Research," *Information and Organization*, 21(3), 161–176.

Rongrui Du., Zezhong, Xiao., and Qiwu, Zhou. 2009. "The Management Accounting Research and Review in China," *Accounting Research*, 9, 72–80.

Yin, R. K. 2009. *"Case Study Research: Design and Methods."* Thousand Oaks, CA, Sage.

Zhigang, Li. 2004. "An Improved Balanced Score Card with AHP Method for Enterprise's Performance Evaluation," *Value Engineering*, 52–54.

Zhouling, Xing. 2012. "A Research of High-performance Human Resources Management System and Organization's Performance: Case Study of China's ChiNext Companies," *Management Review*, 24(07), 91–98.

Chapter 6

Research from the Perspective of Resource Orchestration on How Marginal Enterprises Reconfigure the Digital Ecosystem: A Case of Duch 3D Printing in China

Zhengyan Cui

School of Economics and Management
Beihang University
4363401@163.com

Taohua Ouyang

School of Economics and Management
Beihang University
taohuaouyang@hotmail.com

Abstract

Since digital technologies have brought opportunities for marginal enterprises to rise, it deserves attention from the academia about how marginal enterprises reconfigure ecosystems. This thesis has a case study of Duch Group (Duch) in 3D printing from the perspective of resource orchestration. It deeply investigates the dynamic process of how marginal

95

enterprises reconfigure the ecosystem by digital technologies and attain the core position. It is found that the marginal enterprises, adhering to the "point–line–surface" principle, successively reconfigure the manufacturing process, industry chain, and ecosystem by implementing actions of structuring, bundling, and leveraging on the key resources such as digital technologies to attain the core position. This research benefits both academics and practitioners by contributing to cumulative theoretical developments and by offering practical insights.

Keywords: Digital ecosystem, Resource orchestration, Marginal enterprise, Reconfigure, 3D printing.

Introduction

The emerging digital technologies represented by Internet technologies have changed enterprises' value-creating ways and competition basis, gradually moving the mode of production from being supply-oriented to demand-oriented (Luo Min and Li Liang-yu, 2015). The competition and innovation have been extended to the entire ecosystem, rather than among individual enterprises (Adner and Kapoor, 2015). The digital technologies have brought innovations, new designs, and learning modes to the ecosystem (Selander *et al.*, 2013). These changes, on one hand, challenged the core enterprises in the ecosystem (Christensen and Bower, 1996). For example, Kodak and Nokia descended from hegemons dramatically. On the other hand, these changes have also brought opportunities for the marginal enterprises to rise (Liu Linqing *et al.*, 2015). For instance, LETV, starting from providing marginal businesses, such as free videos, has gradually grown to be the core enterprise integrating "platforms, contents, terminals, and apps."

What are the underlying reasons behind those phenomena? How did the enterprises rise from margin to core applying digital technologies? The existing studies of the ecosystem focus on how the core enterprises evolve and how they govern the ecosystem (Wareham *et al.*, 2014; Adner and Kapoor, 2015), while there is lesser research focus on how the marginal enterprises build the ecosystem and grow to be the core (Yoo *et al.*, 2010; Selander *et al.*, 2013; Thomas *et al.*, 2014). The above phenomena also show that enterprises are not born to be the core. They usually have to rise from the marginal position in the ecosystem (Liu Linqing *et al.*, 2015).

The core enterprises dominate the entire business ecosystem (Teece, 2007), for they have control over the core resources (Perrigot and Pénard, 2013). So the main question is how to further leverage the key resources to maintain core positions. Resource orchestration emphasizes the need to orchestrate key resources in a dynamic environment and create value from those resources to generate sustainable competitive advantages (Sirmon *et al.*, 2011). The resource orchestration theory therefore is helpful to solve the above question.

In light of this, this thesis, based on resource orchestration theory, has a case study of Duch Group (hereinafter referred to as Duch), a leading enterprise in 3D printing. The author had a deep research of how marginal enterprises in the old ecosystem reconfigure it by orchestrating key resources like digital technologies and rise to the core position. This research provides guidance for marginal enterprises to reconfigure the ecosystem and acquire the core position by emerging digital technologies.

Literature review and framework analysis

Digital ecosystem and focal enterprises

In management research, "ecosystem" usually refers to a network com-posed of interconnected organizations surrounding a core enterprise (Teece, 2007; Adner and Kapoor, 2015) or platform (Gawer and Cusumano, 2002). The concept of ecosystem can help us understand that in business context, an enterprise should be regarded as one part of an ecosystem spanning multiple industries, rather than an individual in one single industry (Moore, 1993; Adner and Kapoor, 2015). The digital technologies will both help integrate the focal enterprises in the ecosystem to a large extent and help organizations better perceive and respond to environment changes (Tan *et al.*, 2009).This is an important factor driving the ecosystem into a digital one (Yamakami, 2010). The digital ecosystem bundles different interest groups by digital technologies (Tan *et al.*, 2009), forming stable or unstable federations based on common interests among focal enterprises (Koshutanski *et al.*, 2007).

According to the different dependency relations among focal enterprises in the ecosystem, the enterprises can be divided into three groups: keystone, dominators, and niche players (Lansiti and Levien, 2004a). The roles of keystone and dominators are mainly performed by core enterprises which can promote or hold back the sound development of business ecosystems (Lansiti and Levien, 2004b). The niche players, performing as participants, are marginal in the ecosystem. Depending on the core enterprises, they do not perform the key functions such as building or managing the network. This is because, firstly, the marginal enterprises are small and do not have the strong power to maintain the ecosystem development. Secondly, the resources and capabilities of the marginal enterprises are usually confined to some narrow professional area with which the other enterprises cannot create values (Lansiti and Levien, 2004a). So the marginal enterprises in this thesis are defined as subsidiary and supplementary enterprises mainly providing auxiliary or additional products.

The previous research of ecosystem mainly attaches importance to the evolution of core enterprises and ecosystem governance (Tiwana *et al.*, 2010; Ghazawneh and Henfridsson, 2013; Wareham *et al.*, 2014), hardly focusing on how the marginal enterprises build ecosystems and grow to be the core (Yoo *et al.*, 2010; Selander *et al.*, 2013; Thomas *et al.*, 2014). So it deserves our efforts to investigate these questions.

Resource orchestration

The resource-based view mainly explores the relations between resource properties and enterprises' competitive advantages, but ignores the studies of how managers utilize resources and how resources form and evolve (Wright and Stigliani, 2013; Sirmon *et al.*, 2011). So the resource-based view cannot explain why enterprises owning the same resource basis have different competitive positions (Kor *et al.*, 2007). Sirmon *et al.* (2011), on the basis of the static resource-based view, introduced a dynamic view and came up with the resource orchestration theory that managers' dynamic management of resources is the basis of enterprises' core capabilities and competitive advantages. Resource orchestration involves three actions: (1) Resource structuring: structure the focal resources by acquiring, accumulating, and divesting resources and then match them with the external environment; (2) resource bundling: establish core capabilities by stabilizing, enriching, and pioneering resources; (3) resource leveraging: take the advantages of market opportunities and create values by mobilizing, coordinating, and deploying resources (Sirmon *et al.*, 2011).

The resource orchestration theory subdivides the components of strategic resource management (Cui and Pan, 2014) and emphasizes that managers' dynamic role of resources exerts more influences on competitive advantages than resources themselves (Bridoux *et al.*, 2013). This also explains why owning same resources, some enterprises have superior performance to that of the others (Sirmon *et al.*, 2008). But the existing research of resource orchestration focuses on its components and its influences on the strategies or life cycles of enterprises (Sirmon *et al.*, 2011; Cui and Pan, 2014) while lacking in-depth discussions of how resource orchestration affects the dynamic evolution of enterprises.

Research methodology

Method and case selection

There are two reasons why the case study method is adopted. Firstly, the research aims to answer "how" marginal enterprises reconfigure the ecosystem and rise from the marginal position in the old ecosystem to the core in the new one. Since it belongs to the category of the "how" question, the case study method appears to be more appropriate (Yin, 2013). Secondly, since this study is going to reveal how marginal enterprises reconfigure the ecosystem by resource orchestration, a question the existing literature has not fully explained, the case study method will be more efficient than quantitative research in finding causalities (Ouyang Taohua, 2004; Yin, 2013).

There are also two reasons why Duch is taken as the case sample of this research. The first reason is that Duch is both the leading enterprise in the industry and the typical marginal enterprise which has risen to the core, complying with the principle that the case should be significant and representative (Patton, 1987). Secondly, the previous research of ecosystems does not attach enough importance to the interactions between resource orchestration and ecosystem reconfiguring of marginal enterprises, while Duch is closely related to the effective utilization of resources such as digital technologies while reconfiguring the ecosystem. So studying Duch's reconfiguring of ecosystems from the perspective of resource orchestration can improve the relevant theories of resource orchestration and ecosystem (Glaser and Strauss, 2009).

Data collection

Data were primarily collected from the following three sources: (1) semi-structured interviews conducted in November 2015, and interviewing a total of 13 informants (Table 1); (2) internal archival materials such as corporate annual reports, rules and regulations; and (3) public sources, including books, news, and publications written about Duch. The reason for collecting data from multiple sources was to establish a unique perspective incorporating both organizational "insiders" and "outsiders" points of view (Evered and Louis, 1981) and to triangulate the themes and conclusions (Miles and Huberman, 1984; Yin, 2013).

Table 1. Interview List and Topics

Position/Departments	The Number of Interviewees	Time Duration (hours)	Keywords
President	1	2.5	Strategic Estimate, Strategic Plan
International Trade Department	4	5	Product Sales, Customer Demands
Mold Development Department	3	3	Product R&D, Customer Feedback
Prototype Manufacturing Department	2	2	Customer Demands, Product Innovation
3D Printing Manufacturing Base	3	4	Product R&D, Technological Innovation

Data analysis

Data analysis was conducted simultaneously as data collection to take advantage of the flexibility that the case study method offers (Eisenhardt, 1989). Based on the collected data, to facilitate the investigation of digital ecosystem evolution with different resource orchestration actions, we divided the events and activities into three distinct phases: the gaining phase, integration phase, and expansion phase. The preliminary theoretical model was validated and revised accordingly by three independent steps.

First, the collected data were broken down into themes (Walsham, 2006), examined, compared for similarities and differences, and categorized (Corbin and Strauss, 2014), until a final set of themes was developed. This "open coding" method was conducted to eliminate unrelated data within the value of comments collected and its potential for variance (Corbin and Strauss, 2014). Second, we ensure that every piece of evidence which was used in the construction of the case study is triangulated by at least two sources of data (Yin, 2013) for the sake of eliminating bias in our interpretation. Third, we checked the alignment of existing theories, data, and the emergent model (Eisenhardt and Graebner, 2007) repeatedly. The data analysis followed an iterative process of shifting our research focus among empirical data, relevant literature, and the emerging model until theoretical saturation was reached (Pan and Tan, 2011).

Case description

Duch Group (Duch) was established in 1996. Starting business from rapid prototyping and extending its industry chain both upward and downward, it has now developed into an enterprise focusing on design and R&D and integrated equipment supply, R&D, sales and service all in one. By 2016, Duch had possessed eight wholly owned subsidiaries, covering nine ecosystems, namely smart products, aeronautics & astronautics, military equipment, cultural and creative products, environment-friendly equipment, medical apparatus, biotechnology, 3D printing design and development, and automobile design. Duch has become the leading enterprise with the largest scale and soundest supporting services for industrial design in the domestic industry. The process of the Duch reconfiguring ecosystem can be divided into three phases: the gaining phase, integration phase, and expansion phase.

Gaining phase: 3D printing technologies upgrade the manufacturing process

In 2003, Duch noticed that 3D printing would match the individualized market demands, but at that time, this technology had not been widely used. So Duch set up a specialized R&D team and cooperated with European teams who mastered the core technology of 3D printing to develop 3D control software and 3D printing equipment.

In 2012, Duch established the Vistar International 3D Printing Space and put the 3D printing technologies it had incubated for years into production line. The manufacturing process of 3D printing is 90% shorter than that of CNC machining. This is because, different from the complicated process of CNC, 3D printing only needs you to input orders to the computer and will transform design into products both quickly and accurately. Also, 3D printing is feasible in all kinds of product forms, breaking the technological limitations of CNC. So 3D printing has improved the productivity and resource efficiency. Besides, based on its accumulated craftsmanship, Duch added another procedure — surface treatment in the final stage, complementing 3D printing products' weakness of having bumpy surfaces, however many 3D printing enterprises do not attach importance to this aspect.

Acquiring 3D printing technologies, Duch who in the past could only produce molds has attained manufacturing abilities and shortened the manufacturing process. The corroborating evidence is presented in Table 2.

Integration phase: Digital technologies link all parts of the industry chain

In 2012, Duch planned to establish a 3D printing base. Applying 3D printing and Internet technologies, Duch could link customers with its internal design and manufacturing resources through two platforms: its client and base. Its client, with smart transforming software, can transform customer needs and ideas into production orders readable to 3D printers, enabling

Table 2. Gaining Phase: Resource Orchestration Actions and the Dynamic Evolution of Digital Ecosystems

Gaining Phase		Supporting Data
	Involving manufacturing	3D printing enables us to go beyond producing molds and to manufacture products more quickly
The effectiveness of reconfiguring the digital ecosystem	Shortening manufacturing process	The production process of CNC machining is divided into parts where design, manufacturing, and post-processing are independent. But 3D printing has integrated these parts and carried them on simultaneously, both simplifying structures and saving time
		In 2003, we cooperated with many European organizations to co-develop the control codes and equipment for 3D printing, trying to reduce costs. When 3D printing sprang up in China, we have already taken a leading position both in terms of technologies and costs
Resource orchestration actions	Acquiring, accumulating, and divesting	Since we produced prototypes for various global industries, we have accumulated many design resources and concepts in new materials, new craftsmanship, and new technologies. The capacities of 3D printing are three times as many as that of traditional CNC and the human resources' 3D uses are 90% less than that of CNC. So we have been making efforts to replace CNC machining with 3D printing

customers to perform as product designers. The base then will receive the production orders which will be put into production immediately. By doing so, Duch can reduce the storage cost, shorten production lead time, and achieve entire automation and instant sharing of information.

In 2013, Duch led to build a platform called "Pursuing Dream Alliance" through which Duch collected the resources of global designers and helped to realize their designs into samples for free. Then Duch would complete the first-round financing for the samples through crowdfunding sites

(Duch has established crowdfunding relations with Kickstarter, Taobao Crowdfunding, JD Finance, etc.) on the platform. This can complement Duch's weakness of lacking design professionals. Meanwhile, Duch has also combined this with the original offline sales channel, selling 3D printing products both online and offline. The "Pursuing Dream Alliance" has both explored external design resources and extended the sales channels.

In order to be less dependent on the vendors of 3D printing materials and equipment, Duch cooperated with both domestic and international professional manufacturers and developed the raw materials of 3D printing at half the price. Duch has also innovated the introduced 3D printing equipment, both improving the various machine models and reducing the equipment costs. After reducing the costs of raw materials and equipment, Duch sold these products through market segmentation and extended Duch's sources of profits and business scopes. This helped Duch enjoy cost advantages and improve its competitiveness.

The digital technologies, such as 3D printing and the Internet, enabled Duch to go beyond the traditional businesses, like design and mold making. Targeting customer needs, Duch has both integrated the stages of the industry chain, namely design, production, material supply, sales, logistics, and clients, and omitted storage and other procedures, shortening the original industry chain. The supporting evidence of the above content is presented in Table 3.

Expansion phase: 3D printing technologies expand the ecosystem boundaries

For manufacturing technology and material development, 3D printing is disruptive. Duch has a good command of 3D printing technologies, enabling it to utilize its expertise in design and extend the technologies to more ecosystems, like aeronautics and astronautics, auto spare parts, etc.

Duch is the only enterprise in industrial design having the qualification of military design, but in the past, it only did some businesses in appearance verification commissioned by some aeronautic and astronautic enterprises. Since the all-in-one manufacturing method of 3D printing can improve the products' structural stability and can be dealt with complicated products, this manufacturing method brought opportunities

Table 3. Integration Phase: Resource Orchestration Actions and the Dynamic Evolution of Digital Ecosystems

Integration Phase		Supporting Data
The effectiveness of reconfiguring the digital ecosystem	Shortening the industry chain	Duch integrated the R&D, production and sales of 3D printing, omitting the unnecessary links.
	Integrating the segments of the industry chain	Our idea is to form a closed-loop ecological chain for industrial design.
Resource orchestration actions	Pioneering and enriching	We have connected many global designers through "Pursuing Dream Alliance." The designers can print their products directly on this platform and conversely, their ideas can enrich our design library.

for Duch to design and produce aeronautic and astronautic products. 3D printing, however, cannot meet the demand that aeronautic and astronautic products must resist high temperature. So in order to solve this problem, Duch cooperated with external material vendors to co-develop high-temperature-resistant spray paints. This paint sprayed on the surface of 3D printing products can enhance the thermal resistance, meeting the demand that aeronautic and astronautic products must be solid and high-temperature-resistant. The 3D printing technology can be applied in the production of airplane parts, such as the wings, cradle heads, fuel tanks, and shields. Duch thus has received more orders from military enterprises, such as China Avionics Systems Co., Ltd. Table 4 contains supporting data to the above content.

Case analysis

The objective of this research is to build a model of how marginal enterprises reconfigure the ecosystem (refer to Figure 1). Analyzing Duch from the perspective of resource orchestration opens the black box of how traditional enterprises rise from the marginal position in the old ecosystem to the core

Table 4. Expansion Phase: Resource Orchestration Actions and the Dynamic Evolution of Digital Ecosystems

	Expansion Phase	Supporting Data
The effectiveness of reconfiguring the digital ecosystem	Enhancing original business boundaries	Applying 3D printing technologies, we have upgraded the traditional house decoration in its ways, materials, and craftsmanship
	Expanding business boundaries	Our design should be radiated to various areas, instead of being confined to cell phones or household appliances like refrigerators
Resource orchestration actions	Coordinating, pioneering, and deploying strategies	Considering that the all-in-one manufacturing method of 3D printing can enable the products to better match the designs, we started to cooperate with auto enterprises in the manufacturing of spare parts, such as bumpers, dashboards, and power unit shields

Phases	Gaining Phase	Integration Phase	Expansion Phase
Resource orchestration actions	**Acquiring** external R&D resources of digital technologies, **accumulating** internal design resources and **divesting** the production links of CNC 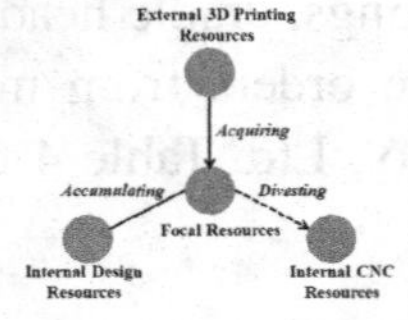	**Pioneering** external potential design resources and **enriching** internal platform resources 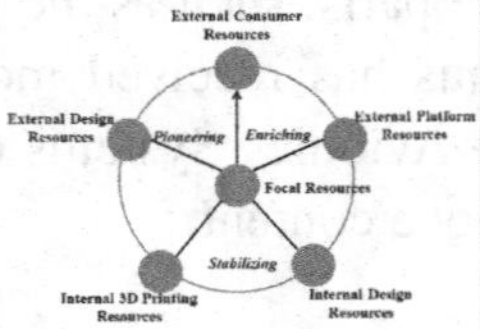	**Converting** internal manufacturing experience, **pioneering** business scopes and **deploying** new businesses in the ecosystem 
The process of reconfiguring the ecosystem	Reconfigure the manufacturing process	Reconfigure the industry chain	Reconfigure the boundary of the ecosystem
Outcome	Reconfigure to form a new ecosystem and transit from the marginal position in the old ecosystem to the core of the new one		

Figure 1. A Process Model of Resource Orchestration in Digital Ecosystem Evolution

Note: The Hollow Black Dots Represent Newly Added Resources.

in the new one. It can be found from this case that orchestrating key resources such as digital technologies, Duch has gradually completed its reconfiguring of the ecosystem.

Gaining phase: Resource orchestration contributes to reconfigure manufacturing process

In the traditional industry chain, industrial design is narrowly defined as appearance design. Holding a small share of the industry chain, the enterprises of industrial design are in the subsidiary and supplementary position. Duch, focusing on industrial design, was at the marginal place. As the customized age has come, the changes of the external environment have stimulated the enterprises to make changes, bringing opportunities for the enterprises featured by customized industrial designs to rise.

After realizing the external change tendencies, Duch implemented resource orchestration actions, including acquiring external 3D printing technologies, accumulating internal design resources, divesting redundant links, etc. (Sirmon *et al.*, 2007, Cui and Pan, 2014), to improve enterprise technical strength and match the external environment, then completed the reconfiguring of the manufacturing process (refer to Figure 2). Resource orchestration both equips Duch with customized manufacturing capacity (i.e. to design and shorten the manufacturing process) and provides the foundation for subsequently orchestrating resources to reconfigure the industry chain (Sirmon *et al.*, 2011).

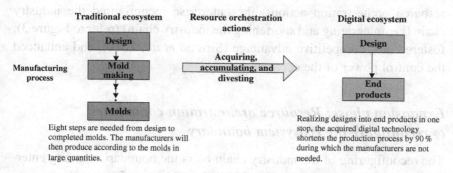

Figure 2. Resource Orchestration Propels Enterprises to Reconfigure the Manufacturing Process

Integration phase: Resource orchestration contributes to reconfigure the industry chain

The enterprises need to extend their own businesses for rising from the marginal position to the core of the industry chain (Jiang Xingming, 2014). The connectivity of digital technology enables many enterprises to connect their own businesses with external independent organizations or resources (Eamonn, 2015). In order to solve the problems that the segments of the industry chain are separated from each other and the customer needs cannot be satisfied one-off, Duch, applying digital technologies such as 3D printing and the Internet, started to extend its business to the upstream and downstream industry chain.

The 3D printing base enables Duch to transform customer designs into its own design resources through which Duch can help enterprises design and optimize products and co-create product values with them (Nambisan and Baron, 2007). The "Pursuing Dream Alliance" could integrate the resources of external designers into its own design platform, complementing Duch's weakness of lacking design professionals and integrating online and offline sales.

In a word, Duch, utilizing digital technologies, bundled the internal and external resources, both old and new, and also pioneered external potential design resources which enabled internalization (Sirmon *et al.*, 2011). By doing so, Duch has enriched its platform resources, strengthened its core competitiveness (Sirmon *et al.*, 2011), extended enterprise external relations (Gawer and Cusumano, 2002) for supporting continued growth (Jawahar and McLaughlin, 2001). By implementing a series of resource orchestration actions, the enterprise reconfigured the industry chain (i.e. integrating and shortening the industry chain) (refer to Figure 3), fostered new competitive advantage (Sirmon *et al.*, 2010), and enhanced the control power of the ecosystem.

Expansion phase: Resource orchestration contributes to reconfigure the ecosystem boundary

The reconfiguring of the industry chain blurs the boundaries among enterprises (Mao Yunshi and Ding Lan, 2006). Instead of confining to the original businesses, enterprises should leverage and transform the existing resources

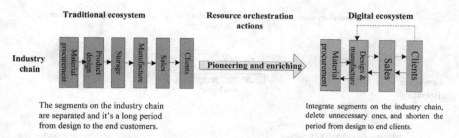

Figure 3. Resource Orchestration Propels Enterprises to Reconfigure the Industry Chain

and generate more comprehensive "solutions" to serve customers' rising expectations (Eamonn, 2015) and find new profit sources (Agarwal and Gort, 2002).

Owing to the fact that industrial design is in itself trans-boundary (Li Wanjun, 2014), Duch's traditional products are usually related to the cultural and creative industry and the industry of environmental protection equipment. Since the 3D printing technology plays a disruptive role in manufacturing technology and material development, Duch combined the existing craftsmanship with this printing technology. By doing so, Duch has met the demands of the aeronautic & astronautic and automobile enterprises, expanded the business scopes of its products, and acquired new profit sources.

Duch deployed and pioneered its business to more ecosystems (Sirmon *et al.*, 2011) by converting its internal craftsmanship and combining it with 3D printing technology (refer to Figure 4). This has both expanded the boundary of the new ecosystem (i.e. strengthening and expanding the ecosystem boundary) to exert greater influence and strengthened its position as the core of the new ecosystem (Smith *et al.*, 1985).

In summary, adhering to the "point–line–surface" principle, Duch has implemented resource orchestration actions on key resources such as digital technologies to carry out three steps successively: "upgrading the vertical production process, reconfiguring the manufacturing process to achieve end-to-end connectivity," "reconfiguring the industry chain to expand the horizontal business scope" and "reconfiguring the ecosystem boundaries." This has changed the situation where the segments of traditional industry chains are separated and reconfigured a new ecosystem focusing on industrial design with an integrated vertical industry chain

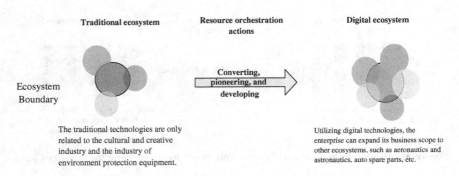

Figure 4. Resource Orchestration Propels Enterprises to Reconfigure the Ecosystem Boundary

and expanded boundaries. Meanwhile, Duch has also risen from the marginal position in the old ecosystem to the core of the new one.

Conclusion

Theoretical and practical contributions

This case study highlights implications for researchers and practitioners. For researchers, firstly, this case study has complemented the existing theories by opening the black box of how resource orchestration drives marginal enterprises to reconfigure the digital ecosystem. The existing studies of resource orchestration focus on its components (Sirmon *et al.*, 2011) while not attaching enough importance to how resource orchestration influences the dynamic evolution of enterprises. It is found by analyzing this case that the marginal enterprises cannot reconfigure the ecosystem except by orchestrating focal resources and different resource orchestration outcomes are displayed in different phases. Secondly, this research has built the model of how marginal enterprises reconfigure the ecosystem. Research on this question is in shortage (Yoo *et al.*, 2010; Thomas *et al.*, 2014), and this thesis will complement the ecosystem theories by building a model of how marginal enterprises reconfigure the ecosystem through the "point–line–surface" principle.

This study also provides practical implications. The emerging digital technologies have brought both opportunities and challenges to traditional enterprises. If they cannot develop independently and extend their businesses to multiple industries, the marginal enterprises, affected by "non-independence", cannot free themselves from being controlled by the core enterprises. The case study of Duch has opened the black box of how marginal enterprises reconfigure the ecosystem by resource orchestration, providing theoretical guidance for them about how to rise. The enterprises need to effectively orchestrate the key resources like digital technologies to hold a more important position in the ecosystem.

Limitation

This research casts light on how marginal enterprises reconfigure the ecosystem from the perspective of resource orchestration and also puts forward some conclusions of both theoretical and practical values. But it also has some shortcomings. The research objectives are traditional and mature enterprises. They have adequate R&D resources and craftsmanship which will help them solve the problems in reconfiguring the ecosystem. But for the small-scale emerging enterprises, while building or reconfiguring the ecosystem, are the conclusions of this research still applicable? So we will further collect and analyze enterprise cases of other kinds and reveal the reconfiguring process and mechanism of Chinese enterprises in a systematic manner.

References

Adner, R., and Kapoor, R. 2015. "Innovation Ecosystems and the Pace of Substitution: Reexamining Technology S curves." *Strategic Management Journal*, 3, 1–24.

Agarwal, R., and Gort, M. 2002. "Products and Firm Life Cycles and Firm Survival." *American Economic Review*, 92, 184–190.

Bridoux, F., Smith, K. G., and Grimm, C. M. 2013. "The Management of Resources Temporal Effects of Different Types of Actions on Performance." *Journal of Management*, 39(4), 928–957.

Christensen, C. M., and Bower, J. L. 1996. "Customer Power, Strategic Investment, and the Failure of Leading Firms." *Strategic Management Journal*, 17(3), 197–218.

Corbin, J., and Strauss, A. 2014. *"Basics of Qualitative Research: Techniques and Procedures for Developing Grounded Theory,"* Thousand Oaks, CA, Sage Publications.

Cui, M., and Pan, S. L. 2014. "Developing Focal Capabilities for E-Commerce Adoption: A Resource Orchestration Perspective." *Information & Management*, 52(2), 200–209.

Eisenhardt, K. M. 1989. "Building Theories from Case Study Research." *"Academy of Management Review,"* 14(4), 532–550.

Eisenhardt, K. M., and Graebner, M. E. 2007. "Theory Building from Cases: Opportunities and Challenges." *Academy of Management Journal*, 50(1), 25.

Evered, R., and Louis, M. R. 1981. "Alternative Perspectives in the Organizational Sciences: 'Inquiry from the Inside' and 'Inquiry from the Outside.'" *Academy of Management Review*, 6(3), 385–395.

Gawer, A., and Cusumano, M. A. 2002. *"Platform Leadership: How Intel, Microsoft, and Cisco Drive Industry Innovation."* Harvard Business School Press, Boston.

Ghazawneh, A., and Henfridsson, O. 2013. "Balancing Platform Control and External Contribution in Third-party Development: The Boundary Resources Model." *Information Systems Journal*, 23(2), 173–192.

Iansiti, M., and Levien, R. 2004a. The Keystone Advantage: What the New Dynamics of Business Ecosystems Mean for Strategy, Innovation, and Sustainability. *Personnel Psychology*, 20(2), 88–90.

Iansiti, M., and Levien, R. 2004b. "Strategy as Ecology." *Harvard Business Review*, 82(3), 68–81.

Jawahar, I. M., and McLaughlin, G. L. 2001. "Toward a Descriptive Stakeholder Theory: An Organizational Life Cycle Approach." *Academy of Management Review*, 26, 397–414.

Jiang Xingming 2014. "Industrial Transformation and Upgrading Connotation Way Research." *Inquiry into Economic Issues*, 12, 43–49.

Kor, Y. Y., Mahoney J. T., and Michael, S. C. 2007. "Resources, Capabilities and Entrepreneurial Perceptions." *Journal of Management Studies*, 44(7), 1187–1212.

Koshutanski, H., Ion M., and Telesca, L. 2007. "Distributed Identity Management Model for Digital Ecosystems," In *The International Conference on Emerging Security Information, Systems, and Technologies (SECUREWARE 2007)*, Valencia, pp. 132–138. Doi: 10.1109/SECUREWARE.2007.4385323.

Li Wanjun. 2014. "Discuss the Spanning Design of Industrial Design," *Art Education Research*, 24, 95–95.

Liu Linqing, Tan Chang, Jiang Shi-song, and Lei Hao. 2015. "Li Feng's Process of Platform Leadership Achievement: A Resource Dependence Perspective." *China Industrial Economics*, (1), 134–146.

Luo Min, and Li Liang-yu 2015. "The Age of the Internet Business Model Innovation: Value Creation Perspective." *China Industrial Economics*, 1, 95–107.

Mao Yunshi, and Ding Lan. 2006. "Technological Advancement and the Blur of Industrial Borderlines: Strategic Reactions of Corporation and Meanings of Governmental Policies," *Journal of Sun Yatsen University*, 46(4), 109–113.

Miles, M. B., and Huberman, A. M. 1984. "Drawing Valid Meaning from Qualitative Data: Toward a Shared Craft," *Educational researcher*, 13(5), 20–30.

Moore, J. F. 1993. "Predators And Prey: A New Ecology of Competition." *Harvard Business Review*, 71(3), 75–83.

Nambisan, S., and Baron, R. A. 2007. "Interactions in Virtual Customer Environments: Implications for Product Support and Customer Relationship Management." *Journal of Interactive Marketing*, 21(2), 42–62.

Ouyang Taohua. 2004. "Case Study Method in the Field of Business Administration." *Nankai Business Review*, 7(2), 100–105.

Pan, S. L., and Tan, B. 2011. "Demystifying Case Research: A Structured–Pragmatic–Situational (SPS) Approach to Conducting Case Studies." *Information and Organization*, 21(3), 161–176.

Patton, M. Q. 1987. *"How to Use Qualitative Methods in Evaluation,"* Thousand Oaks, CA, Sage.

Perrigot, R., and Pénard, T. 2013. "Determinants of E-Commerce Strategy in Franchising: A Resource-Based View." *International Journal of Electronic Commerce*, 17(3), 109–130.

Selander, L., Henfridsson, O., and Svahn, F. 2013. "Capability Search and Redeem across Digital Ecosystems." *Journal of Information Technology*, 28(3), 183–197.

Sirmon, D. G., Gove, S., and Hitt, M. A. 2008. "Resource Management in Dyadic Competitive Rivalry: the Effects of Resource Bundling and Deployment." *Academy of Management Journal*, 51(5), 919–935.

Sirmon, D. G., Hitt, M. A., Arregle, J.-L., and Campbell, J. T. 2010. "Capability Strengths and Weaknesses in Dynamic Markets: Investigating the Bases of Temporary Competitive Advantage." *Strategic Management Journal*, 31(13), 1386–1409.

Sirmon, D. G., Hitt, M. A., Ireland, R. D., and Gilbert, B. A. 2011. "Resource Orchestration to Create Competitive Advantage Breadth, Depth, and Life Cycle Effects." *Journal of Management*, 37(5), 1390–1412.

Smith, K. G., Mitchell, T. R., and Summer, C. E. 1985. "Top Level Management Priorities in Different Stages of the Organizational Life Cycle." *Academy of Management Journal*, 28, 799–820.

Tan, B., Pan, S. L., Lu, X., and Huang, L. 2009. "Leveraging Digital Business Ecosystems for Enterprise Agility: the Tri-Logic Development Strategy of Alibaba. com." In *ICIS 2009 Proceedings*, p. 171.

Teece, D. J. 2007. "Explicating Dynamic Capabilities: the Nature and Microfoundations of (Sustainable) Enterprise Performance." *Strategic Management Journal*, 28(13), 1319–1350.

Thomas, L., Autio, E., and Gann, D. 2014. "Architectural Leverage: Putting Platforms in Context," *Academy of Management Perspectives*, 28(2), 198–219.

Tiwana, A., Konsynski, B., and Bush, A. A. 2010. "Research Commentary-Platform Evolution: Coevolution of Platform Architecture, Governance, and Environmental Dynamics." *Information Systems Research*, 21(4), 675–687.

Walsham, G. 2006. "Doing Interpretive Research." *European Journal of Information Systems*, 15(3), 320–330.

Wareham, J., Fox, P. B., and Cano Giner, J. L. 2014. "Technology Ecosystem Governance." *Organization Science*, 25(4), 1195–1215.

Yamakami, T. 2010. "A Mobile Digital Ecosystem Framework: Lessons from the Evolution of Mobile Data Services, In *2010 13th International Conference on. IEEE*, Hoboken, New Jersey, pp. 516–520.

Yin, R. K. 2013. "*Case Study Research: Design and Methods*." Sage Publications, London.

Yoo, Y., Henfridsson, O., and Lyytinen, K. 2010. "Research Commentary — The New Organizing Logic of Digital Innovation: An Agenda for Information Systems Research." *Information Systems Research*, 21(4), 724–735.

Chapter 7

Red Collar Group: Transform Towards Smart Manufacturing

Jing (Elaine) Chen

Beihang Univerisity
37 Xueyuan Road, Beijing
China

Shan L. Pan

University of New South Wales
UNSW Sydney NSW 2052
Australia

Qingfeng Zeng

Shanghai University of Finance and Economics
777 Guoding Road, Shanghai
China

Abstract

Red Collar Group (RCG) is an apparel manufacturer specialized in personalized suits. It took over 10 years for the company to achieve smart manufacturing, so the company could produce personalized suits in the same production line with the efficiency of mass manufacturing. This chapter introduces the key actions carried out by RCG to achieve its transformation, namely, accumulate data systematically, establish standards for data collection, and redefine business processes.

Keywords: Smart manufacturing, Big data, Transformation, Case, Digital enablement.

Red collar group (RCG)

Founded in 1995, RCG is an apparel manufacturer headquartered in Jimo, Shandong, P. R. China (see Figure 1). With around 5,000 employees and an annual revenue of over 300 million USD, the company is now a major producer of high-grade personalized suits in the global market, serving tailor shops all over the world.

Just like any other traditional manufacturer, RCG started its business by taking bulk orders from clients, for instance, an order of 800 sets of uniforms. It took the company over 10 years to acquire the expertise in making clothes, and being capable of producing the personalized suits represents the mastery of such expertise — it takes over 300 procedures to complete a set of suits; and for each procedure, customers may have

Figure 1. The End Product Corner of Personalized Suits

hundreds of options. Given such high complexity, personalized suits production traditionally is highly expensive and time consuming. Specifically, it takes 3–6 months' manual work to complete one set of suits, and a highly skilled production line of personalized suits can only complete five sets each day, even with a very limited range of options.

Mr. Daili Zhang, the founder of RCG, has been challenging such a tradition of producing personalized suits for over 10 years. He believes in the business potential of personalized suits in response to the growing market need on customization, and he also believes in the possibility to be a game changer in the digital era. Specifically, as the digital technology advancements enable organizations to perform more efficiently, effectively, and intelligently, the previously highly time-consuming and labor-intensive customized operations could be carried out in a much economic way. Under Zhang's vision, RCG embarked on a bold adventure in 2003 in order to transform its traditional production line towards the mode of smart manufacturing.

After 12 years endeavor, the company as now become a role model in smart manufacturing. RCG is able to provide a wide range of customization options to customers and deliver the products 7 days after the order placement at only 1.1 times the cost of mass production. Moreover, the company can produce over 3,000 sets of personalized suits each day. How did RCG achieve it?

Red collar's transformational journey

Accumulate data systematically

The transformation started from the systematic accumulation of data across the whole business process along the adoption of a series of enterprise systems.

Initially, the company adopted an enterprise resource planning (ERP) system to manage order production in 2002, so that the company started to accumulate operational data along the business processes. Then the company developed an order placement system for personalized clothes, and gradually made it an online platform to take orders in 2007. In order to meet the need of customization, the company gradually accumulated a large database regarding all the possible options, such as the catalogue of textile with technical parameters, the catalogue of styles (for instance, different styles of collar or neckline), etc. Meanwhile, the order information documented in the order placement system as well as the later developed Warehouse Management Systems (WMSs), are also critical data resources.

By doing so, the company had gradually prepared the necessary raw data for smart manufacturing mode, and had developed its own understanding of the business process under such modes.

Establish standards for data collection

In addition to the data accumulation, the company needed to establish standardized data collection approach for the traditionally non-standardized business process, in particular, taking the body measurements for personalized suits as well as clothing pattern making.

Taking body measurements is a critical step for producing fitted suits, and it is even more so for producing personalized suits. With accurate body measurements, tailors can design the right patterns of cloth to be cut out for sewing. Traditionally, only very experienced tailors are competent to do the measurements and pattern making, and the whole process of each order can only be done one by one manually, which severely hinders the efficiency of order production.

To address this issue, RCG created its own body measurement approach after a long period of trial-and-error. Instead of the non-standardized method that can only be operated by experienced tailors but cannot be well replicated, the new approach generates a set of standardized data comprising 22 parameters. Such a standardized approach can be learned simply by taking a 7-day training course.

Moreover, with a standardized body measurement, the company can better reuse previous clothing patterns. Since all the business process data, including the clothing patterns of each order and its corresponding measurements, have been documented digitally, it would be possible to repeat the clothing patterns if the size matches. Accordingly, the company implemented a Business Logics (BLs) system in order to match the measurements and its clothing patterns. Meanwhile, the company developed an advanced size chart with over 9,600 sizes based on its standardized measurement approach in contrast with the typical 8-size chart (i.e. from XXS, XS… to XXXL). Accordingly, the clothing patterns are also better categorized.

Redefine business processes

With the aforementioned data sets and standards, RCG started to redefine its business process. For instance, based on the standardized body measurement approach, catalog of clothing patterns, and BL systems, RCG reversed the sequence between taking measurements and making clothing patterns. Traditionally, a tailor's shop needs to take all the measurements of the customer, and then make the clothing patterns accordingly. However, with the large dataset and powerful Computer Aided Design (CAD) technology, when providing a new style for sales, RCG generates the clothing patterns of each size for its huge size charts. The time-consuming manual pattern making process (it could take up to a month in the past) was then replaced by a series of information queries that could be automatically done within 5 minutes.

Figure 2. RCG's Production Line with Intensive Usage of IT

Moreover, the company leveraged on its enterprise systems and Radio-Frequency Identification (RFID) technology to reconstruct its production line. Based on the enterprise systems, which record the detailed information of every piece of material used for an order, a worker no longer simply repeats the same operations on the same materials for the bulk orders. Instead, every order a worker operated on may involve different materials and different actions. Each piece of material is transmitted with an RFID label to remark related order information. With a smart hanging system developed by the company, these personalized materials can be automatically, accurately, and efficiently delivered to the worker in charge of operating. Once the worker scans the RFID label, the detailed instruction on the operations will be shown on the screen for the workers to follow (see Figure 2). In such ways, the whole production line turned out to be highly flexible and could produce personalized suits at the speed of mass manufacturing.

Acknowledgments

Funding for this research was provided by China's NSFC (71529001).

Chapter 8

Data Connection: Scene Marketing Creates Demand

Daojun Sun

Case Center of the Economic and Management School
Communication University of China
No.1 Dingfuzhuang East Street, Chaoyang District
Beijing, 100024, P. R. China
sundaojun@cuc.edu.cn

Yanyan Wang

Case Center of the Economic and Management School
Communication University of China
No.1 Dingfuzhuang East Street, Chaoyang District
Beijing, 100024, P. R. China
1143996771@qq.com

Chunhu Cui

Case Center of the Economic and Management School,
Communication University of China
No.1 Dingfuzhuang East Street, Chaoyang District
Beijing, 100024, P. R. China
1642974622@qq.com

121

Abstract

Tea is one of the flagship products in the Chinese beverage market. After more than a decade's rapid growth, excessive production capacity of the tea beverage market triggered slow growth and performance decline, especially when China's economy entered a new normal. Some brands chose to stay out of the market and some struggled. However, Master Kong tea beverage, which is the object of this research, acts in positive innovation, and strives to explore new marketing methods and modes, creates new demands and pursues new growth points by observing changes of the consumer market by virtue of big data. Based on the analysis of Master Kong's practice, the author creatively indicated the basic logic of building marketing scenes through data connection, put forward three dimensions for scene construction, that is, time, space, and relationship. Thus, the scene consists of three elements: experience, connection, and community. Data performs connection function in scene construction.

Keywords: Scene marketing, Scene dimension, Scene element, Data connection.

Introduction

This chapter has briefly proposed that firms could build market scenes through data connection and create new needs based on the scene. To illustrate this, we adopt the case of Master Kong, who has collaborated with Baidu Map to convince consumers that Master Kong green tea is highly relevant for a healthy lifestyle and a achieved huge marketing success. In this case, Master Kong created a sentiment through experience process by connecting time, space, people, things, and other elements closely with fundamental facilities (smartphone, sensor, cloud computing, and big data, etc.), and consequently creates great experience feelings and promotes spontaneous shared wide spreading. It is believed that this topic (scene marketing building through data connections) and case study are really novel and interesting, in which how scene marketing using big data could help firms to achieve better marketing performance is discussed.

Market trend requires new growth

In 2014, Master Kong, a tea beverage brand that took a leading part in the Chinese tea beverage market, had deteriorating performances (detailed in Figure 1) for 50 months successive (detailed in Figures 1 and 2). With the slow growth of soft beverage, it seemed that Master Kong could not turn the tide no matter how it tried and tried. According to Master Kong's internal analysis and diagnosis, the Chinese tea beverage market had ushered in more than a decade's rapid growth since it was listed in 2001 and consequently Master Kong held the leading position through the strategic consciousness of quantity. Nevertheless, the tea beverage market appeared to face difficulties such as slow growth and excess production capacity in 2012 just as other traditional manufacturing industries, so transformation and upgrading became an inevitable choice for Master Kong. Confined to traditional market competition, the road for development would become increasingly narrow!

China has a long history of tea consumption, which lays a cultural foundation for the long existence of the tea beverage market; meanwhile,

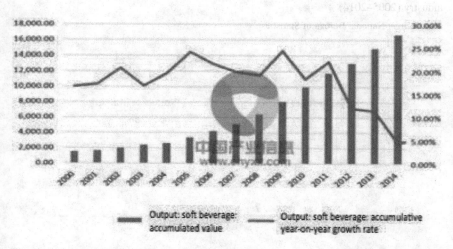

Figure 1. Accumulative output (10,000 t) and year-on-year growth rate of soft beverage industry (2000–2014)

Data source: National Bureau of Statistics.

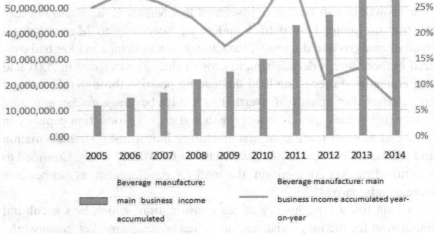

Figure 2. Accumulated income (10,000 Yuan) and year-on-year growth rate of beverage industry (2005–2014)

Data source: National Bureau of Statistics.

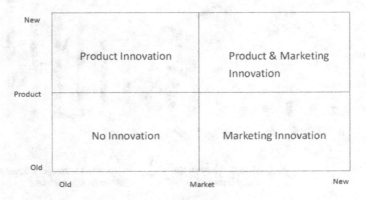

Figure 3. Market Growth Model

innovation of tea beverages is limited, that is, production innovation is very difficult for the tea beverage market. Thus, Master Kong can strive to create new demands and expand new markets through marketing innovation (as shown in Figure 3).

Precision insight based on big data

Consumer characteristics

According to Baidu indexes, Master Kong green tea has a consumer group aged 20–39 in first-tier and second-tier cities, where male consumers cover 71%. Promotion marketing focuses on behavioral demands of young male consumers after 80s and 90s.

According to the investigation of the Beijing Hylink Advertising Digital Marketing Institute, the generations after 80s and 90s have a high degree of dependency on social network, they leaf through smartphones more than 43 times every day, more than 60% of them are moderately

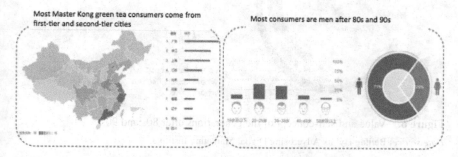

Figure 4. Baidu indexes of Master Kong green tea consumer insight

Data source: Baidu Marketing Institute.

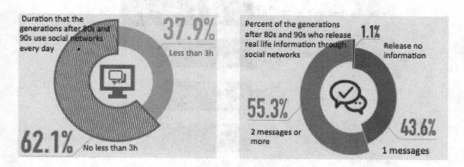

Figure 5. Social networking attributes of the generations after 80s and 90s

Date source: Beijing Hylink Advertising Digital Marketing Institute.

severe users who browse social networks at least 3 hours every day, that is, they spend no less than 20% of time on "surfing" social networks every day. As a result, such media habits as demand immediacy, information fragmentization and social contact activation are reflected.

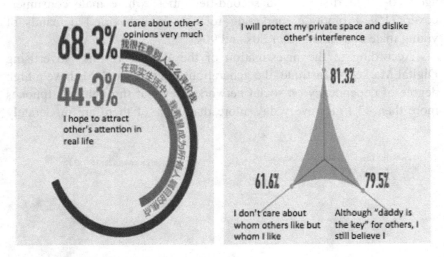

Figure 6.   Value and self-concept of the generations after 80s and 90s

Date source: Beijing Hylink Advertising Digital Marketing Institute.

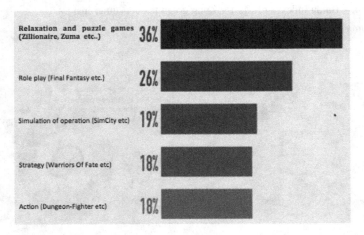

Figure 7.   Top five favorite games of the generations after 80s and 90s

Date source: Beijing Hylink Advertising Digital Marketing Institute.

The generations after 80s and 90s prefer to believe in personal efforts and hope to be independent. Although they still have dreams like youths, they lead a utilitarian and real life; meanwhile, they have been protected by families and get used to be concerned and recognized. All these are typical intergenerational characteristics between the generation after 80s and the generation after 90s.

The generations after 80s and 90s show a great interest in involvement and personal experience. According to investigation of Beijing Hylink Advertising Digital Marketing Institute, top five favorite games for the generations after 80s and 90s are relaxation and puzzle, role-play, simulation of operation, strategy, and action, which reflect their demands for involvement and integration.

Market opportunity

(1) All-people healthy life style and fitness trends are advocated: According to investigation of Baidu Marketing Institute, health and health maintenance have been a public topic among different age groups in recent years. Particularly, such keywords as "weight loss, fitness, calorie, Mermaid Line and Firm-abs" were widely spread among the generations after 80s and 90s and health became the key topic (Yang Yi and Guan Yu, 2010).

(2) Marketing expansion of fragmented time: The generations after 80s and 90s can hardly pay attention. Practice has proved that an effective way of attracting attention is to design an application, an activity or a game; all-media coverage of fragmented environments is also an important means of attracting attention.

(3) Scene marketing: It is a scene that consumers are attracted to participate in an application, an activity or a game by health concept, that is, consumers are encouraged to experience health and play roles. (Yu Mengni, 2015).

(4) Consumer awareness and recognition of Master Kong: Master Kong's rich brand assets can win the trust from consumers to participate in activities.

Marketing thought

Based on consumer and market insights, a conclusion was drawn that, even though Master Kong green tea had a solid market base in the Chinese soft beverage market, major consumers changed their life styles and hobbies, and the ways of cognizing product value and selecting products were very different from those of the generations after 60s and 70s, which were the primary causes of contraction in demand and descent in achievements. Thus, Master Kong realized that marketing innovation should focus on two aspects:

First, Master Kong should "play" with the generations after 80s and 90s, attract them to get involved and create a trust relationship based on interaction among media, brand, and consumers with the aim of establishing a new and valuable identity-based activity system.

Second, Master Kong should spread the concept of "Master Kong healthy life style" to consumers through customized marketing programs and improve brand awareness and social value.

Third, Master Kong needs to rebuild relations with consumers. According to Jenkins's point of view, because in the new market economy, marketing is moving from the existing media channels to a part of people's daily lives, people's activities began to be more and more shared, rather than those that are designed to grab attention (Jenkins, 2006).

Marketing practice based on mapping media

Under the impetus of Marketing Department, Master Kong's marketing company and Baidu established a Master Kong green tea innovative marketing team and proposed an O2O scene marketing program based on life style and value orientation of the generations after 80s and 90s: "green tea green and healthy walking" promotion activity:

Concepts

All-people deambulation (walking), correlate Master Kong green tea with healthy and low-carbon life style, enhance brand value, and popularize brand reputation.

Contents

- Play with consumers through Baidu map, grasp the need for travelling, respond to healthy and low-carbon life style, join activities through navigation, integrate time segments, acquire and share prizes.
- Master Kong and Baidu map carry out O2O scene marketing and popularize Master Kong green tea in the navigation process combined with young people's need for walking navigation.

Processes

Step 1

Enter Baidu map (see Figure 8).

Integrate new version, promote healthy walking through soft marketing.

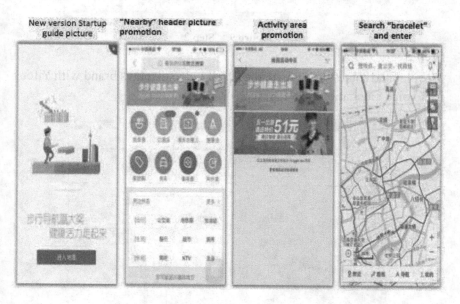

Figure 8. Step 1

Step 2

Enter walking navigation module for route planning, then "follow me" can be customized (see Figure 9).

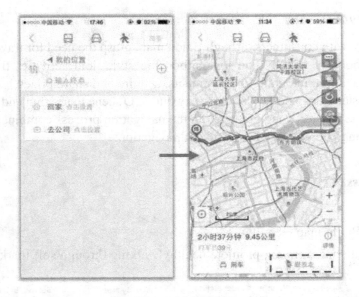

Figure 9.   Step 2

Step 3

The planned route turns green, the scroll video displays brand with Yifeng
Li's voice navigation (see Figure 10).

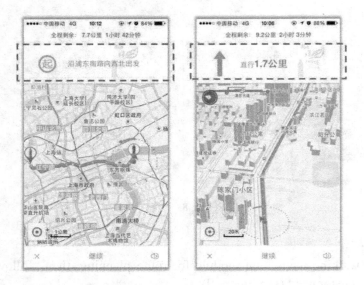

Figure 10.   Step 3

Step 4

Enter activity page, share results, exchange credits, and attract users via media transmission (see Figure 11).

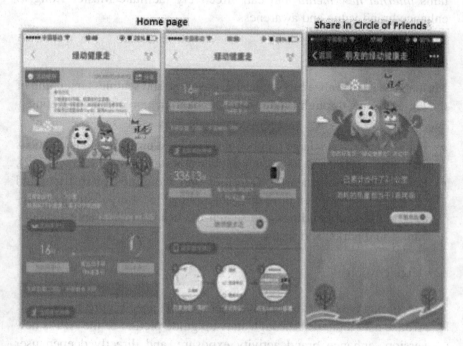

Figure 11. Step 4

Guide resource

- SEM
- Post-bar first picture
- Post-bar sticky post
- Baidu map official WeChat
- Master Kong green tea official MicroBlog
- Metro/platform side advertising
- TV advertising

Media advantages of Baidu map

Baidu map can provide innovative scene marketing through LBS and scene design. Different from traditional media, such scene marketing contains *internet new media* and can effectively facilitate Master Kong to enhance brand value and awareness.

(1) High precision

Master Kong can realize high-precision coverage and seamless matching of the target groups through Baidu map and maximize precision marketing.

- Baidu map covers a large number of users, most users are the generations after 80s and 90s aged 20–39, where male users cover 78% (see Figure 12).
- Baidu map covers nearly 400 cities and thousands of districts and counties. Users can enquire the geographical location of streets, shopping malls, and buildings and search the nearest restaurants, schools, banks, and parks, and so on.

(2) High coverage

- Baidu map is one of the popular mobile APPs (see Figure 13).
- Arouse user's interest through start-up guide picture of the APP's new version, enhance brand activity exposure, and directly deepen user impression.

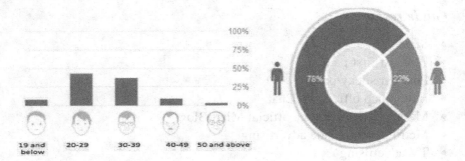

Figure 12. Baidu indexes of Baidu map target users

Data source: Baidu Marketing Institute.

排名	APP名称	2015年02月活跃用户数 (万)
1	微信	38711.06
2	QQ	29497.53
3	百度	14406.89
4	QQ浏览器	11655.29
5	搜狗手机输入法	11005.95
6	淘宝	10458.87
7	百度地图	10334.33
8	UC浏览器	9215.47
9	360手机卫士	8589.44
10	腾讯新闻	8352.18

Figure 13. Ranking list of mobile APPs in February 2015

Data source: Baidu Marketing Institute.

- Supported by many media and resource products subordinate to Baidu, grasp target groups enhance activity experience through map navigation scene marketing, enable users to feel Master Kong green tea's healthy and rational life attitude, popularize social networks through users, and attract more attention to activities.

Marketing effect

Advertiser appeal matching degree

Spread a healthy life style and enhance brand awareness and social value of Master Kong green tea through "green and healthy walking" activity.

Cover target groups accurately, help users to gradually establish the relevance between walking and Master Kong green tea and provide Master Kong green tea with a new market of walking consumption.

Social influence

(1) Influence

Cover target groups accurately through Baidu's high-quality media resources, effectively promote Master Kong green tea's "green and healthy walking" activity combined with hot topics, and popularize brand value and concept.

(2) Public opinion and praise

Walking is an all-people deambulation that not only is conducive to health and low-carbon environmental protection, but also spreads a healthy life style and enhances brand value and public praise.

Goal attainment degree

According to data, the activity reaches the expected effect and realizes a high coverage degree of target groups, a high degree of involvement, and a high attention.

The number of participants is predicted to be 120 million, but the actual number reaches 240 million, the interaction rate reaches up to 201% and is far higher than the expected value.

Effect Demonstration

(1) Extremely high user attention

Since Master Kong green tea's green and healthy walking activity was launched in April 2015, the average daily retrieval rate has soared and reached the peak in June (see Figure 14). It maintained a high user attention and the mobile user attention reached above 70%. Compared with Uniform green tea's bike riding activity in 2013, the retrieved data showed a low user attention.

"Green and healthy walking" activity enables Master Kong green tea to realize perfect combination between walker's instant demands and brand concept through Baidu map walking navigation.

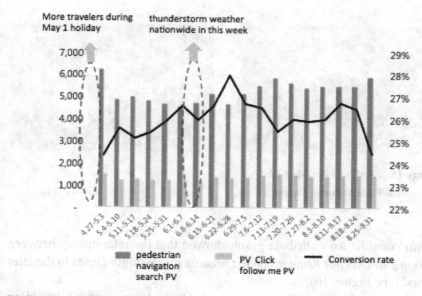

Figure 14. Activity effect data I

Data source: Baidu Marketing Institute.

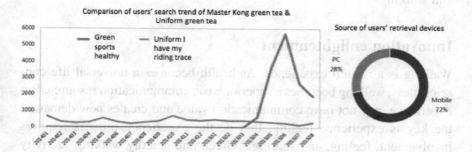

Figure 15. Activity effect data II

Data source: Baidu Marketing Institute.

(2) Relevance between walking and Master Kong green tea has been greatly enhanced

"Green and healthy walking" activity enables users to gradually establish the relevance between walking and Master Kong green tea (see Figure 15).

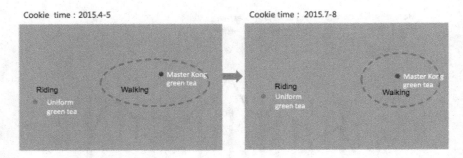

Figure 16. Activity effect data III
Data source: Baidu Marketing Institute.

Baidu compass user attribute graph showed that the relationship between walking and Master Kong green tea became increasingly closer in the later period (see Figure 16).

However, Uniform green tea had a higher relevance with bike riding (which was launched 3 years ago), so Master Kong should carry out more marketing activities in order to enhance the relevance between brands and walking.

Innovation enlightenment

Walking is a natural experience. As health becomes a universal life consciousness, walking becomes a superior basic communication resource. But experience may not have communication value and creates new demands, the key is experience feeling, that is, the experience process requires involvement, feeling, and sharing. "Green and healthy walking" activity closely connects time, space, people, things, and other elements and creates a sentiment through experience process and fundamental facilities (smartphone, sensor, cloud computing, and big data, etc.), and consequently creates great experience feelings and promotes spontaneous shared wide spreading; consumers gain the initiative in the walking process. The passion that participants create stories and spare no efforts to publicizing the leading role is self-evident. We gain enlightenments from Master Kong's practice as follows:

1. Customization: Focus on user needs, design and activity enable young people to "play" together: grasp young TA's traveling demands through entry-level mobile APP-Baidu map, gather attention segments through walking navigation, trigger social sharing through reward mechanism after users complete navigation, and participate in activities.

2. Integration into daily life: Walking is an all-people deambulation that is conducive to health and low-carbon environmental protection. According to time fragmentization of city dwellers and considering the need for fitness of the generations after 80s and 90s, commuters can increase or decrease the walking time voluntarily and will be rewarded through accumulated steps of the bracelet so that users can spread a healthy life style and the brand value personally.

3. Scene construction: With mature technologies, scene-marketing strategies should be constructed in three aspects, that is, time, space, and relationship. In this chapter, consumer's commuting route or walking route at their leisure constituted a scene through LBS technique, brand and commercial activities became a part of consumer life, resulting in strong experience feelings and impulse sharing as well as "extraordinary" propagation effects. Suppose time, space, and relationship constitute a scene, then experience, connection, and community create a scene. Based on people-oriented idea, the role of brand changes: mobile internet constitutes a scene based on experience, connection, and community, and brand becomes a participant of the scene.

4. O2O interaction: The activity is carried out from April to August in spring and summer. Walkers will feel thirsty and thus the consuming willingness is triggered, besides, the activity stretches across two peak tourist seasons May Day and summer vacation. Master Kong green tea has mature brand awareness and wide marketing channels, so most stores along the walking route sell Master Kong green tea or beverage series, in other words, marketing activities provide an offline consumer environment attentively and implicitly.

5. Data connection: A brand new closed-loop marketing system is constructed through mobile Internet technologies such as LBS, mobile APP display, cloud computing, WeChat Payment, and big data as well as "scene construction + field service." It can enhance brand's service ability to create and contact with users and create an integrated scene

application experience for users on the spot. Moreover, it facilitates to develop user habit of participating in and experiencing commercial activities through Scan and Shake, and even encourages users to shop online "unintentionally" and realizes effective connectivity between users and merchants. Finally, it realizes connectivity between consumers and connectivity between consumers and the society in the experience process, makes experience sharing and interaction a fashion, creates new demands, and expands new markets.

References

Henry Jenkins. 2006. *"Convergence Culture: Where Old and New Media Collide."* New York University Press, USA.

Yang Yi, Guan Yu. 2010. "A Comparative Study Of 80s and 90s Consumer Behavior," *Daguan Ads: Theory Edition*, 4, 75–85.

Yu Mengni. 2015. "A Study on Scene Marketing on Mobile Internet Era," China: *Management Observation*, 17, 173–175.

Chapter 9

Establishing an Ecosystem for Digital Entrepreneurship: A Case of Zhongguancun

Jiamin Yin

Department of Information Systems
School of Computing, National University of Singapore
heather_yin@163.com

Wenyu (Derek) Du

Management Science and Engineering Department
School of Business, Renmin University of China
duwenyu@rbs.org.cn

Abstract

The emergence of digital entrepreneurial ecosystems (DEE) has brought broad economic and social consequences, such as creating jobs, attracting investment capital, and revitalizing digital economy. Thus, many countries nowadays hope to establish DEE to gain a competitive edge in the global business world. However, research on DEE has lagged behind practice and little is known about its underlying orchestration processes. In this study, we apply extant literature on DEE, self-organization, and resource orchestration to analyze the case of Zhongguancun DEE in China. By interviewing 52 participants in Zhongguancun DEE, three orchestration processes (i.e. opportunity appropriability, resource sharing, and ecosystem stability) that are pivotal to the prosperity of self-organizing DEE are proposed. To our knowledge, our research is one of first studies revealing effective orchestration strategies within DEE. Apart from academic significance, our findings could provide insightful references for entrepreneurial and political practitioners as well.

Keywords: Digital entrepreneurial ecosystem, Orchestration, Resource sharing, Opportunity appropriability, Ecosystem stability.

Introduction

Today, novel digital technologies are bringing new opportunities for digital entrepreneurs to create high-tech ventures in the digital entrepreneurial communities around the globe (Bharadwaj *et al.*, 2013; Davidson and Vaast, 2010; Del Giudice and Straub, 2011). On a macro level, these communities bring broad social consequences by creating new job opportunities, attracting venture capital and revitalizing local economy (Engel, 2015). To illustrate, despite sluggish global economy, Silicon Valley still witnesses robust growth in digital start-ups, angel investors, and incubators, serving as the engine of local economic growth (Piscione, 2013). Thus, many countries are currently considering to establish digital entrepreneurship communities to boost economic development (Engel, 2015; Isenberg, 2010). Despite hot in practice, research on digital entrepreneurship "has lagged behind practice (Shen *et al.*, 2015, p. 1)" and little attention has been paid to this phenomenon (Grégoire and Shepherd, 2012). *Information Systems Journal* (ISJ) has even launched a special issue to call for more research on digital entrepreneurship (Shen *et al.*, 2015).

More importantly, most of the research in this area focuses on a micro level and mainly emphasizes on how individual entrepreneurs (Fischer and Reuber, 2014) and businesses (Bharadwaj *et al.*, 2013) are enabled by digital technologies to pursue opportunities. Yet, due to limited resources being available, entrepreneurs often have to leverage resources and capabilities beyond organizational boundaries in the process of building a new venture (Stevenson, 1985). Thus, the existence of digital entrepreneurial ecosystem (DEE) is important for the emergence and growth of success-ful digital start-ups since it could provide a supportive structure and culture to provide actors with an access to needed resources and informa-tion (Adner and Kapoor, 2010; Spigel, 2015). Thus, it is imperative for us to develop a fine-grained understanding of DEE in this chapter.

In addition, although many countries are interested in establishing DEE to promote digital economy, little is known about its orchestration processes, which is one of the major challenges faced by an entrepre-neurial ecosystem due to its self-organizing nature (Hurmelinna-Laukkanen *et al.*, 2012). Without a central hub firm, autonomous actors within ecosystems would independently make decisions based on their own needs and interests. Under this circumstance, goals of individual actors are very likely to conflict with the collective goal of the whole network (Hoda *et al.*, 2013). Thus, how to align differing goals among actors to achieve synergistic effects on the ecosystem level is of great significance for entrepreneurial ecosystem governance.

Dhanaraj and Parkhe (2006) have examined how a hub firm orches-trates an innovation network before. However, network control from a central actor is nearly impossible within DEE. Thus, self-orchestration processes arising from a collective of independent actors is required for the sustainable ecosystem development, which are still treated as a black box in previous studies. *Strategy Entrepreneurship Journal* (SEJ) has even called for papers on entrepreneurship ecosystems in a special issue (Autio *et al.*, 2015). Specifically, they invite more research on "what are the best strategies for entrepreneurial ecosystem orchestration" (Autio *et al.*, 2015, p. 2). As such, we contend that future research in this area is needed to reveal the underlying orchestration processes through which actors successfully govern their self-organizing entrepreneurial communities.

To address the above-mentioned research gaps, the research question this study aims to answer is: "how to orchestrate a digital entrepreneurial ecosystem?" Using a case study methodology, our study conducts 52 on-site face-to-face interviews in Zhongguancun DEE and could make contributions in a number of ways. First, our chapter addresses the paucity of study on digital entrepreneurship on an ecosystem level by examining Zhongguancun DEE as a whole. Second, our study could shed light on ecosystem dynamics by deriving specific propositions on how to effectively orchestrate a self-organizing DEE. Third, our findings could contribute to orchestration literature on a network level by opening the black box of orchestration under an ecosystem context. Apart from its academic significance, our study could also provide insightful references for policymakers on how to intentionally promote the growth of DEE and for entrepreneurship communities on how to coordinate with each other to better explore and exploit digital entrepreneurial opportunities within DEE.

Literature review

Digital entrepreneurship ecosystem

Venkataraman (1997) proposes a framework for entrepreneurship and defines its domain as "how, by whom, and with what effects opportunities to create future goods and services are discovered, evaluated, and exploited." In the digital economy, novel digital technologies are providing new opportunities for entrepreneurs and disrupting competition rules (Bharadwaj *et al.*, 2013) by reducing the costs of information flow (Schultze and Leidner, 2002). Nonetheless, conceptualization of digital entrepreneurship remains rather elusive and lacks a coherent theory (Shen *et al.*, 2015). In this study, we follow Davidson and Vaast (2010) by defining digital entrepreneurship as "the pursuit of opportunities based on the use of digital media and other information and communication technologies."

Existing research on digital entrepreneurship mainly focuses on a micro level (Shen *et al.*, 2015). To illustrate, individual-level research states that digital technologies could influence decision-making behavior of entrepreneurs (Autio *et al.*, 2011; Shepherd *et al.*, 2014). Organization-level researches examine the role of digital technologies in fostering agility capabilities, transforming business strategies, and enhancing firm performance (Bharadwaj *et al.*, 2013; Sambamurthy *et al.*, 2003). However, recent research points out that digital technologies could extend inter-firm relationships into business networks (Bharadwaj *et al.*, 2013), illustrating the importance of interactions of participants to value creation and extraction in an ecosystem context.

Nonetheless, previous research on ecosystem in entrepreneurship literature is rather varied (Autio, *et al.*, 2015, p.1). Moore (1993) first coins the term "ecosystem" to describe how a network of participants cooperate and compete with each other around an innovation. Spigel (2015) further defines an entrepreneurial ecosystem as "combinations of social, political, economic, and cultural elements within a region that support the development and growth of innovative start-ups and encourage nascent entrepreneurs and other actors to take the risks of starting, funding, and otherwise assisting high-risk ventures (p. 2)." In this chapter, we study the DEE as a whole and refers it as an EE that enables digital entrepreneurs to pursue opportunities inherent in digital technologies. Due to the vast number of opportunities generated from digital technology, the number and diversity of new ventures in DEE are far greater than those from traditional EE (David and Vaast, 2010). With fiercer competition and fast-changing technologies, inter-firm relationship among these digital start-ups fascinates us.

On the basis of Spigel's (2015) research, we identify the following major actors within DEE: digital entrepreneurs, potential employees of digital start-ups, local mature IT companies, nearby universities and research institutions, accelerators, investment institutions, and local government. It is inter-organizational coordination and collaboration among these actors that enable individual actor to leverage resources and capabilities beyond their control, simultaneously enhancing competitiveness of themselves and the whole ecosystem (Thomas and Autio, 2012). Specifically, inter-firm social networks benefit entrepreneurs by facilitating resources and information mobilization across organizational boundaries (Hoang and Antoncic, 2003) and fostering innovation capability of mature firms (Weiblen and Chesbrough, 2015).

Ecosystem orchestration

As noted before, with the absence of formal hierarchical control, orchestration processes are required to align differing interests among autonomous actors within self-organizing DEE. Since no single actors within DEE could exploit opportunities without resorting to external organizations, we study the self-orchestration on a network level in this chapter. Previous researches on network-level orchestration have been applied in the context of innovation networks (Dhanaraj and Parkhe, 2006), crowdsourcing platforms (Feller *et al.*, 2012) and R&D networks (Hurmelinna-Laukkanen *et al.*, 2012). DEE are similar to these forms of organizations since they all bundle and leverage dispersed resources to foster innovation capability (Dhanaraj and Parkhe, 2006; Feller *et al.*, 2012; Hurmelinna-Laukkanen *et al.*, 2012). Another similarity lies in that all these networks lack a formal hierarchy (Dhanaraj and Parkhe, 2006; Feller *et al.*, 2012; Hurmelinna-Laukkanen *et al.*, 2012). However, all these researches focus on the orchestration processes steered by a hub firm. In this chapter, we take the self-organizing nature of DEE into consideration and study self-orchestration processes steered by a collective of individual actors.

In the context of DEE, the first orchestration task involves how to discover and exploit opportunities (Davidson and Vaast, 2010). This is because if actors could not derive fair value from their opportunities, they would feel demotivated and may participate in other ecosystems instead. Moreover, due to the differences in prior knowledge and external environmental changes, digital entrepreneurs differ in opportunity identification and exploitation (Shane and Venkataraman, 2000; Venkataraman, 1997). Thus, diverse resources enable digital entrepreneurs with diverse demands and goals to profit from opportunities. On the other hand, actor interdependence within ecosystems could drive value co-creation and appropriation through combining complementary resources and capabilities in a novel way (Adner and Kapoor, 2010; Thomas and Autio, 2012), which contributes to new entrepreneurial opportunities discovery and exploitation (Nieto and Alvarez, 2014), investment capital acquisition (Shane and Cable, 2002), new venture creation (Carolis *et al.*, 2009).

Moreover, effective opportunity exploitation within DEE depends on utilizing resources beyond boundaries (Stevenson, 1985). According to resource orchestration framework, actors could create resource-based competitive edge under dynamic environment by structuring (acquiring, accumulating, and divesting), bundling (stabilizing, enriching, and pioneering) and leveraging (mobilizing, coordinating, and deploying) dispersed resources (Sirmon *et al.*, 2007, 2010). Additionally, actors could rely on interorganizational coordination and collaboration to access needed knowledge and information from others to achieve a synergistic effect (Tsai, 2002). Such sharing routines is further facilitated by reciprocity norm, trust, and network identification within ecosystems (Kankanhalli *et al.*, 2005; Poppo *et al.*, 2008).

Finally, a successful DEE would achieve dynamic stability (Wareham *et al.*, 2014) to balance between retaining existing participants and attracting newcomers. A stable environment ensures actors to reap long-term benefits from their investments, while dynamic capability helps actors adapt to a volatile environment. Specifically, agility could help capture entrepreneurial opportunities inherent in shifting market demands and digital technology advancements (Sambamurthy *et al.*, 2003).

Methodology

Our study follows the interpretive case study methodology (Klein and Myers, 1999) for the following two reasons. First, it is especially appropriate for answering our "how" research questions (Walsham, 1995). Second, inter-organizational dynamics within DEE are too complex and require exploratory research (Pan and Tan, 2011; Siggelkow, 2007) to lay a foundation for future quantitative studies.

Based on our research objective, we select Zhongguancun DEE in Beijing as case DEE since it is the largest and most successful DEE in China and has been regarded as the Silicon Valley of China. In 2015, firms in Zhongguancun DEE have attained a total revenue of $198.21 billion and industrial output value of $55.20 billion, increasing by 11.2% and 16.6%, respectively, over 2014 (Liu, 2015). It has also witnessed the emergence of 8,577 new digital start-ups, 16,095 intellectual property applications, and $6.84 billion investment last year (Liu, 2015).

We conducted a total of 52 on-site face-to-face interviews in Zhongguancun DEE from May to August in 2015. Each interview was digitally recorded and lasted around 60–90 minutes. Our interviewees cover a wide range of critical actors in DEE with demographic background diversity (age, education, working experience, etc.) so that our data could be more representative, improving the reliability of our study. An overview of interviewee information and some selected examples could be seen in Appendix A (Table A.1.). Our interview questions were designed to be open-ended, semi-structured and exploratory in nature. Interviews yield over 400 pages of transcripts and field notes. Apart from interview data, we also collected approximately 150-page documents on Zhongguancun DEE, including web-based blogs, news and articles and internal archival reports published by the actors within Zhongguancun DEE. We have also participated in a number of discussion forums and salons in Zhongguancun DEE (e.g., the 2015 annual meeting of incubator AAMA).

We collected and analyzed our data at the same time. We mainly use open coding and selective coding (Strauss and Corbin, 1993) in our data analysis processes. Through data analysis, we found three major orchestration strategies adopted by actors within DEE. The findings could be seen in the case description and analysis section.

Case description and analysis

In this section, we describe the case of Zhongguancun DEE and analyze three orchestration processes within DEE, which are managing opportunity appropriability, resource sharing, and ecosystem stability.

Managing opportunity appropriability

Within DEE, the major objective of entrepreneurs is to derive as much economic value as possible from discovered opportunities. Thus, the first DEE orchestration task involves opportunity appropriability. Appropriability is used to describe "an innovator's ability to capture the profits generated by an innovation (Teece, 1986)." In this chapter, we extend this construct into digital entrepreneurship literature and suggest that the prosperity of the DEE depends on how it enables participants to derive more value through digital start-up creation (Pitelis and Teece, 2010). Our study reveals that opportunity appropriability could be achieved by (1) provision of diverse resources, and (2) value co-creation among actors.

Resource diversity

Due to differences in prior information, individual digital entrepreneurs vary in the opportunity discovery, evaluation, and exploitation processes (Venkataraman, 1997). That is, entrepreneurs would respond differently to same technology due to differences in education and experience.

In addition, novel digital technologies, fast-changing market environments and regulatory changes also create multiple opportunities for entrepreneurs (Shane and Venkataraman, 2000). Thus, resource diversity could help actors exploit opportunities.

First, Zhongguancun DEE aggregates a diverse set of skilled business and technical talents (e.g., accountants, consultants, HRs, lawyers, etc.) where start-ups could easily find employees with complementary expertise here. Quite a few of our interviews indicate the major reason they join in Zhongguancun DEE is to recruit technical or market specialists that are needed to found a new venture.

Second, investment capital is also vital for the growth and expansion of digital start-ups. In Zhongguancun DEE, diversity of preferences of investors and investment institutions help offer more specialized support for start-ups with diverse focuses. For example, investor Mr. Kang said he is particularly attentive to the projects related to O2O restaurants and has already successfully invested in several projects in this field. Apart from diversity in investment focus, Zhongguancun DEE also provide diverse types of investment capital (e.g., angel investment, venture capital, industry investment fund, IPO, etc.) to cater to the needs of digital start-ups in different development stages.

Third, local government launches diverse policy initiatives to foster growth of diverse actors as well. Mr. Xuan, a government officer responsible for Zhongguancun ecosystem management, reveals that Beijing government provides multiple financial support for digital entrepreneurs, helping address their fund shortage problem. Apart from financial incentives, government also simplifies bureaucratic regulation processes (e.g., provision of one-stop services for firm registration) to attract digital entrepreneurs. As for incubators, government assists in establishing physical infrastructure and offers huge rent subsidies to alleviate their financial burden.

Moreover, heterogeneity of incubators' business focuses ensures digital start-ups in different fields could receive specialized services in Zhongguancun DEE. For example, IC coffee is an expert in incubating intelligent hardware start-ups while 36 Kr is specializing in assisting B2B digital start-ups. Diversity could also encourage co-opetition among incubators and thus increase their competitiveness. Mr. Wang, the director of incubator 3W Coffee, notes that apart from competing for investment and promising projects, incubators would also collaboratively organize events and often recommend promising start-ups to each other.

Value co-creation

Resource diversity alone could not ensure participants to derive value from digital opportunities. Value co-creation is also significant for actors to seize lucrative digital opportunities by leveraging cross-boundary resources through inter-firm interaction. For example, entrepreneur Mr. Zhang told us that he has worked as a programmer for years. It is his collaboration with a physical doctor that leads to the discovery and exploitation of opportunities in mobile health.

Additionally, actors could establish co-marketing alliances to enhance their competitiveness. Mr. Wang, the founder of a mobile socialization app, has mentioned that he and his collaboration partners advertised for each other on their own official websites to enlarge existing customer base. Moreover, incubators sometimes collaborate with larger firms to help advertise for its incubated firms. For example, Mr. Xie from Angel Crunch reveals that they advertised for its incubated digital start-ups on Zhubajie, the largest crowd sourcing website in China.

Another common collaborative strategy is to share talents (e.g., programmers and accountants) to reduce labor costs. The director of incubator 3W coffee further notes that "the entrepreneurial teams in our incubator often cooperate with each other. It is quite common to see that employee from one entrepreneurial team assists in another team in solving technical problems." Such talent collaboration practice greatly reduces entrepreneurs' effort and time in searching for appropriate talents and could promote knowledge mobility.

Managing resource sharing

Opportunity appropriation greatly relies on inter-organizational resource sharing, which facilitates actors to structure, bundle, and leverage cross-boundary resources. According to our analysis, resource sharing within DEE is achieved by (1) physical collocation, and (2) establishment of a community of practice.

Physical collocation

A wide range of actors concentrate in Zhongguancun DEE, promoting knowledge mobility by aggregating local talents and serving as a venue for communication

First, nearby renowned universities (e.g., Peking University, Tsinghua University, etc.) and large mature IT firms (e.g., Baidu, Tecent, etc.) cultivate a large number of talents with rich technical expertise and managerial experience, facilitating talent-seeking activities for digital start-ups within DEE. Local incubators also help start-ups access technical or managerial experts through established social networks and self-operated recruitment websites such as Lagouwang, a IT talent recruiting website founded by 3W Coffee. On the other hand, collocation of firms provides rich job opportunities, further promoting knowledge sharing by facilitating worker mobility.

Second, Zhongguancun DEE serves as a venue for actors to communicate with each other by provision of diverse lectures, salons and discussion forums, helping actors sensitize technology frontiers and industry outlooks. One investor indicates that the reason why he comes to Zhongguancun DEE is to "catch up with the recent trends in digital entrepreneurship." Another entrepreneur Mr. Chen also states that he attended activities organized by Zhongguancun to keep up with up-to-date digital technologies, industry landscape, and policy changes.

Community of practice

Physical collocation encourages the emergence of a community of practice, which is referred to as a group of close actors who share information, tasks, activities and physical official space with each other, where learning processes are underpinned by social relations (Lave and Wenger, 1991).

In such a community, both resource contributors and receivers could benefit from this community. For those resource receivers, apparently, they could conveniently access the needed knowledge, information, and skills from others in a community of practice, enhancing their competitive edge.

For those resource contributors, they could also derive both intrinsic and extrinsic rewards from this community. Although some contributors share knowledge for direct compensation, social capital building or expected reciprocal resource exchange, in most cases, they are motivated out of intrinsic rewards. To illustrate, some interviewees indicate that they derive enjoyment and a sense of achievement through helping peers who confront bottlenecks. Other common extrinsic rewards include gaining respect and recognition from peers, sharpening problem-solving skills, and helping advance the whole community. Specifically, Ms. Guo from incubator AAMA notes that they have launched a "cradle plan", where previous experienced members who have successfully founded enterprises voluntarily act as mentors and offer their suggestions and advice for those new members, helping new comers avoid potential pitfalls during venture creation processes (Spigel, 2015). Apart from associations organized by incubators, people sharing similar working experience spontaneously form their own associations (e.g., "Antarctic Circle" founded by those once worked in Tecent), where more seasoned members impart useful suggestions to new members.

Managing ecosystem stability

The third orchestration task faced by Zhongguancun DEE is to enhance ecosystem stability, which could be achieved by (1) incubators that serve as a locus of coordination; and (2) collective identity of actors and shared culture.

Locus of coordination

Despite lack of formal hierarchy, incubators within Zhongguancun DEE serve as the locus of coordination and connect all actors together (Thomas and Autio, 2012). These incubators enhance the collective performance of an ecosystem by bridging among diverse actors.

First, incubators bridge between digital start-ups and potential investors. Mr. Xie from Angel Crunch told us that many digital entrepreneurs are technical experts. They often find it difficult to gain investment due to lack of knowledge and experience in capital market. To solve this problem, incubators such as Angel Crunch help digital start-ups to polish up their business plans and act as a middleman between entrepreneurs and investors.

Incubators also serve as a bridge between start-ups and other third-party entrepreneurial service providers. From our interviews, we learn that incubator HDKC has collaborated with a number of ancillary entrepreneurial service providers to offer free specialized services (e.g., intellectual property protection, accounting, human resources management, social security management, etc.) for digital start-ups in the first 6 months. This practice greatly lowers the barriers of start-up creation by greatly reducing administrative costs and improving managerial skills.

Furthermore, incubators often provide propaganda for incubated start-ups to gain more media exposure. One interviewed entrepreneur mentions that his start-up is incubated by 36Kr, which is a leader incubator in technology media and would offer free propaganda services to its members to help attract more attention from customers and investors. Ms. Zhou from HDKC also notes that they have collaborated with Youku, a major video sharing website in China, to produce a series of documentaries called "entrepreneurs", which involves in-depth conversations between digital entrepreneurs and their investors, advisors and mentors, and enables the masses to have a deeper understanding of the stories of digital entrepreneurs.

Collective identity and shared culture

Finally, ecosystem stability could be achieved by actors' collective identity and shared culture (Spigel, 2015), which motivates actors to strive for a collective goal: the self-sustaining growth of DEE.

Entrepreneurs within Zhongguancun call themselves "makers" since they believe their innovations could make major societal impacts. These "makers" share common personal traits and are often described as energetic, outgoing, adventurous, passionate, and enjoy embracing changes in their lives. They may even share similar past experience. For example, several of our interviewees states that they have previously worked in large internet companies (e.g., Baidu and Alibaba) before and "felt quite bored of such routinized work and thus quit stable jobs to devote themselves into entrepreneurial activities now." Collective traits and experience facilitate people to find congenial companions within DEE. For example, Entrepreneur Ms. Wang reveals that, "The strong entrepreneurial atmosphere here (Zhongguancun DEE) helps me find a lot of like-minded friends."

Shared culture also promotes positive growth of DEE by establishing common rules and values that are conducive to entrepreneurial activities. For example, due to lack of hierarchical control, Zhongguancun DEE has cultivated a sense of fairness, which is conducive for improving creativity capabilities. One of the employees working for a socialisation app start-up reveals that he prefers to work in digital start-ups since he "enjoys the creative and respectful working atmosphere here." Also, the history of entrepreneurship in Zhongguancun DEE fosters an innovation-seeking and risk-taking atmosphere (Spigel, 2015). Therefore, risky entrepreneurial activities seem to be acceptable and even preferable. Entrepreneur Ms. Wang even told us that "some investors even prefer those serial entrepreneurs who have experienced failure before since they are more mature and committed."

Discussion

Based on our analysis of Zhongguancun DEE, our findings on DEE orchestration could be summarized in Table 1. Specifically, we find that opportunity appropriability is achieved by resource diversity and value co-creation. Resource sharing is achieved by physical collocation and establishment of a community of practice. Ecosystem stability is achieved by an established locus of coordination and collective identity and shared culture.

Our findings on opportunity appropriability links value creation and appropriation in ecosystem literature (Thomas and Autio, 2012). First, we admit that apart from individual differences in opportunity discovery and evaluation (Venkataraman, 1997), entrepreneurs also differ in creating and appropriating value from profitable opportunities due to differences in

Table 1. Orchestrating a DEE

Opportunity appropriability		Resource diversity
		Value co-creation
Resource sharing	is achieved by	Physical collocation
		Community of practice
Ecosystem stability		Locus of coordination
		Collective identity and shared culture

resources and capabilities (Teece, 1986; Pitelis, 2012). Thus, we propose the importance of resource diversity in attracting participants. Also, we offer a better understanding of the role of universities (Bishop *et al.*, 2011), mature firms (Semrau and Sigmund, 2012), venture capitalists (Wijbenga *et al.*, 2007) and incubators (Bollingtoft and Ulhoi, 2005) in DEE. In addition, resource diversity alone could not help entrepreneurs exploit opportunities when they are locked within organizational boundaries (Dhanaraj and Parkhe, 2006). It is value co-creation that enables co-specializing actors to take advantage of complementary resources and capabilities (Pitelis, 2012), which is greatly facilitated by interactions of participants (Thomas and Autio, 2012).

Opportunity appropriability depends on bundling and utilizing cross-boundary resources. Thus, we propose resource sharing as the second orchestration task. Also, we challenge the claim that physical collocation is not that important in inter-organizational sharing due to rapid development of digital technologies (Malhotra and Lott, 2001; Schultze and Leidner, 2002). Instead, we argue that collocation still matters for aggregating talents and establishing value-creation social ties in DEE, promoting knowledge mobility among high-tech firms (Presutti *et al.*, 2013). Specifically, actors could benefit greatly from local specialists and knowledge spillovers (Kolympiris *et al.*, 2011), especially taking nearby renowned universities and large IT firms into consideration (Bishop *et al.*, 2011). Additionally, collocation of participants in one region provides a venue for peer communication. To an extent, collocation in DEE plays a role similar to academic conferences, aggregating scholars around the world to exchange their perspectives on latest research progresses (Garud, 2008). Thus, the advantage brought by agglomeration of actors could still not be entirely replaced by the emergence of virtual digital communities.

Physical collocation also lays a foundation for a community of practice by facilitating the accumulation of social and relational capital. We confirm that such a community improves inter-organizational information flow and shapes agility in responding to problems and opportunities (Cross *et al*, 2006). Specifically, we provide empirical evidence for the role of mentors and incubators in linking small start-ups with large incumbent firms (Spigel, 2015). This is especially important since digital start-ups could benefit from resource and experience shared by large established firms.

As for the third orchestration task, our research is consistent to previous research (Dhanaraj and Parkhe, 2006; Thomas and Autio, 2012; Wareham *et al.*, 2014) in that an ecosystem composed of diverse actors with conflicting interests could not evolve without stability. Also, we point out that although DEE lacks a dominating hub firm, a small number of incubators serve as nodes in DEE and connect a larger number of participants, enhancing the competitive edge of the whole ecosystem (Thomas and Autio, 2012). Also, through the coordination of incubators, actors benefit from entrepreneurial risk spreading through alignment of interests, which is important in retaining existing actors and attracting newcomers.

More importantly, we reveal that a DEE orchestration framework should at least contain economic, social, and cultural attributes. According to our analysis, opportunity appropriation attracts actors and encourages their interaction through providing economic incentives (value co-creation based on a diverse set of complementary resources). As for resource sharing, it promotes resource mobility and exploitation of cross boundaries through inter-organizational socialization processes, which is facilitated by collocation of firms and a community of practice. Incubators provide a supportive governance infrastructure to create both economic and social values for the whole DEE. Last but not least, a supportive entrepreneurial culture is important in fostering digital innovations and ensuring health development of the whole digital ecosystem (Spigel, 2015).

Theoretical and practical implications

With an attempt to unveil DEE orchestration processes, our study makes three theoretical contributions. First, we shift the focus on digital entrepreneurship research to an ecosystem level, rather than at an individual (Fischer and Reuber, 2014) or organization level (Bharadwaj *et al.*, 2013). In essence, we emphasize that single actors alone in DEE could not access and leverage resources needed to create a new venture, but a collective action of actors could (Stevenson, 1985).

Second, our research answers the call by Autio *et al.*, (2015) by examining entrepreneurial ecosystems dynamics. Specifically, our findings open the "black box" of effective strategies in EE orchestration (Autio *et al.*, 2015) and provide a richer understanding of dynamic inter-organizational relationships in DEE.

Third, by considering the self-organization nature of DEE, we move from the orchestration processes of hub firms to that of a collective of actors. That is, we "tease out the unique contributions a hub firm makes (Dhanaraj and Parkhe, 2006)" within an inter-organization networks that lack hierarchical authority. Thus, our research could enrich understanding in orchestration process at a network level. Additionally, by demonstrating how autonomous actors with self-interests collectively create and extract value from DEE, our study could also complement self-organization theory.

As for practical implications, our research provides valuable practical insights by offering a DEE orchestration framework. Additionally, prior entrepreneurship literature disproportionately concentrates on the DEE in developed nations and our research be especially valuable for DEE in an emerging economy (Bruton *et al.*, 2013). DEE in emerging economies often face far more difficulties compared with those in developed countries, such as lacking abundant investment capital and a global talented workforce. Under this circumstance, our chapter demonstrates the role of governmental regulation in lowering the barrier of digital venture creation and investment attraction.

Limitations and directions for future research

We acknowledge that our study has limitations as well. First, since we only collect data from one single DEE in China, generalizability of our propositions to DEE in other industries and countries should be viewed with caution.

Second, as for opportunity appropriability, this paper emphasizes that actors are motivated to participant in DEE since they can generate more value compared with creating ventures alone. However, we do not discuss the allocation of value in this chapter. This is because most of digital start-ups do not make much profit and may even suffer from loss in the initial phase. Since fair distribution of value is vital to keep participants in DEE (Dhanaraj and Parkhe, 2006), we hope future research could address more on this issue among actors in DEE.

Conclusions

Currently, start-ups enabled by digital technologies prosper in DEE around the world, which bring huge social and economic impacts to the whole society. In this Chapter, we examine how to orchestrate DEE using the case study of Zhongguancun DEE. Our central argument in this paper is that three orchestration processes, which are managing opportunity appropriability, resource sharing, and ecosystem stability, respectively, are necessary to the prosperity of self-organizing DEE. In conclusion, our Chapter could provide a richer understanding in digital entrepreneurship on an ecosystem level and guide digital entrepreneurial communities and governments hoping to advance digital economy to deal with challenges in DEE orchestration.

Acknowledgment

This research is supported by the National Natural Science Foundation of China (71402187).

References

Adner, R., and Kapoor, R. 2010. "Value Creation in Innovation Ecosystems: How the Structure of Technological Interdependence Affects Firm Performance in New Technology Generations," *Strategic Management Journal*, 31(3), 306–333.

Autio, E., George, G., and Alexy, O. 2011. "International Entrepreneurship and Capability Development-Qualitative Evidence and Future Research Directions," *Entrepreneurship Theory and Practice*, 35(1), 11–37.

Autio, E., Nambisan, S., Wright, M., and Thmas, L. 2015. "Call for Paper for a Special Issue: Entrepreneurial System," *Strategic Entrepreneurship Journal*. Available at: http://onlinelibrary.wiley.com/store/10.1002/(ISSN)1932-443X/asset/homepages/SEJ-Entrepreneurial_Ecosystems.pdf?v=1&s=4548d7b62c28292b826ef7d74eae7bfcd396f34a&systemMessage=Please+be+advised+that+we+experienced+an+unexpected+issue+that+occurred+on+Saturday+and+Sunday+January+20th+and+21st+that+caused+the+site+to+be+down+for+an+extended+period+of+time+and+affected+the+ability+of+users+to+access+content+on+Wiley+Online+Library.+This+issue+has+now+been+fully+resolved.++We+apologize+for+any+inconvenience+this+may+have+caused+and+are+working+to+ensure+that+we+can+alert+you+immediately+of+any+unplanned+periods+of+downtime+or+disruption+in+the+future.&isAguDoi=false

Bharadwaj, A., Sawy, O. A. E., Pavlou, P. A., and Venkatraman, N. 2013. "Digital Business Strategy: Toward a Next Generation of Insights," *MIS Quarterly,* 37(2), 471–482.

Bishop, K., D' Este, P., and Neely, A. 2011. "Gaining from Interactions with Universities: Multiple Methods for Nurturing Absorptive Capacity," *Research Policy,* 40(1), 30–40.

Bollingtoft, A., and Ulhoi, J. P. 2005. "The Networked Business Incubator-Leveraging Entrepreneurial Agency?" *Journal of Business Venturing,* 20(2), 265–290.

Bruton, G. D., Filatotchev, I., and Si, S. 2013. "Entrepreneurship and Strategy in Emerging Economies," *Strategic Entrepreneurship Journal,* 7(3), 169–180.

Carolis, D. M. D., Litzky, B. E., and Eddleston, K. A. 2009. "Why Networks Enhance the Progress of New Venture Creation: The Influence of Social Capital and Cognition," *Entrepreneurship Theory & Practice,* 33(2), 527–545.

Cross, R., Laseter, T., and Parker, A. 2006. "Using Social Network Analysis to Improve Communities of Practice," *California Management Review,* 49(1), 32–60.

Davidson, E., and Vaast, E. 2010. "Digital Entrepreneurship and Its Sociomaterial Enactment," in *Proceedings of the 43rd Hawaii International Conference on System Sciences (HICSS),* IEEE Computer Society, Honolulu, HI, pp. 1–10.

Del Giudice, M., and Straub, D. 2011. "Editor's Comments: IT and Entrepreneurism: an On-again, Off-again Love Affair or a Marriage?" *MIS Quarterly,* 35(4), 3–7.

Dhanaraj, C., and Parkhe, A. 2006. "Orchestrating Innovation Networks," *Academy of Management Review,* 31(3), 659–669.

Engel, J. S. 2015. "Global Clusters of Innovation: Lessons from Silicon Valley." *California Management Review,* 57(2), 36–65.

Feller, J., Finnegan, P., and Hayes, J. 2012. "'Orchestrating' Sustainable Crowdsourcing: A Characterisation of Solver Brokerages," *Journal of Strategic Information Systems,* 21(3), 216–232.

Fischer, E., and Reuber, R. A. 2014. "Online Entrepreneurial Communication: Mitigating Uncertainty and Increasing Differentiation Via Twitter," *Journal of Business Venturing,* 29(4), 565–583.

Garud, R. 2008. "Conferences as Venues for the Configuration of Emerging Organizational Fields: The Case of Cochlear Implants," *Journal of Management Studies,* 45(6), 1061–1088.

Grégoire, D. A., and Shepherd, D. A. 2012. "Technology-Market Combinations and the Identification of Entrepreneurial Opportunities: An Investigation of the Opportunity-Individual Nexus," *Academy of Management Journal*, 55(4), 753–785.

Hoda, R., Noble, J., and Marshall, S. 2013. "Self-organizing Roles on Agile Software Development Teams," *IEEE Transactions on Software Engineering*, 39(3), 422–444.

Hoang, H., and Antoncic, B. 2003. "Network-based Research in Entrepreneurship: A Critical Review," *Journal of Business Venturing*, 18(2), 165–187.

Hurmelinna-Laukkanen, P., Olander, H., Blomqvist, K., and Panfilii, V. 2012. "Orchestrating R&D Networks: Absorptive Capacity, Network Stability, and Innovation Appropriability," *European Management Journal*, 30(6), 552–563.

Isenberg, D. J. 2010. "The Big Idea: How to Start an Entrepreneurial Revolution," *Harvard Business Review*, 88(6), 40–50.

Kankanhalli, A., Tan, B., and Wei, K. K. 2005 "Contributing Knowledge to Electronic Knowledge Repositories: An Empirical Investigation," *MIS Quarterly*, 29(1), 113–143.

Klein, H. K., and Myers, M. D. 1999. "A Set of Principles for Conducting and Evaluating Interpretive Field Studies in Information Systems," *MIS Quarterly*, 23(1), 67–94.

Kolympiris, C., Kalaitzandonakes, N., and Miller, D. 2011. "Spatial Collocation and Venture Capital in the US Biotechnology Industry," *Research Policy*, 40(9), 1188–1199.

Lave, J. and Wenger, E. 1991. "Legitimate Peripheral Participation in Communities of Practice. Situated Learning: Legitimate Peripheral Participation." Cambridge University Press, Cambridge.

Liu, Y. Y. 2015. "Zhongguancun Releases Half Year Operations Report," *China Daily*, (July 9), http://www.chinadaily.com.cn/m/beijing/zhongguancun/2015-07/09/content_21229422.htm. Last accessed: July 12, 2017.

Malhotra, A. and Lott, V. 2001. "Radical Innovation Without Collocation: A Case Study at Boeing-Rocketdyne," *MIS Quarterly*, 25(2), 229–249.

Moore, J. F. 1993. "Predators and Prey: A New Ecology of Competition," *Harvard Business Review*, 71(3), 75–86.

Nieto, M., and González-Álvarez, N. 2014. "Social Capital Effects on the Discovery and Exploitation of Entrepreneurial Opportunities," *International Entrepreneurship & Management Journal*, 10(4), 1–24.

Pan, S. L., and Tan, B. 2011. "Demystifying Case Research: A Structured–pragmatic–situational (SPS) Approach to Conducting Case Studies," *Information & Organization*, 21(3), 161–176.

Piscione, D. P. 2013. "*Secrets of Silicon Valley: What Everyone Else Can Learn from the Innovation Capital of the World*," St. Martin's Press, New York.

Pitelis, C. N., and Teece, D. J. 2010. "Cross-border Market Co-creation, Dynamic Capabilities and the Entrepreneurial Theory of the Multinational Enterprise," *Industrial and Corporate Change*, 19(4), 1247–1270.

Pitelis, C. 2012. "Clusters, Entrepreneurial Ecosystem Co-creation, and Appropriability: A Conceptual Framework," *Industrial & Corporate Change*, 21(6), 1359–1388.

Poppo, L., Zhou, K. Z., and Rhu, S. 2008. "Alternative Origins to Interorganizational Trust: An Interdependence Perspective on the Shadow of the Past and the Shadow of the Future," *Organization Science,* 19(1), 39–55.

Presutti, M., Boari, C., and Majocchi, A. 2013. "Inter-organizational Geographical Proximity and Local Start-ups' Knowledge Acquisition: A Contingency Approach," *Entrepreneurship & Regional Development,* 25(5–6), 446–467.

Sambamurthy, V., Bharadwaj, A., and Grover, V. 2003. "Shaping Agility through Digital Options: Reconceptualizing the Role of Information Technology in Contemporary Firms," *MIS Quarterly,* 27(2), 237–263.

Schultze, U., and Leidner, D. E. 2002. "Studying Knowledge Management in Information Systems Research: Discourses and Theoretical Assumptions," *MIS Quarterly,* 26(3), 213–242.

Semrau, T., and Sigmund, S. 2012. "Networking Ability and the Financial Performance of New Ventures: A Mediation Analysis among Younger and More Mature Firms," *Strategic Entrepreneurship Journal,* 6(4), 335–354.

Shane, S., and Venkataraman, S. 2000. "The Promise of Entrepreneurship as a Field of Research," *Academy of Management Review,* 25(1), 171–184.

Shane, S., and Cable, D. 2002. "Network Ties, Reputation, and the Financing of New Ventures," *Management Science,* 48(3), 364–381.

Shen, K., Lindsay, V., and Xu, Y. 2015. "Information Systems Journal Special Issue on: Digital Entrepreneurship," *Information Systems Journal.* Available at: http://onlinelibrary.wiley.com/store/10.1111/(ISSN)1365-2575/asset/home-pages/ISJ_SI_Digital_Entrepreneurship.pdf?v=1&s=696d716f21e6137e1fbe3 2f3b0fd4afee81c9618&systemMessage=Please+be+advised+that+we+experi enced+an+unexpected+issue+that+occurred+on+Saturday+and+Sunday+Janua ry+20th+and+21st+that+caused+the+site+to+be+down+for+an+extended+pe riod+of+time+and+affected+the+ability+of+users+to+access+content+on+W iley+Online+Library.+This+issue+has+now+been+fully+resolved.++We+apol ogize+for+any+inconvenience+this+may+have+caused+and+are+working+to+e nsure+that+we+can+alert+you+immediately+of+any+unplanned+periods+of+d owntime+or+disruption+in+the+future.&isAguDoi=false&isAguDoi=false

Shepherd, D. A., Williams, T. A., and Patzelt, H. 2014. "Thinking About Entrepreneurial Decision Making: Review and Research Agenda," *Journal of Management,* 41(1), 11–46.

Siggelkow, N. 2007. "Persuasion with Case Studies," *Academy of Management Journal*, 50(1), 20–24.

Sirmon, D. G., Hitt, M. A., and Ireland, R. D. 2007. "Managing Firm Resources in Dynamic Environments to Create Value: Looking Inside the Black Box," *Academy of Management Review*, 32(1), 273–292.

Sirmon, D. G., Hitt, M. A., Ireland, R. D., and Gilbert, B. A. 2010. "Resource Orchestration to Create Competitive Advantage Breadth, Depth and Life Cycle Effects," *Journal of Management*, 37(5), 1390–1412.

Spigel, B. 2015. "The Relational Organization of Entrepreneurial Ecosystems," *Entrepreneurship Theory and Practice*, 41(1), 49–72.

Strauss, A. L., and Corbin, J. M. 1993. "The Articulation of Work Through Interaction," *The Sociological Quarterly*, 34(1), 71–83.

Strauss, A., and Corbin, J. 1998. "*Basics of Qualitative Research: Grounded Theory Procedures and Techniques.*" Sage, Newbury Park, CA.

Stevenson, H. 1985. "The Heart of Entrepreneurship," *Harvard Business Review*, 73(2), 85–94.

Teece, D. J. 1986. "Profiting from Technological Innovation: Implications for Integration, Collaboration, Licensing and Public Policy," *Research Policy* 15(6), 285–305.

Thomas, L. D. W., and Autio, E. 2012. "Modeling the Ecosystem: A Meta-Synthesis of Ecosystem and Related Literatures," in *DRUID Conference*, CBS, Copenhagen, Denmark.

Tsai, W. 2002. "Social Structure of 'Coopetition' within a Multiunit Organization: Coordination, Competition, and Intraorganizational Knowledge Sharing," *Organization Science*, 13(2), 179–190.

Venkataraman, S. 1997. "The Distinctive Domain of Entrepreneurship Research: An *Editor's* Perspective," in *Advances in entrepreneurship, firm emergence, and growth (3)*, J. Katz and R. Brockhaus (eds.), JA, Greenwich, CT, pp. 119–138.

Walsham, G. 1995. "Interpretive Case Studies in IS Research: Nature and Method," *European Journal of Information Systems*, 4(2), 74–81.

Wareham, J., Fox, P. B., and Cano Giner, J. L., 2014. "Technology Ecosystem Governance," *Organization Science*, 25(4), 1195–1215.

Weiblen, T., and Chesbrough, H. W. 2015. "Engaging with Startups to Enhance Corporate Innovation," *California Management Review*, 57(2), 66–90.

Wijbenga, F. H., Postma, T. J. B. M., and Stratling, R. 2007. "The Influence of the Venture Capitalist's Governance Activities on the Entrepreneurial Firm's Control Systems and Performance," *Entrepreneurship Theory & Practice*, 31(2), 257–277.

Appendix A: Interviewee Information

Table A.1.　An Overview of Interviewe Information (N = 52)

Actors (Number of interviewees)	Information about selected interviewees
Entrepreneurs (N = 16)	Mr. Zhang, aged 30, who once worked in IT companies such as Alibaba, Sogou, and Baidu, is now the founder of a firm focusing on the mobile health care. He also has entrepreneurial experience in agriculture e-commerce and P2P financing
	Mr. Xu has successfully created an IT company which is still running. He also has entrepreneurial experience in mobile medical care and sports
	Founder of an entrepreneur training firm, who was once an employee of Midea (one of the largest household appliance firms in China).
	Ms. Wang is a serial entrepreneur now focuses on creating a mobile app on fashion
Employees (N = 3)	Mr. Li, who was a programmer in Baidu before, is now working for a start-up developing a social networking mobile app
	Mr. Liu, aged 22, is an undergraduate from Wuhan and now works for 58 City, one of the largest online recruitment firms in China. He is preparing to setup his own start-up, an online music score sharing, in the near future;
Incubators and accelerators (N = 10)	Mr. Sun is the founder of incubator Yangcongtou, an entrepreneurial service platform focusing on entrepreneurship in culture-related industry or in O2O restaurants
	Mr. Wang is the director of 3W coffee, an incubator focusing on incubating IT entrepreneurship firms. It also has its own coffee shop, accelerator, training program, and angel fund
	Ms. Guo and Mr. Bu are the secretary-general and director of incubator AAMA, respectively. AAMA focuses on aggregating and upbringing Asians leaders in the field of business and technology

(Continued)

Table A.1. (*Continued*)

Actors (Number of interviewees)	Information about selected interviewees
Third-party service providers (N = 7)	Mr. Xie is a manager of Angel Crunch, a platform bridging start-ups and investors Mr. Guo, is the partner of a law service firm that specializes in start-up registration, contract drafting, patent appliance, etc. The manager of E-Capital, a financial advisory firm that has set up a special team to serve start-ups
Investors (N = 10)	Mr. Xu is an investor and a member of incubator Heimahui; he also has entrepreneurship experience Mr. Kang is an investor, who also acts as an entrepreneurship coach to guide the growth of start-ups at the same time Mr. Hao is the founder of a small-scale investors association and a member of incubator No. 66 Growth House
Government and state-owned company (N = 6)	Mr. Xuan is now an associate director of Zhongguancun Technology Ecosystem Management Committee Ms. Zhou is an employee in Haizhi Kechuang (HZKC), a stated controlled incubator responsible for InnoWay operation Founder of Senior Services Informatics Development Committee (SSIDC), affiliated with China Association of Social Welfare and responsible for fostering innovation in senior health care in China

Chapter 10

Meeting New Friends via Habitual Use of Mobile Instant Messaging (MIM) Apps: System Fit & Cultural Preference

Charlie Chen

Walker College of Business, Appalachian State University
287 Rivers St, Boone, NC, USA, 28608,
chench@appstate.edu

Peter Ractham

Thammasat Business School, Thammasat University
2 Prachan Road, Phra
Borom Maha Ratchawang,
Bangkok, Thailand, 10200
peter@tbs.tu.ac.th

Abstract

Mobile instant messaging (MIM) is one of the most popular mobile applications used for communication services worldwide. People use it to chat, talk, and video call with their friends and family. This study looked at the perceived communication control, mobility, and perceived subjective norm (PSN) of MIM apps and investigated if they are a task-technology fit that helps users to develop new friendships, and if this affects their intention to adopt the apps. The study found that MIM's features could enhance the interconnectivity, convenience, mobility, playfulness, and communication of its users. MIM users can use the apps to control their communication within the networks in order to retain their current friendships, as well as create new ones.

Keywords: M-Commerce, Mobile instant messaging (MIM), IT culture, Mobile application.

Introduction

The number of smartphone users in the U.S. has surpassed that of PC users. In some countries, such as China, the percentage of users who access the internet via smartphones has actually exceeded those who access the web by using PCs. This ubiquity of smartphones has transformed the lifestyle of young adults by providing them with a more mobile lifestyle. About 97% of smartphone users now use text services and mobile instant messaging (MIM) is the most frequently used application (PewResearch Center, 2015). In fact, some 36% of U.S. smartphone owners use MIM apps, such as WhatsApp, imessage or Kik (PewResearch Center, 2015), which are emerging as the dominant global communication medium. This is because of their hedonic, interoperability (Oghuma *et al.*, 2015), temporal (Wang and Zhu, 2014) and nomadic features. As MIM continues to proliferate and evolve with more features, users are assimilating them into their mobile lifestyle.

MIM is currently transforming one-to-one communication into one-to-many communication. Although MIM has drastically increased communication efficiency, it also poses serious security risks because "security is only as strong as the weakest link". Most MIM app users have not received any rigorous security training and its instant connectivity makes security control worse. There are a number of major issues related to the use of MIM apps, including SMS spam, SMiShing, extortion, kidnapping, identify theft, terrorism, Trojan horses, viruses and malware. These emerging security threats are in contrast to the perceived benefits of MIM apps, which are communication control and increased mobility. There is also the question of how susceptible users are to peer pressure, and if they adopt MIM apps to make new friends. Also, research on how a young person or in this case the digital native generation adapt to MIM apps is still lacking. This study proposes an integrative research model to investigate whether MIM apps are a fit technology that helps users to develop new friendships.

The remainder of the chapter is organized as follows: we will first review the literature that is related to perceived communication control, mobility and the perceived subjective norm (PSN) in the context of MIM apps. There will then be further discussion about the MIM apps' influence on task-technology fit and whether users adopt them because they help to develop new friendships. We will propose our hypotheses at the end of the literature review, followed by the research methodology and data analysis sections. The results of the analysis will then be reported in order to validate our proposed hypotheses and the theoretical and practical implications drawn based on the analysis results. This study will be concluded with both the limitations of the research, as well as future research directions.

Literature review

MIM apps equip young adults with communication control capacity

Communication control capacity (CCC), which is the ability of users to control the length, content, and pace of communication, has had a strong effect on how MIM apps are used to develop online friendships (Sheer, 2011). These apps have continued to evolve since MIM's introduction with many rich media, such as free voice and video calls, stickers, group chat, notifications, photos and video sharing, temporary snap pictures and movies, adding new friends and self-representation. A growing number of users prefer to use MIM for customer support services because they are more flexible and provide greater control of the communication process (Eddy, 2014). While MIM is becoming popular amongst youths, it annoys many people from other age ranges and can make their work unproductive (Frankola, 2015). For instance, the messages in MIM apps are organized chronologically. As messages are exchanged frequently, their number can increase exponentially to the point where they become unmanageable.

If users try to cut into an ongoing conversation, their messages can easily be out of sync with existing messages. As a result, users who are not following the messages closely can feel overwhelmed. These users often feel that they lose their capacity to control communication and choose to skim through volumes of messages instead, or just leave the chat room.

Despite these potential drawbacks, MIM apps continue to thrive amongst young smartphone users. A recent study has found that mobile phone users are showing symptoms of mobile dependency. This is particularly the case for MIM users who are highly sociable. Many of them experience anxiety, loss, and social withdrawal if they cannot access their MIM apps (Lin *et al.*, 2015). It is plausible that young adults may feel that MIM apps provide them with a capacity for better communication control. Therefore, it is important to understand whether young adults feel that they can properly control MIM apps in order to assist them with the process of making new friends, increasing their social networking activities, and meeting friends of the opposite sex. Therefore, we propose that the following hypothesis.

H1: MIM are applications with a good fit for young adults who wish to control their communication capacity.

MIM apps meet the mobility needs of young adults

MIM are applications that fit the mobile lifestyle of young adults. Instead of calling each other, the majority of them choose to use MIM apps to call, share pictures, music and videos (Lin and Li, 2014). In addition, the perceived ease of use and playfulness of MIM apps are two important factors that affect the intention of users to adopt them (Yoon *et al.*, 2015). Most MIM apps have emoticons or stickers because they are easy to use and fun to play with, allowing users to quickly express their emotions with cute, self-explanatory pictures. This means the information sender and receiver can quickly understand each other, without spending too much time or effort on texts or audio-based explanations.

Privacy is another reason that youths choose to adopt MIM, rather than traditional phone and short messaging services. Some MIM apps, such as Instagram, enable users to share time-limited private messages and pictures. Information senders can see whether the recipients are online and where they are 24/7 by using the MIM's locational feature. These global applications are not limited to any geographical barriers created by telecom companies in different countries. Group chat is another popular feature that is used to enhance communication efficiency. All of these features enable MIM users to efficiently and instantly communicate with each other, independent of time and place (Mallat *et al.*, 2009). MIM apps are popular with youths because they can meet their growing demand for a more mobile lifestyle. Therefore, we propose the following hypothesis.

H2: MIM are applications with a good fit for the mobile lifestyle of youths.

SN has a positive effect on the adoption of MIM Apps that develop and maintain friendships

SN is the perceived importance of a referent's decision to adopt certain behaviors (Kaushik *et al.*, 2015). Previous studies have also shown that SN has a significant influence on a person's decision to adopt the new technology (Mou and Lin, 2015). SN exhibits a similar influence on the decision of young people to adopt MIM apps (Shim and Shin, 2016; Liu *et al.*, 2011). However, many novelty technologies, such as time-limited messages, hidden messages, and MIM anonymity, enable users to conceal their identity when they use MIM-based communication. These technologies could potentially decrease SN's influence on a young adult's decision to adopt MIM apps.

A holistic understanding of MIM apps can be examined from three different perspectives: technological purposes, subscription methods (e.g., free or pay), and networking purposes (Pedersen *et al.*, 2002). This study is more interested in understanding the two primary networking purposes for youths to adopt MIM apps, which are (1) maintaining existing relationships and (2) developing new relationships.

Maintaining friendships is considered to be an instrumental part of communications and has the purpose of completing a specific task (e.g., making a friend laugh by sharing a funny video or telling other friends about the latest news) (Nysveen *et al.*, 2005). A recent study about the purpose of using MIM apps, such as Snapchat, showed that they are primarily used for maintaining good relationships with close friends and family, via selfies or picture doodling features (Piwek and Joinson, 2016).

In contrast, MIM apps can quickly help to develop new friendships via group-based communications (Zhou and Lu, 2011a). For instance, a user can meet up with a new friend and they can both quickly share their MIM accounts with each other. Once this new friendship is established, the new friend can quickly invite the user to join any social groups that he/she has established. The user can then immediately access new friends in these new social groups. It is plausible that the user can take advantage of this and other MIM features, and so start making new friends from these groups. Thus, we propose the following hypothesis.

H3: Subjective norms have a positive influence on the adoption of MIM apps by youths to develop new relationships.

MIM apps are good fit technologies for developing new friendships

Some MIM apps enable users to meet and interact with potential friends nearby who share common things, such as their location, access time, activities, and interests. Mobile social scenarios can also be accurately constructed, based on their encounter history on mobile social networks (Li *et al.*, 2015). A growing number of young adults have been using MIM apps to obtain contextual, real-time recommendations from their friends (e.g., what they should buy, where to get it and from whom). A study has shown that contextual recommendations can increase the users' utilitarian, hedonic, and social values and thereby increase their intention to adopt a mobile social reviews platform (Shen *et al.*, 2013). Old friends often help people to make new friends in the physical world. MIM apps can provide a timely, personalized digital profile of new friends, via old friends in the existing social network, and thereby increase the chances of making more new friendships. Therefore, MIM apps are good fit technologies for developing new friendships. Therefore, we propose the following hypothesis.

H4: MIM apps are good fit technologies for developing new friendships.

MIM apps with a high degree of fit can increase the likelihood of users using them to develop new friendships

MIM apps can capture valuable information (e.g., text records, location, community structure, relationships, members in the network and influencers) about a person's social network relationships. Many companies are using social network analysis methods to identify influential users who have a high impact on others (Han *et al.*, 2014). The adoption of MIM apps may also have similar patterns if influential users find them useful to develop new friendship and become agents in encouraging others to adopt those apps. Thus, we propose the following hypothesis.

H5: MIM apps with a high degree of fit can increase the likelihood of users adopting them to develop new friendships.

The above discussion leads to our research model (Figure 1), which has seven constructs and six relationships.

Research methodology

We conducted a field experiment methodology because it had the merits of "gaining insight *into the methods of instruction*". A survey

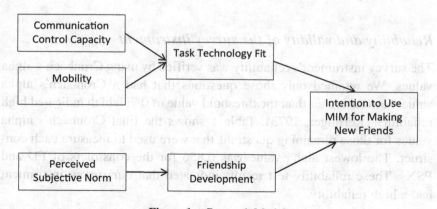

Figure 1. Research Model

research method was adopted in order to understand users' perceptions about the most popular MIS apps, LINE, and their intention of adopting them. All of the questions used to measure the reach construct were modified from previously published journal papers. Table 1 includes all of the questions that were used to measure each variable. The survey instrument adopted a 7-point Likert's scale with 1 = "strongly disagree" and 7 = "strongly agree". This study used Sheer's 2011 survey instrument to measure the CCC. The mobility construct was measured by using Mallat *et al.*'s 2009. The construct of the task technology fit (TTF) was measured by using Zhou *et al.*'s (2010) study. In addition, the friendship development (FD) construct was measured by using Sheer's 2011 study.

We posted our survey on a bulletin board of a public university in Taiwan. The users of the bulletin boards were students and faculty teachers at the university. Four prizes were prepared for subjects who participated in the study. The first prize was a $17 gift card from 7 to 11, the popular convenience store in Taiwan. The second prize was a $10 gift card, followed by $7 and $3 gift cards for the third and fourth prizes. The prizes were drawn after the 1-week deadline.

A total of 89 subjects participated in the study. About 40.45% of these subjects were aged 23 to 29-years-old, followed by 38.2% of them aged 18- to 22-years-old, 19.1% aged 31- to 39-years-old and the remaining 2.25% were aged 40-years-old and over. Females represented 51.69% of the total subjects and males 48.31%.

Reliability and validity of the survey instrument

The survey instrument's reliability was verified by using Cronbach's alpha values. We retained only those questions that had a Cronbach's alpha value that was higher than the threshold value of 0.7, which indicated high reliability (Kerlinger, 1973). Table 1 shows the final Cronbach's alpha values for those remaining questions that were used to measure each construct. The lowest alpha value was 0.856 for the constructs of FD and PSNs. These reliability test results indicated that our survey instrument had a high reliability.

Table 1. Reliability Test Results

Constructs	Questions	Cronbach's Alpha Values
CCC	• I feel I have full control in what I intend to communicate on LINE • I can control the communication pace on LINE • I can control the length of the communication time on LINE • I can control my own image well on LINE • I can control the use of features at will on LINE • I can control whether to respond to oncoming messages on LINE	0.886
Mobility (MOB)	• Using LINE is independent of time • Using LINE is independent of place • Communicating with someone using LINE is convenient because it is usually with me	0.856
PSN	• People are important to me and I think I should use this LINE • People whose opinions I value would prefer me to use this LINE • People I look up to expect me to use this LINE	0.965
TTF	• TTF1: In helping complete my tasks, the functions of LINE are enough • TTF2: In helping me complete my tasks, the functions of LINE are appropriate • TTF3: In general, the functions of LINE fully meet my communication needs	0.904
FD	• LINE helps me to meet new people • LINE helps me to develop friendships with new people • LINE helps me to obtain others' personal information I am interested in • LINE helps me to know others well	0.887
CI	• I plan to keep using this LINE in the future • I intend to continue using this LINE in the future • I expect my use of this LINE to continue in the future	0.897

Table 2. Construct Validity Tests: Discriminant and Convergent Analysis

	CCC	FD	INT	MO	PSN	CI
CCC	0.799					
FD	0.541	0.762				
INT	0.489	0.366	0.967			
MO	0.490	0.279	0.558	0.902		
PSN	0.543	0.465	0.328	0.338	0.882	
CI	0.647	0.414	0.544	0.516	0.525	0.911

Moreover, we tested the convergent and discriminant validity of our survey instrument in order to ensure the existence of high construct validity. Table 2 shows the correlation matrix with the square roots of the Average Variance Extracted (AVE) values, as reported on the diagonal of the matrix. The square roots values are larger than their cross-correlations. This shows that the variance that can be explained by each construct is larger than the measurement error variance. It is therefore clear that the survey instrument has a high discriminant validity. In addition, all the items loaded are greater than 0.5 on their associated constructs, indicating that all the questions have a high validity (Wixom and Watson, 2001). The evidence of high discriminant and convergent validity ascertains that the survey instrument used in this study has a high construct validity. Therefore, we used the revised survey instrument to conduct the full-scale study with confidence.

Hypothesis test results

The smart PLS was used to perform the structural equation modelling (SEM) analysis. This analysis calculated the estimated path coefficients, path significance, and $R2$ values. All six proposed hypotheses were supported at $p < 0.01$. As shown in Table 3, Hypothesis 1 (H1) was supported, indicating that CCC had a significantly positive effect on the increase in user perception about the degree of TTF for using MIM to develop new friendships. H2 was supported, indicating that the MO feature had a positive effect on the increase of TTF to use MIS to develop new friendships. CCC and MO together can explain 47% ($R2$ value) of the variance in the

Table 3. SEM Test Results

Hypothesized Paths	Path Coefficients (β)	*T*-statistics
H1: CCC → TTF**	0.518	17.877
H2: MO → TTF**	0.263	7.665
H3: PSN → FD**	0.356	11.078
H4: TTF → INT**	0.473	43.025
H5: FD → INT**	0.171	4.904

** $p < 0.01$

TTF factor. H3 was supported by indicating that PSN had a positive effect on the use of MIM for making new friends. H4 was supported, indicating that MAS had a positive cultural effect on the use of MIM to make new friends. Both PSN and MAS together can explain 31.1% of the variance in the FD factor. H5 was supported, indicating that the TTF had a positive effect on the CI of using MIM to get to know others. Success of MIM apps in making new friends could encourage users to continue using them. TTF and FD together can explain 32% of the variance in the CI factor.

Discussion

MIM apps empower users to represent themselves with different tools (e.g., texts, emoticons, stickers, personal profile, QR code, Shake, Friend Radar, and Drift Bottle) while making new friends. Texts and asynchronous media have important control communication capacities (Hiltz and Turoff, 1993) and MIM apps combine both instantaneous and asynchronicity features. Users can freely switch between these two features by using a wide variety of communication tools. For instance, MIM users can use video chat with each other for urgent communications. In contrast, users can engage in conversations with a limited time interval and release the pressure and stress (Walther, 1996). Users of MIM apps can also decide whether to interact with others, how soon and for how long. During each conversation, MIM users can also decide how much information to disclose to new friends. If trust has not been established yet, users can conceal their true identity to decrease the risks of self-disclosure (Henderson and Gilding, 2004). This study shows that MIM apps are effective in helping users make new friends because of their high CCC.

Mobility is an important mechanism for both making new friends and maintaining old friendship. A study shows that most new connections occur at an immediate geodesic distance (Collet and Hedstrom, 2013). MIM apps enable users to discover potential new friends nearby, and their mobility feature can increase this possibility of making new friends. This study confirms the importance of mobility for users who choose MIM apps in order to make new friends.

The FD processes involve three phases: making a new friend, getting to know them, and becoming a close friend (Canary *et al.*, 2008). Breaking the ice when meeting a stranger and then making them a new friend is particularly challenging for most people because of the lack of trust between both parties (Millar and Rogers, 1976). This study finds that perceived SN is an important factor that contributes to people adopting MIM apps to make new friends, as many users may feel the pressure of not participating in new social groups and MIM apps can help them to expand their social network. The social pressure or SN is evident in the adoption of MIS apps to make new friends, and this finding affirms that SN could help to determine the behavioral intention of users to build new friendships via MIM apps (Colman, 2015).

Cultural differences need to be considered when information systems are adopted (Lee and Kramer, 2013).

Information Technology can be used to expand the users' social network (Buhalis and Law, 2008). Furthermore, an IT application can both create and foster communication between existing friendships, as well as expanding them to nearby nodes (Huckfeldt, 1983). The users' communication line for both existing and new networks can also be enhanced by features found in IT applications, such as MIM apps. Therefore, because these apps and their features are fit to enhance both existing and new friendships, it is a fit technology for users to develop new friendships.

MIM apps are widely available on today's smartphones (Lee, 2015) and it is their ease-of-use and the ubiquitous network between MIM users that play an important role in their popularity. Many other useful features also contribute to the apps' usage. Once users are attached to the network, the cost of leaving it is higher than actually staying connected to the network (Hampton and Wellman, 2001). Hence, the MIM app has a positive impact on increasing the intentions of both old and new users to develop new friendships.

Limitations and future research directions

This study has a number of limitations that could be improved upon by future research. Firstly, the sample is from one country and does not represent the general population. Secondly, we only surveyed the most popular MIM app, LINE, and did not cover other popular services, such as WhatsApp or WeChat. These limitations could be further explored in future research. Future studies could also expand beyond just one culture and explore various types of popular MIM Apps.

Conclusion

This research explored how the features and usage of popular IT applications, such as MIM apps, fit in terms of helping young adult users to find new friends. MIM features can enhance the interconnectivity, convenience, mobility, playfulness, and communication of its users. In addition, MIM users can use the app to control their communication within networks in order to both retain current friends and create new friendships. This research also found that SN plays an important part in MIM users continuing to use the service. Although there has been past studies into MIM app adoption, this research helps to increase understanding of how the MIM app system fits in helping young adults to find new friends and networks.

References

Buhalis, D. and Law, R. 2008. "Progress in Information Technology and Tourism Management: 20 Years on and 10 Years after the Internet — The State of eTourism Research," *Tourism Management*, 29(4), 609–623.

Canary, D. J., Cody, M. J., and Manusov, V. L. 2008. "*Interpersonal communication: A goals Based Approach.*" Macmillan, London.

Collet, F. and Hedström, P. 2013. "Old Friends and New Acquaintances: Tie Formation Mechanisms in an Interorganizational Network Generated by Employee Mobility," *Social Networks*, 35(3), 288–299.

Colman, A. M. 2015. *"Theory of Reasoned Action,"* A Dictionary of Psychology. Oxford University Press, Oxford.

Eddy, N. 2014. "Consumers like Using Text Messages to Solve Customer Service Issues," *eWeek*. Retrieved from November 21. 15. http://www.eweek.com/networking/consumers-like-using-text-messages-to-solve-customer-service-issues.html.

Frankola, K. 2015. "Has Instant Messaging become more Annoying than Email? 5 Steps for more Productive Pining." *Huff Post Business*. Retrieved from November 21, 15. http://www.huffingtonpost.com/karen-frankola/has-instant-messaging-become-more-annoying-than-email-5-steps-for-more-productive-pinging_b_6815700.html.

Hampton, K. and Wellman, B. 2001. "Long Distance Community in the Network Society Contact and Support Beyond Netville," *American Behavioral Scientist*, 45(3), 476–495.

Han, X., Cuevas, A., Crespi, N. Cuevas, R., and Huang, X. 2014. "On Exploiting Social Relationship and Personal Background for Content Discovery in P2P Networks," *Future Generation Computer Systems*, 40, 17–29.

Henderson, S. and Gilding, M. 2004. "'I've Never Clicked this Much with Anyone in My Life': Trust and Hyperpersonal Communication in Online Friendships," *New Media & Society*, 6(4), 487–506.

Hiltz, S. R. and Turoff, M. 1993. *"The Network Nation: Human Communication via Computer,"* Mit Press, Cambridge, Massachusetts.

Huckfeldt, R. R. 1983. "Social Contexts, Social Networks, and Urban Neighborhoods: Environmental Constraints on Friendship Choice," *American journal of Sociology*, 89(3), 651–669.

Kaushik, A. K., Agrawal, A. K., and Rahman, Z. 2015. "Tourist Behaviour Towards Self-service Hotel Technology Adoption: Trust and Subjective Norm as Key Antecedents," *Tourism Management Perspectives*, 16, 278–289.

Kerlinger, F. N. 1973. *Foundations of Behavioral Research*, New York: Holt, Rinehart and Winston, Inc., pp. 445–452.

Lin, T. T., Chiang, Y. H., and Jiang, Q. 2015. "Sociable People Beware? Investigating Smartphone Versus Nonsmartphone Dependency Symptoms among Young Singaporeans," *Social Behavior and Personality: An International Journal*, 43(7), 1209–1216.

Lee, E. M. and Kramer, R. 2013. "Out with the Old, in with the New? Habitus and Social Mobility at Selective Colleges," *Sociology of Education*, 86(1), 18–35.

Lee, W. J. 2015. "The Effects of Smartphone Addiction Drivers on Work Performance," In *21st Americas Conference on Information Systems, Puerto Rico*. http://aisel.aisnet.org/amcis2015/GlobalIssues/GeneralPresentations/1/.

Li, H., Chen, Y., Cheng, X., Li, K., and Chen, D. 2015. "Secure Friend Discovery Based on Encounter History in Mobile Social Networks," *Personal and Ubiquitous Computing*, 19(7), 999–1009.

Lin, T. T. and Li, L. 2014. "Perceived Characteristics, Perceived Popularity, and Playfulness: Youth Adoption of Mobile Instant Messaging in China," *China Media Research*, 10(2), 60–71.

Liu, Z., Min, Q., and Ji, S. 2011. "A Study of Mobile Instant Messaging Adoption: Within-Culture Variation," *International Journal of Mobile Communications*, 9(3), 280–297.

Mallat, N., Rossi, M., Tuunainen, V. K., and Öörni, A. 2009. "The Impact of Use Context on Mobile Services Acceptance: The Case of Mobile Ticketing," *Information & Management*, 46(3), 190–195.

Millar, F. E. and Rogers, L. E. 1976. "A Relational Approach to Interpersonal Communication," In Miller, G. R. (ed.), Explorations in Interpersonal Communication. Oxford, England, Sage.

Mou, Y., and Lin, C. A. 2015. "Exploring Podcast Adoption Intention via Perceived Social Norms, Interpersonal Communication, and Theory of Planned Behavior," *Journal of Broadcasting & Electronic Media*, 59(3), 475–493.

Nysveen, H., Pedersen, P. E., and Thorbjørnsen, H. 2005. "Intentions to Use Mobile Services: Antecedents and Cross-service Comparisons," *Journal of the Academy of Marketing Science*, 33(3), 330–346.

Oghuma, A. P., Chang, Y., Libaque-Saenz, C. F., Park, M. C., and Rho, J. J. 2015. "Benefit-Confirmation Model for Post-adoption Behavior of Mobile Instant Messaging Applications: A Comparative Analysis of KakaoTalk and Joyn in Korea," *Telecommunications Policy*, 39(8), 658–677.

Pedersen, P. E., Methlie, L. B., and Thorbjornsen, H. 2002. "Understanding Mobile Commerce End-user Adoption: A Triangulation Perspective and Suggestions for an Exploratory Service Evaluation Framework," In *System Sciences, 2002. HICSS. Proceedings of the 35th Annual Hawaii International Conference on*, P. 8.

PewResearch Center 2015. "Mobile Messaging and Social Media 2015." PewResearch Center, Retrieved from November 21, 15. http://www.pewinternet.org/2015/08/19/mobile-messaging-and-social-media-2015/.

Piwek, L. and Joinson, A. 2016. "'What do they Snapchat About?' Patterns of Use in Time-limited Instant Messaging Service," *Computers in Human Behavior*, 54, 358–367.

Sheer, V. C. 2011. "Teenagers' Use of MSN Features, Discussion Topics, and Online Friendship Development: The Impact of Media Richness and Communication Control," *Communication Quarterly*, 59, 82–103.

Shen, X. L., Sun, Y., and Wang, N. 2013. "Recommendations from Friends Anytime and Anywhere: Toward a Model of Contextual Offer and Consumption Values," *Cyberpsychology, Behavior, and Social Networking*, 16(5), 349–356.

Shim, H., and Shin, E. 2016. "Peer-group Pressure as a Moderator of the Relationship Between Attitude Toward Cyberbullying and Cyberbullying Behaviors on Mobile Instant Messengers," *Telematics and Informatics*, 33(1), 17–24.

Walther, J. B. 1996. "Computer-mediated Communication Impersonal, Interpersonal, and Hyperpersonal Interaction," *Communication Research*, 23(1), 3–43.

Wang, Q. and Zhu, Y. 2014. "Temporal Pattern of Communication: Messaging Within a Mobile Social Networking App," *Journal of Electronic Commerce in Organizations (JECO)*, 12(4), 57–68.

Wixom, B. H., and Watson, H. J. 2001. "An Empirical Investigation of the Factors Affecting Data Warehousing Success," *MIS Quarterly*, 25(1), 17–41.

Yoon, C., Jeong, C., and Rolland, E. 2015. "Understanding Individual Adoption of Mobile Instant Messaging: A Multiple Perspectives Approach." *Information Technology and Management*, 16(2), 139–151.

Zhou, T., Lu, Y. B., and Wang, B. 2010. "Integrating TTF and UTAUT to Explain Mobile Banking User Adoption," *Computers in Human Behavior*, 26(4), 760–767.

Zhou, T., and Lu, Y. 2011. "Examining Mobile Instant Messaging User Loyalty from the Perspectives of Network Externalities and Flow Experience," *Computers in Human Behavior*, 27(2), 883–889.

Chapter 11

Exploring the Development of China's Mobile Payment from the Perspective of Resource-based Platform Strategies

Jiang Yu

Institute of Policy and Management
Chinese Academy of Sciences, Beijing, 100190, P. R. China
yujiang@casipm.ac.cn

Wenmiao Hu

Institute of Policy and Management
Chinese Academy of Sciences, Beijing, 100190, P. R. China

Yue Zhang

Institute of Policy and Management
Chinese Academy of Sciences, Beijing, 100190, P. R. China

Abstract

China has witnessed the rapid development of mobile payment as the revolutionary idea of digitalizing has potentially reshaped many industries including payment. Various practitioners are involved in this emerging industry like Internet giants, mobile network operators, card associations, and banks. These mobile payment platform providers have walked their own way while developing the platforms. We

179

formulate the framework in this chapter to analyze how the different platform providers determined their platform strategies by leveraging their key resources at the different stages of platform development. Three development stages including technological innovation, platform deployment, and platform scaling have been identified. The framework illustrates resource-based platform strategies in the context of China's mobile payment development. Multiple case studies have been conducted to validate the framework we have formulated for the resource-based platform strategies of China's mobile payment platform providers.

Key words: China Mobile Payment, Resources based, Platform Strategies.

Introduction

The revolutionary idea of digitizing has potentially shattered the previous service model and the stability of the industrial organization. Digital convergence has attracted much attention yet no universally accepted understanding of it has been revealed (Tilson *et al.*, 2010b). Digital convergence with mobile technologies has sparked numerous digital innovations in the payment industry (Ondrus and Lyytinen, 2011).

At the same time, "Platform economy" has come with dramatical power in the business world. Most groundbreaking innovations of many companies like Amazon, Google, and Alibaba are not products or services alone; they are the platforms on which these products and services are built.

Inspired by the research work of Hanseth and Lyytinen (2010) that the development of platforms embraces evolutionary dynamics, this chapter is aimed at studying resource-based platform strategy variations during the development of the mobile payment platform since for each mobile payment dominator or provider, the resources they have obtained are not the same and thus result in different platform strategies and platform performance. Thus, we formulate the following research question: *how do resource-based platform strategies determine the success of mobile payment platform?* This Chapter will be conducted as follows: first, we present and discuss prior research on platform, platform strategy, RBV, and service innovation theories. Researches on mobile payment have also been reviewed to help the theoretical framework formulation. Then we formulate the theoretical framework of the resource-based platform strategy at different stages of mobile payment platform development followed by analysis of multiple cases of four different mobile payment platform providers. Finally, our findings and conclusions will be presented.

Literature review

Vargo and Lusch (2004) defined service as "the application of specialized knowledge skills through deeds, processes, and performances for the benefit of customers". As service is increasingly provided through digital technology (Yoo *et al.*, 2010), service system innovations are offered new opportunities. Service system is seen as "socio-technical assemblages of distributed, heterogeneous, and resource-integrating actors whose relationships are governed by shared institutional logics, standards, and digital technology" (Orlikowski and Scott, 2008; Eaton *et al.*, 2015).

Besides, Lusch and Nambisan (2015) have offered the definition of service innovation as limitations of the perspectives other scholars have adopted like digital innovation (Yoo *et al.*, 2010), digital infrastructure (Tilson *et al.*, 2010), and software-based platform (Tiwanan *et al.*, 2010) in need of a broader conceptualization of service innovation. Thus, they defined service innovation as rebundling of diverse resources that create novel resources which are beneficial (i.e. value experiencing) to some actors in a given context; this almost always involves a network of actors, including the beneficiary (e.g., the customer).

As continuing developments of digital technology have offered new opportunities for service innovation (Yoo *et al.*, 2012), three views are summarized by Eaton *et al.* (2015) to focus on the different opinions of scholars on digital innovation. The first view as the generative view focuses on the generative aspect of digital technology and the dynamics of innovations is changed. The second view as the infrastructure view notes the growing scale and scope of information infrastructures, which supports diversified forms of services and service innovation (Hanseth and Lyytinen, 2010; Hanseth *et al.*, 2010). The third view as the integrative view tries to characterize service systems enabled by digital technology as multisided markets (Eisenman *et al.*, 2006) and platforms (Gawer, 2009; Tiwana *et al.*, 2010).

The term "platform" widely being referred to in the management field as a word means foundation of components around which an organization can create a related but differentiated set of products (or services) (Cusumano, 2010). Platform research within management also highlights the classifications of it. Gawer (2014) classified platforms as internal platforms, supply-chain platforms, industry platforms, and two-sided platforms. It is also increasingly recognized that external application developers may play a significant role in platform innovation (Messerschmitt and Szyperski, 2003; Evans *et al.*, 2006; Bosch, 2009) and serve as the basis for software leadership (Gawer and Cusumano, 2002).

Boundary resource is proposed by Ghazawneh and Henfridsson referring to the software tools and regulations that serve as the interface for the arm's length relationship between the platform owner and the application developer (Ghazawneh and Henfridsson, 2012). They established constructs of boundary resource model of resourcing and securing to show the structural arrangement of service systems enabled by digital technology and how it helps firms to ease the tension between the control and generativity issues.

However, in the following work of Eaton *et al.* (2015), they pointed out that Ghazawneh and Henfridsson (2012) failed to explain how boundary resources come into being and how they evolve over time so Eaton *et al.* (2015) extended the work of Ghazawneh and Henfriddon seeking to understand the underlying mechanisms by which boundary resources come into being and evolve over time with the in-depth embedded case study of Apple's IOS service system.

Researches on platform are also demonstrated as a focal topics in many specific fields of management including strategic management, organizational management, and innovation management. As for the platform itself, scholars have studied different types of platforms, and the important attributes of a successful platform. As for platform strategies, different types of platform strategies have been studied. Some have focused on the competition and collaboration between different platforms. Some have conducted in-depth researches on specific attributes of a platform from several perspectives, like openness, quality, architecture, etc.

However, neither many researches to study the evolutionary dynamics of platform in the settings of mobile payment nor researches from the perspective of resources of platform have been conducted.

Theoretical framework

We propose our framework to analyze the phenomena in China's mobile payment industry about how mobile payment platform providers determine their platform strategies through leveraging their key resources at the different stages of the development of the platform.

Diversified *technological innovations* begin to reshape the traditional payments industry. New innovative mobile payment solutions are constantly emerging. While *Platform deployment* matters a lot at the next stage of the mobile payment platform development. Once the platform reaches the critical mass, *platform scaling* is ignited, more partners are attracted and more heterogeneous services are offered, which in turn increases the reach of the platform (Henfridsson and Bygstad, 2013; Ondrus *et al.*, 2015).

In this chapter we refer to *boundary resources* as the software tools and regulations, hardware components and operating systems and applications that serve as the interface and functionality support for mobile payment between the platform owners and any other relevant stakeholders, including SDK and APIs of App-based payment platform, POS terminals, NFC (near-field communication) related components and devices, etc. We refer to *common resources* as the installed base of the platform that is potentially able to become mobile payment service beneficiaries, including App users, POS adopted merchants, and payment service tailored mobile phone users, etc.

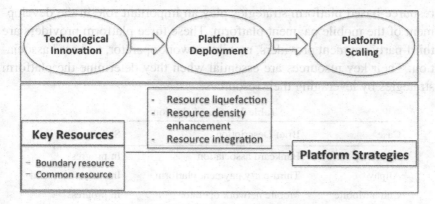

Figure 1.   Theoretical Framework

Resource liquefaction refers to the decoupling of information from its related physical form or devices that store, transmit, or process it (Normann, 2001). Whether the degree of resource liquefaction relatively influences the decision making on technology and standards, mobilizing external contributions, etc. needs much to be desired. *Resource density enhancement* refers to the need to mobilize contextually relevant knowledge (resource) in the most effective and efficient way. *Resource integration* refers to integration of resources that are not only market facing but also nonmarket facing where, and innovations and resources are mutually combined for more innovative possibilities (Lusch and Nambisan, 2015).

Methodology

In this chapter, we aim to understand how mobile payment platform providers determine the platform strategies by leveraging their key resources. We would like to study the development of different mobile payment platforms in China to see their evolutionary dynamics. Our choice is to conduct multiple case studies. Yin (2001) describes a case study as the ideal research design when the researcher asks *why* and *how* questions to understand a phenomenon. We aim to conduct multiple case studies to summarize some general instrumental experiences for platform providers. We aim to achieve this understanding by using multiple cases in answering the research question *"How do resource-based platform strategies determine the success of mobile payment platforms?"*

We have chosen the three cases because they explicitly clarify why resource-based platform strategies play an important role in the development of the mobile payment platform. These three platform providers are third-party payment providers, mobile network operator, and card association. Their key resources are essential when they determine the platform strategies by leveraging their resources.

Table 1. Case Selection

Case	Brief Description	State
UnionPay	Bankcard association	In progress
Alipay	Third-party payment platform	Initially successful
China Mobile	Mobile network operator	In progress

The relevant theory is used to analyze the phenomenon about different types of platform strategies in different industries and how RBV has been applied to many fields of research. By using multiple cases, we get data from different mobile payment platform providers and this enables us to understand the phenomenon from different angles.

Data has been collected from many different sources including both first-hand and second. Interviews were conducted with more than 10 managers and staff in mobile payment related companies, from POS terminal manufacturers, and mobile payment service providers like Alipay, and different merchants. Other sources of second-hand data came from homepages of the firms, consultancy reports, news reports, government regulations, and so on.

Case studies

Before we go to the three cases to combine our theoretical framework with real cases in mobile payment development, we would like to make a brief introduction to the mobile payment platform and its value chains.

As shown in Figure 2, the upstream part of the value chain falls into what enables the mobile payment platform itself including infrastructure providers like banks and mobile network operators and card associations, component suppliers, etc.

The downstream part of the value chain includes mobile payment platform complement producers and other intermediaries between the platform owner and end-users. End-users here consist of two groups of users including consumers and merchants. Downstream complements are bundled by the mobile payment platform's end-users to customize it to their unique needs.

Case 1: UnionPay

Stage I: Technological innovation

Early 2008, China UnionPay (CUP) collaborated with five commercial banks to launch a mobile phone payment pilot project in Shanghai using the Nokia 6131i cellphone with NFC technology. In the following years, different mobile payment products like HandPay, NFC–SD cellphone

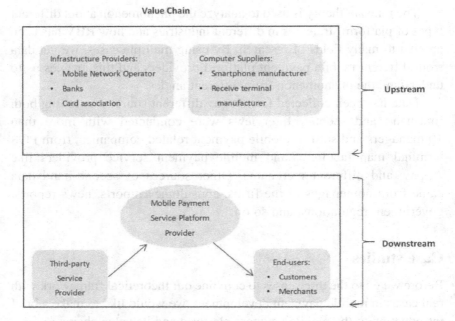

Figure 2. Upstream and Downstream Parts of Mobile Payment Platform Value Chains

payment standardized product, NFC–SIM cellphone with Samsung have been launched. Until the end of 2012, UnionPay's 13.56 MHz NFC solution was adopted by PBC as the official standard for mobile payment.

CUP operates the inter-bank transaction settlement system and possesses huge the installed base of UnionPay bankcard and POS terminals. Boundary resources of CUP mainly could be seen as the clearing and settlement system, and the widespread installed POS terminals. Mobile payment transactions are supported by the clearing and settlement system. POS terminals serve as the boundary for merchants to adopt mobile payment. CUP has chosen the NFC technology to enable mobile payment leveraging its boundary resources. In order to build the mobile payment platform, combing its own resources CUP chose to start with upstream collaboration by standard domination and then reached the goal of mobilizing external contribution from the upstream value chain.

Stage II: Platform deployment

In 2013, CUP, Bank of China, and China Mobile co-announced that the NFC cellphone payment products based on the TSM mobile payment platform are officially put into commercial banks. Later, 10 national commercial banks accessed the TSM[1] platform in succession and began to promote pilot projects in 14 cities to aiming at expanding the business scope of NFC mobile payment products. In 2014, CUP has also forged collaborations with some smartphone manufacturers like Nubia.

At the stage of platform deployment, CUP invested quite a lot to speed the POS terminal transformation. As for consumers, CUP has cooperated with many smartphone manufacturers to promote smartphones with NFC function.

In December 2015, UnionPay and over 20 commercial banks launched Cloud QuickPass based on NFC smartphones. This new mobile payment method is based on HCE and Token technology on android system and there is no need to unlock the smartphones, open App when making payments. Later, UnionPay announced cooperation with Apple.

Before CUP went forward hand in hand with ApplePay, much collaboration with upstream part was reached in order to realize better platform deployment and as for consumers, CUP did not have direct access to consumers. It was also not easy for CUP to mobilize smartphone manufacturers to invest heavily on promoting NFC function if the NFC infrastructure has not been deployed. Although CUP has a large installed base of POS terminal adopted merchants, and cardholders as what we called common resources, to accomplish the platform deployment successfully requires cross-side network effects where both merchants and consumers are important. Common resources transition comes first at this stage through resource density enhancement. The need to mobilize different brands of smartphones in the most effective and efficient way requires a strong brand having amazing reputation among consumers. The collaboration with ApplePay seems a good way out. However, there still

---

[1] Trusted service manager (TSM): the trusted service manager enables service providers to distribute and manage their contactless applications remotely by allowing access to the secure element in NFC-enabled handsets. https://en.wikipedia.org/wiki/Trusted_service_manager.

Table 2.   Key Points of the UnionPay Case

The Stages of the Development of Mobile Payment Platform

	Technological Innovation	Platform Deployment	Platform Scaling
Key Resources	Boundary resources • POS terminals • Mobile payment standards	Common resources • POS terminal adopted merchants • UnionPay cardholders • Iphone users	—
Resource Leverage	Resources liquefaction • POS terminal transformation • Dominant standards	Resource density enhancement • Collaborations with many smartphone brands • HCE with ApplyPay	—
Platform Strategies	Boundary resources design	Common resources transition	—

needs time to prove if this resource-based platform strategy of common resources transition by resource density enhancement works.

As for the stage of platform scaling, we have to say that CUP has not reached this stage until the time of writing this chapter.

Case 2: China Mobile

China Mobile Hebao is a comprehensive mobile payment business provided for individual and business customers. With NFC smartphones and the NFC–SIM cards, users can enjoy convenient online payment services like online shopping, fee charging, etc.

Stage I: Technological innovation

Early 1999, China Mobile did begin to launch pilot projects on mobile payments business. Before 2009, China Mobile launched SIMpass card, which integrates RFID chip on a normal SIM card. In 2009, China Mobile began to launch 2.4G RF–SIM cards based on Bluetooth technology to integrate RFID function on SIM card. Later in 2012, China Mobile determined NFC–SWP solution as the settled one. In 2013, China Mobile officially launched mobile wallet business based on NFC-SWP solution.

As one of the three mobile network operators in China, China Mobile has control on communication network, and the large installed base of SIM card users. China Mobile is already the provider of services relating to mobile devices such as cellphones and smartphones. This has given the mobile network operator special access to an immense customer base. After several choices of mobile payment solutions, China Mobile has chosen NFC–SWP solution, which demands the combination of SIM card and NFC-enabled mobile phones.

Stage II: Platform deployment

Since the NFC–SWP solution demands the support of both SIM cards and mobile phones, China Mobile has invested a lot on these two aspects. China Mobile subsidizes the manufacturers for original NEC-USIM cards deployed.

Table 3. Key points of the China Mobile Case

	The Stages of the Development of Mobile Payment Platform		
	Technological Innovation	Platform Deployment	Platform Scaling
Key resources	Boundary resources • NFC-SIM cards • Communication network	Common resources • SIM card users • Exclusive Contract smartphone users	—
Resources leverage	Resource liquefaction • Dominant Standards (failed) • NFC–SWP solution chosen	Resource density enhancement • Public transportation as starting point • Subsidy for NFC related manufacturers • Subsidy for NFC terminal sellers and buyers (users)	—
Platform strategies	Boundary resource combination	External contribution mobilization	—

In 2016, China Mobile continues promoting NFC by "developing 100 city bus mobile application, 100 school and enterprise one-card mobile application to enrich the NFC application scenarios and build the NFC ecosystem".[2] Besides, "Public transportation application is the pilot product of China Mobile in 2016. We will provide our 800 million clients with the portal to public transportation application".

For mobile network operators, they would not be willing to be partners for voice and data services only as a channel. The mobile payment function and the additional services would lead to increased sales and the market development of further sources of revenue. However, from going through the path of China Mobile's promoting NFC-enabled products and services, at least for now, they have not effectively leveraged their key resources to better realize platform deployment.

Case 3: Alipay

Alipay has an almost 50% market share in third-party online payments and over near 80% market share in third-party mobile payments in China.[3] Alibaba's e-commerce and its large user base has been the strong backing for Alipay.

Stage I: Technological innovation

Alipay Wallet (APP) was launched in June 2009. It has chosen QR code as the main technology to let customers in the Alipay Wallet.

The biggest benefit of QR code for mobile payment compared to NFC-enabled mobile payment is that there is no need for replacing the SIM card or installing security element. It was designed for millions of small businesses to provide them with low-cost devices without additional payment services.

With the trend of mobile Internet daily life, Alipay grasped the good timing to launch the mobile application APP. The QR code mobile payment is effectively integrated into the mobile application and acts as the mobile payment technological innovation to help Alipay extend their

---

[2] http://tech.163.com/16/0122/15/BDUOMPN0000915BD.html. Last accessed: July 25, 2017.
[3] Citi Research, "how fintech is forcing banking to a tipping point," 2016.

online payment services to offline payments. This backend technology helps Alipay to enter the mobile payment market very fast to grasp the good timing. The online platform has helped the mobile platform to cultivate and educate users, which makes the latter platform acquire the users smoothly with its mobility.

Stage II: Platform deployment

Alipay is the preferred payment solution on Taobao and Tmall as the large user base is easy to transfer from PC to mobile terminals. With the launch of the mobile application Alipay Wallet, it offers an integrated mobile payment platform to consumers and small businesses.

In 2013, Alipay established strategic alliance with Kuaidi (mobile app for online transportation network). At the end of 2013, Alipay mobile payment users exceeded 0.1 billion and Alipay Wallet announced to be an independent brand. Especially on the day of 12th December, Alipay launched large-scale promotion campaign among 20,000 offline stores, with 50% discount promised for using Alipay Wallet. This triggered another strong wave of Alipay Wallet App download and its mobile payment service adoption.

At this stage of platform deployment, based on its user base of Taobao, and Tmall, these portions of users are easy to be transferred into mobile payment users. We think this can be seen as platform envelopment strategies of complements. The envelopment of complements is most likely to succeed with high overlap in the platform's user base and these complements are reciprocally specific to each other (Eisenmann *et al.*, 2011). All Taobao and Tmall users are also Alipay users, and vice versa. This overlap facilitates share of user base and mutually boosts more service innovation.

Stage III: Platform scaling

In August 2014, Alipay announced that over 60 APIs from 7 categories were available for third-party service providers for creating more mobile payment scenarios for users on its open platform.

This open platform of Alipay provides free APIs and interface guide for third-party applications that need payment function inside. The industry solution covers from catering, integrated general merchandise, to

Table 4. Key Points of the Alipay Case

	The Stages of the Development of Mobile Payment Platform		
	Technological Innovation	Platform Deployment	Platform Scaling
Key resources	Boundary resources • Convenient payment portal with QR code backend technology • Online payment platform IS capabilities	Common resources • Taobao and Tmall users (Alipay online payment users)	Boundary resources • Free APIs on the platform Common resources • Offline merchants • APP users
Resources leverage	Resource liquefaction • QR code technology chosen • App-based payment solution	Resource density enhancement • Stepped into O2O • Vigorous promotion among offline merchants	Resource integration • Free APIs offered • Individual-centric functional architecture
Platform strategies	Fast entry	Envelopment of compliments	Multiple actors mobilization

entertainment business. Merchants themselves rely on the payment ability of Alipay through its open platform to complete traditional service online and improve the efficiency. Third-party service providers can provide diversified marketing service for merchants on the open platform and help merchants identify potential customers and reduce overall operating costs.

At this stage of platform scaling, more and more services based on mobile payment are offered to the users, which have increased the usage frequency of users and their loyalty. More and more third-party service providers joined to help diversify the services. More and more collaborations from different industries have been reached to jointly scale the mobile payment platform.

Discussions

At the stage of technological innovation, based on its own boundary resources, different mobile payment platform providers will choose different platform build strategies. The platform strategy direction can be divided into two types: from upstream to downstream and from downstream to upstream. Providers that start with massive boundary resources will choose to dominate the standards to gain the leading position. Providers that have massive common resources and innovation enough to transfer the user base will choose to quickly go to the stage of platform deployment. Service innovation is a very important driving factor, both at the stage of platform deployment and platform scaling.

Alilpay has chosen QR code technology as the mobile payment solution considering its ease of use, convenience, and good compatibility within mobile App etc. to quickly capture the market share of mobile payment by cultivating the usage habit of consumers. Unlike CUP and China Mobile, Alipay has not invested too much on mobile payment technological innovations; they have moved to the stage of platform deployment very fast and gained the late-mover advantage. Alipay has effectively leveraged their installed user base to achieve mobile payment platform envelopment. As for Alipay, since all Taobao and Tmall users are Alipay users, user base overlap is highly symmetrical. Alipay has their focal function — Alipay for online shopping, which has to a large extent helped retain the users and transferred them to mobile payment.

Once the positive network effects were ignited, Alipay went to the stage of platform scaling quite smoothly and fast. Both merchants and consumers have joined their mobile payment platforms and external contributions from service providers are gaining momentum to help realize the self-strengthening of the platform. More and more solutions and services are offered to merchants and customers, which in turn will attract more of them, more resources will be invested in and the virtuous circle has began.

The resource-based platform strategies of Alipay is more focused on the downstream part of mobile payment value chian, which has proved that the downstream part is more important than the upstream part since the key factor of the success of a mobile payment platform falls on the installed base of end-users.

However, we could not jump to the conclusion that CUP and China Mobile went totally wrong when cultivating the mobile payment platform. If we look at the key resources CUP and China Mobile have, the choice of NFC solutions makes sense for them. To build the mobile payment platform from scratch requires multiple actors to join together to promote. Opening a platform enlists new allies committed to its defense. Many benefits must be balanced against the fact that opening a platform exposes its creator to increased competition. The coopetition relationships among different practitioners are too complicated to unite their powers together.

This chapter focused on how mobile payment platform providers leverage their key resources to boost the development of its mobile payment platform. In the different stages of the platform development, different resource-based platform strategies are considered and carried out. Extending the notion of resource-based platform strategies, the process of managing platform strategies can be viewed as a dynamic capability. Dynamic capability demands recombining resources to generate new value-creating strategies (Eisenhardt and Martin, 2000). Ambidexterity acts as a dynamic capability to reconfigure assets and exiting capabilities to gain long-term competitive advantages (O'Reilly and Tushman, 2007). In this regard, dynamic capabilities in platform development can be another angle to study the platform phenomena in various industries.

Conclusion

In this Chapter, we explore the phenomena in China's mobile payment industry from the perspective of resource-based platform strategies. By leveraging key resources of the mobile payment platform providers themselves, different platform strategies are determined at the different stages of the platform development. Boundary resources and common resources are the two main key resources we discussed in this chapter. At the stage of technological innovation, boundary resources are leveraged most to build or enter the mobile payment platform. At the stage of platform deployment, common resources are key factors for platform providers to realize the initial success. Platform scaling is not easy to reach unless platform deployment is successful.

This chapter mainly analyzed two kinds of resources that the mobile payment platform providers leveraged. This may lead to omitting other key resources that also play an important role during the platform development. The categories of resources could be more specific to complete the analysis concerning the resource-based view of the platform providers.

The unique context of China has set many limits for the development of the mobile payment industry. In this chapter, we did not spend much time on analyzing the influence that institutional environments have on its development. Meanwhile, each of these four cases is interdependent with others, the co-opetition relationship among them has also been influential to their choices of platform strategies.

References

Accenture Technology R&D, 2016. People Fisrt: The Primacy of People in a Digital Age, Accenture.

Bosch, T. E. 2009. "Using Online Social Networking for Teaching and Learning: Facebook Use at the University of Cape Town," *Communication: South African Journal for Communication Theory and Research*, 35(2), 185–200.

Bygstad, B. 2010. "Generative Mechanisms for Innovation in Information Infrastructures, Information and Organization."

Citi Rearch, 2016. "How fintech is forcing banking to a tipping point, Citi Global Perspective & Solutions."

Cusumano, M. A. 2010. *"Staying power: Six Enduring Principles for Managing Strategy and Innovation in an Uncertain World (Lessons from Microsoft, Apple, Intel, Google, Toyota, and More),"* Oxford University Press, Oxford, England.

Dahlberg *et al.*, 2015. "A Critical Review of Mobile Payment Research," *Electronic Commerce Research and Applications.*

Dennehy and Sammon, 2015. "Trends in Mobile Payments Research: A Literature Review," *Journal of Innovation Management.*

Eaton, B., Elaluf-Calderwood, S., Sorensen, C., and Yoo, Y. 2015. "Distributed Tuning of Boundary Resources: The Case of Apple's iOS Service System," *MIS Quarterly*, 39(1), 217–243.

Eisenhardt, K. M., and Martin, J. A. 2000. "Dynamic Capabilities: What are They?" *Strategic Management Journal*, 21(10), 1105–1121.

Eisenmann, T. R., Parker, G. G., and Van Alstyne, M. W. 2006. "Strategies for Two-Sided Markets," *Harvard Business Review*, 84(10), 92–101.

Eisenmann *et al.*, 2007. "Platform Envelopment," *Strategic Management Journal.*

Evans, M. C., Parsons, E. M., Scott, R. D., Thornhill, T. S., and Zurakowski, D. 2006. "Comparative Flexion after Rotating-Platform vs Fixed-Bearing Total Knee Arthroplasty," *Journal of Arthroplasty*, 21(7), 985–991.

Gawer, A., and Cusumano, M. A. 2002. *"Platform Leadership: How Intel, Microsoft, and Cisco Drive Industry Innovation,"* Harvard Business Review Press, Brighton, Massachusetts.

Gawer, A. 2009. *"Platform Dynamics and Strategies: From Products to Services,"* Chapter 3 of Platforms, Markets and Innovation, Edward Elgar Publishing, Cheltenham.

Gawer, A. 2014. "Bridging Differing Perspectives on Technological Platforms: Toward an Integrative Framework," *Research Policy*, 43(7), 1239–1249.

Ghazawneh, A., and Henfridsson, O. 2012. "Balancing Platform Control and External Contribution in Third-Party Development: The Boundary Resources Model," *Information Systems Journal*, 23(2), 173–192. Available at: http://onlinelibrary.wiley.com/doi/10.1111/j.1365-2575.2012.00406.x/abstract.

Guo and Bouwman, 2015. An Analytical Framework for an m-Payment Ecosystem: A Merchants' Perspective, *Telecommunications policy.*

Hanseth, O., and Lyytinen, K. 2010. "Design Theory for Dynamic Complexity in Information Infrastructures: The Case of Building Internet," *Journal of Information Technology*, 25, 1–19.

Henfridsson and Bygstad, 2011. The Generative Mechanisms of Digital Infrastructure Evolution, *MIS Quarterly*.

Henfridsson, O., and Bygstad, B. 2013. "The Generative Mechanisms of Digital Infrastructure Evolution," *Management Information Systems Quarterly*, 37(3), 907–931.

Homepage of Alipay, https://global.alipay.com/ospay/home.htm. Last accessed: July 1, 2016.

Jun Liu, Robert J. K., Dan M, 2015. "Competition, Cooperation, and Regulation: Understanding the Evolution of the Mobile Payments Technology Ecosystem," *Electronic Commerce Research and Applications*.

Kraaijenbrink *et al.*, 2010. "The Resource-Based View: A Review and Assessment of Its Critiques," *Journal of Management*.

Luo *et al.*, 2016. "ApplyPay is Reshaping the Payment Ecosystem?" Huatai securities.

Lusch, R. F., and Nambisan, S. 2015. "Service Innovation: A Service-dominant Logic Perspective," *MIS Quarterly: Management Information Systems*, 39(1), 155–175.

Messerschmitt, D. G., and Szyperski, C. 2003. *"Software Ecosystem: Understanding an Indispensable Technology and Industry,"* The MIT Press, Cambridge, Massachusetts.

Miao, M. and Jayakar, K, 2016. "Mobile Payments in Japan, South Korea and China: Cross-border convergence or divergence of business models?," *Telecommunications Policy*.

Normann, R. A., and Mintzberg, H. 2001. *"Reframing Business: When the Map Changes the Landscape,"* John Wiley & Sons, Hoboken, New Jersey.

Ondrus, J., and Lyytinen, K. 2011. "Mobile Payments Market: Towards Another Clash of the Titans?" *IEEE Xplore*, 166–172. Available at: http://ieeexplore. ieee.org/search/searchresult.jsp?newsearch=true&queryText=Mobile%20 Payments%20Market:%20Towards%20Another%20Clash%20of%20 the%20Titans%3F.

Ondrus, J., Gannamaneni, A., and Lyytinen, K. 2015. "The Impact of Openness on the Market Potential of Multi-sided Platforms: A Case Study of Mobile Payment Platforms," *Journal of Information Technology*, 30(3), 260–275.

O'Reilly, Charles A. and Tushman, M. 2007. Ambidexterity as a Dynamic Capability: Resolving the Innovator's Dilemma. Stanford University Graduate School of Business Research Paper No. 1963. Available at SSRN: https://ssrn.com/abstract=978493 or http://dx.doi.org/10.2139/ssrn.978493.

Orlikowski, W. J., and Scott, S. V. 2008. "Sociomateriality: Challenging the Separation of Technology, Work and Organization," *Academy of Management Annals*, 2(1), 433–474.

Reuver *et al.*, 2014. "Collective Action for Mobile Payment Platforms: A Case Study on Collaboration Issues between Banks and Telecom Operators," *Electronic Commerce Research and Applications.*

Staykova and Damsgaard, 2015. "The race to dominate the Mobile Payments Platform: Entry and Expansion Strategies," *Commerce Research and Applications.*

Tan *et al.*, 2015. "Leveraging Digital Business Ecosystems for Enterprise Agility: The Tri-logic Development Strategy of Alibaba.com," *Journal of the Association for Information Systems.*

Tilson, D., Lyytinen, K., and Sørensen, C. 2010. "Digital Infrastructures: The Missing IS Research Agenda," *Information Systems Research*, 21(4), 748–759.

Tiwana, A. 2014. *"Platform Ecosystem: Aligning Architecture, Governance, and Strategy."* Elsevier.

Tiwanan, A., Konsynski, B., and Bush, A. A. 2010. "Platform Evolution: Coevolution of Platform Architecture, Governance, and Environmental Dynamics," *Information Systems Research*, 21(4), 675–687.

Vargo, S. L., and Lusch, R. F. 2004. "Evolving to a New Dominant Logic for Marketing," *Journal of Marketing*, 68(1), 1–17.

Wade and Hulland, 2004. Review: The Resource-Based View and Information Systems Research: Review, Extension, and Suggestions for Future Research," *MIS Quarterly.*

Wang Songbo, 2015. "Focusing on the New Trend of Mobile Payment," Founder Securities.

Yin, R. K. 2001. *"Case Study Research: Design and Methods,"* 2nd edn., Porto Alegre: Bookman.

Yoo, Y., Henfridsson, O., and Lyytinen, K. 2010. "The New Organizing Logic of Digital Innovation: An Agenda for Information Systems Research," *Information Systems Research*, 21(4), 724–735.

Zhu Zhiyong, 2015. "Paying Attention on Mobile Payment," Aijian Securities.

Chapter 12

Exploring Service Dominant Logic and Business Model for IT Firms to Transition to the Cloud Era: A Focus Group Study

Jau-Rong Chen

Ming Chi University of Technology, Taiwan, R.O.C.
kellychen@mail.mcut.edu.tw

Abstract

Increasingly, IT firms are turning to cloud services as a new way of creating and capturing value. The challenge faced by current IT firms is not limited to development of new cloud service. It is simultaneously about the deployment and usage of existing resources and capability to develop new value offerings for forms of value creation. This chapter argues that due to the paucity of research on the emergent potential dominant logic in the cloud era for IT firms, our understanding of the critical resource allocation decision process through which cloud-related product development is limited. The cloud dominant logic provides a novel and valuable theoretical perspective that necessitates a rethinking and re-evaluation of the conventional business practices in the IT industry. This study was carried out within the framework of a Smart System Services Project (SSSP), where this study aims to explore the future opportunities and the mechanisms of cultivation of talent for the Taiwanese IT industry in cloud era. The SSSP incorporates four levels including (1) strategic planning, (2) process redesign, (3) technical architecture assessment, and (4) agile system deployment, and aims to focus on the development of the optimal service model-driven system architecture to increase the service value for the Taiwanese IT industry. The findings from the analysis suggested that six cloud dominant logic categories are needed for IT firm business transformation in cloud era positing that they can help scholars and managers analyze, design, and implement breakthrough advances in resource use and allocation decisions.

Keywords: Cloud computing, Service Dominant Logic, Information Technology, Qualitative study.

Introduction

There is a growing emphasis on cloud era and an increasing tendency for IT industry to think and respond agilely. In general, cloud computing refers to both the applications delivered as services over the Internet and hardware and systems software in the data centers that provide those services (Armbrust *et al.*, 2010). Accordingly, it covers every possible sort of online service and the three primary models of cloud services are Software as a Service (SaaS), Platform as a Service (PaaS), and Infrastructure as a Service (IaaS). SaaS model provides the on-demand software such as Gmail or Salesforce.com; PaaS model provides computing platforms (e.g., operating system and database) such as Windows Azure; IaaS model provides computing infrastructure (e.g., physical machines, storage) such as Amazon EC2. Cloud computing continues to gain more mainstream adoption as more companies move into the cloud. Apparently, even some experts have considered that cloud computing is far from mature, but the cloud has arrived and widely acknowledged by IT industry alike as a major force in significantly altering the entire IT landscape. Accordingly, there is an expressed need to pay attention to the coevolution between the emergence of cloud era and the transition of SME IT firms.

Increasingly, IT firms are turning to cloud services as a new way of creating and capturing value. As suggested by Choudhary's (2007), the faster dissemination of new features under cloud-based SaaS can lead to higher quality of IT services. Apparently, the availability of on-demand IT services and the pay-as-you-go pricing model makes it attractive for firms to source many IT services from the cloud (Choudhary and Vithayathil, 2013). Yet, the cloud is a very broad concept and is still vague. That is, despite having a number of business benefits and research scope, there is no universally accepted comprehensive, conceptual definition for cloud computing (Madhavaiah et al, 2012). For example, as cited by Armbrust *et al.* (2010) and Madhavaiah *et al.,* (2012), Oracle's CEO Larry Ellison mentioned that: "the interesting thing about cloud computing is that we've redefined cloud computing to include everything that we already do.... I don't understand what we would do differently in the light of cloud computing other that change the wording of some of our ads." Unfortunately, with its roots in software/ technological IT industry, business logic falls short of seizing the advantages of the cloud business. Apparently, despite its potential benefits, many IT firms struggle to deploy service activities effectively, not least because they fail to change their mindset in their business model. The challenge faced by current IT firms is not limited to the development of a new cloud service. It is simultaneously about the deployment and usage of existing resources and capability to develop new value offerings for forms of value creation (Schneider and Spieth, 2013). To date, for IT firms, there is little knowledge on low cloud computing has fundamentally changed the way IT firms operate. In the absence of this knowledge, the effective leverage of cloud computing technologies is difficult to attain.

A better business model often will beat a better idea or technology and today, innovation must include business models, rather than just technology and R&D (Chesbrough, 2007). Accordingly, the recent rapid advances in cloud computing have highlighted the rising importance of the business model innovation for IT firms. The business model of a company is a simplified representation of its underlying core business logic and strategic choices for creating and capturing value within a value network (Shafer *et al.*, 2005). Business model innovation refers to the search for new logics of the firm and new ways to create and capture value for its stakeholders, (Casadesus-Masanell and Zhu, 2013).

It thereby aims at consciously renewing a firm's core business logic rather than limiting its scope of innovation on single products or services (Schneider and Spieth, 2013). In addition, Prahalad and Bettis (1986) have proposed that the successful management of highly diversified firms can be attributed to the concept of a corporate "dominant logic" that guides all of its business units. Managers' dominant logic refers to "the way in which managers conceptualize the business and make critical resource allocation decisions — be it in technologies, product development, distribution, advertising, or in human resource management" (Prahalad and Bettis, 1986). The concept can be used to refer more broadly to a general management logic that can govern the decision-making processes throughout the firm by producing a mindset or world view that can be shared across all of its business units (Lampel and Shamsie, 2000).

This chapter argues that due to the paucity of research on the emergent potential dominant logic in the cloud era for IT firms, our understanding of the critical resource allocation decision process through which cloud-related product development is limited. The cloud dominant logic provides a novel and valuable theoretical perspective that necessitates a rethinking and reevaluation of the conventional business practices on the IT industry. To address this gap and along with the trend of cloud computing, the aim of this chapter is to explore the potential dominant logic and the logic-driven business model innovation to answer the question: "how will IT firms reconfigure themselves to gazing into the future and to grow cloud competition?" Specifically, the author conducts this study in the context of SaaS, due to a large number of SME IT firms that are now confronted with the impacts of the cloud trend, and where the issue of SME IT transformation becomes relevant and important. The author inductively develops a potential dominant logic for IT firms in the cloud are using qualitative data of a focus group research. The next section of this chapter presents the background for cloud computing and dominant logic and focus group research as well. This discussion provides a guideline for the author to analyze the qualitative data. This is followed by a detailed description of the cases. Subsequently, the analysis and findings of the study are discussed. The chapter concludes by discussing future research directions.

Theoretical background — business model

Business model is referred to as an enterprise's strategic artifact. Furthermore, the term "understand business models" is the representation of the "design or architecture of the value creation, delivery, and capture mechanisms" (Teece, 2010, p. 172) an enterprise employs. Business models provide a powerful way to understand analyze, communicate, and manage strategic-oriented choices among business and technology stakeholders (AI-Debei and Avision, 2010). Casadesus-Masanell and Zhu (2013) suggest that business models as profit functions and additional elements in the business include human resources management policies, the production technologies used, or the marking policies are all part of 'the logic of the firm, the way it operates and how it creates value for stakeholders' and, thus, are all part of a firm's business model, and could be included in the profit function to have a more detailed representation of the firm's business model.

What is more, business models themselves have emerged as a promising unit of analysis and starting point for innovation strategies (Schneider and Spieth, 2013). Cao (2014): a business model should include at least three essential value-based premises including value proposition, value creation and delivery, and value appropriation. Value proposition covers the identification of target clients and a statement of why they should buy a product or service. Value creation and delivery are about the design of the retail value chain. Value appropriation concerns the retail profit formula (PF). Based on Cao's discussion, value creation and delivery is about the management's activities and processes including the retail format, assortment, price, services, promotion, store location, procurement, logistics, information system, human resources (HR), financing/accounting, organization/structure, and relationship with suppliers and consumers.

Based on Johnson *et al.* (2008), a business model consists of four interlocking elements that, taken together, create and deliver value including: (1) customer value proposition (CVP); (2) PF; (3) key resources; and (4) key processes.

(1) CVP can be referred to as a way to create value for the customer. To help target customers get important jobs (customer's fundamental

problem) done (solution by design offering in turn creates value for customer). The components of CVP include target customer, job to be done, and offering.

(2) PF can be referred to as the blueprint that defines how the company creates value for itself while providing value to the customers. The components of PF are including revenue, cost structure, margin model, and resource velocity.

(3) Key resources are needed to deliver the CVP profitably. The components of key resources include people, technology, products, equipment, information, channels, partnerships, and alliance.

(4) Key processes, as well as rules, metrics, and norms. Key processes make the profitable delivery of the CVP repeatable and scalable. Key processes include processes, rule and metrics, and norms.

AI-Debei and Avision (2010) in their work "Towards a service-based business model", provide the following explanations, including value proposition, value architecture, value network, and value finance. Chesbrough (2007) also proposed six common business model parameters. This study based on Chesbrough (2007) has six BM parameters as the theoretical background.

Research method

Focus group

Focus groups have become a popular technique for gathering qualitative data for a wide range of academic and applied research areas (Morgan, 1996) including MIS research (e.g., Prior *et al.*, 2013; Rosemann and Vessey, 2008; O'hEocha *et al.*, 2012; Tremblay *et al.*, 2010).

Focus group referred to as a "focused interview", a discussion group that concentrates on a particular topic or topics, that is facilitated by a trained moderator, and that typically consists of 8 to 12 participants (Byers, *et al.*, 1991).

As reviewed by Strickland (1999), the focus group is particularly useful for the exploration of topics of interest and clarification of content domains and, unlike the individual interview, the focus group capitalizes on group interaction and group norms.

As cited by Överlien *et al.* (2005), the interaction gives the moderator the opportunity to study the processes of collective sense making and to learn the language and vocabulary used by the participants (Frith, 2000), and it is the process which moderators co-construe meaning in focus group interaction (Puchta and Potter, 2002).

Study context

This study was carried out within the framework of a Smart System Services Project (SSSP), where the author tried to explore the future opportunities and the mechanisms of cultivation of talent for Taiwanese IT industry in cloud era. The SSSP incorporates four levels including strategic planning, process redesign, technical architecture assessment, and agile system deployment, and aims to focus on the development of the optimal service model-driven system architecture to increase the service value for Taiwanese IT industry.

The criteria for selecting the participants of each group were based on a determination of who had the experiences and had an interest to take part in the study. Accordingly, study participants were recruited largely based on those government funding support IT firms for promoting cloud industry programs and willing to join the group interaction around the research topic: "how Taiwanese SME IT Firms to Transition to the Cloud Era?"

All participants were scrutinized carefully to ensure that they were IS practitioners with a would be common understanding of the issue addressed in the research and the groups would be quite homogeneous to ensure quality of the data. A total of 20 IT managers and 10 IT scholars decided to participate and were distributed among the two focus groups with 9 and 11 participants in each group. Each focus group interview lasted approximately 2 hours. In the discussion, moderator has to control what topics are discussed and manage group dynamics as well (Morgan, 1996). A semi-structured interview guide was used only to help initiate and guide the interview process. Additional observations were noted immediately after the completion of each interview.

As suggested by Strickland (1999), the focus group is often combined with other approaches such as the grounded theory, and participant observation. Accordingly, in order to achieve this study, the open coding technique of grounded theory (Strauss and Corbin, 1990) was employed in data analysis. Open coding is the part of the analysis concerned with identifying, naming, categorizing, and describing phenomena found in the text. The dominant logic can be identified and categorized and their influence on Taiwanese SME IT firms to transition to the cloud era can therefore be explored.

Findings and discussion

To help target customers get important job

To help self-service customers to fulfill their information requirements and scale their IT investments by providing standardized, high reliable, and intelligent IT services which are requested as required.

Revenue mechanisms

Since anything is a service, customers change their capital expenditure to an operating expense. While cloud service provides the need to go

Emerging Features of Cloud Service BM	Evidences from the Focus Group Studies
Requested as required	"We provide the total solutions for Taiwan Railway. As the result, they put the whole business in the cloud via us. Since we can provide them adequate resources promptly to enable them at that point in time. Now, there is no complains at all. The pipe can be very quickly crossed the bottleneck. Furthermore, regarding resources, they will not have any concerns. In addition there is noted that in the cloud environment, you can see your resource usage. Meanwhile, we do to help them conducting the analysis with the observation of resources, allowing them to make adjustments. (Acer Manager)"

(Continued)

(Continued)	
Emerging Features of Cloud Service BM	**Evidences from the Focus Group Studies**
Embedded IT services	"As I mentioned before, my company provides that service for chain restaurants. Their end users are customers. Customer experience is value and important. As the result, we realize that we are not selling products to our clients any more. We do provide service to them instead. Our company has to fulfill what the clients need. And hopefully, they will be satisfied with our services. However, to financing service industry, it's a new challenge. As in nowadays, we must take this IT service embedded to support our service. Our service is B2B2C. Our clients wouldn't recognize it at all. They just enjoy it. This is the reason why I do think in terms of IT service industry. What we face is a new challenge. We have to find a new way to overcome it. (IT Service Manager)."
Customer self-service	Our first product is called a cloud i-report. When we prompt our i-report, I find it is similar with knowledge management, including seized by the multi-distribution, image take, do a discussion, and forward. However, we do make things easy to use, and simple now. We provide user friendly and value-added interface. We don't even need to provide education or training to our clients as they can enjoy our service on they own. Our i-report can be seen as customer self-service and actually APP or our clients' easy deployment (Soft Deputy)"
	"Our customers download on their own. We do not need to help them to install our service. What they need to do is open an account via our cloud services. We offer service to relatively small business, probably three to five stores this scale, so they do not need too complex information platform. As the result, we find that depolying whole service process are very convenient in the cloud service plus APP (Industrial Manager)"

beyond single offering, it also provides service architecture (as virtual supermarkets), shared-service profit pricing model and also provides service automation to reduce cost. Service might be measured by a number of transactions or number of users.

Emerging Features of Cloud Service BM	Evidences from the Focus Group Studies
Service logic	"With the recent prevalence of cloud, we are now providing our latest service - SAS, security as a service. What our clients need to concern is their daily job. We take care of their security business (Deputy General Manager)"
Undemand Data Model	"We are deal with structured data. In addition, we also provide our service to deal with unstructured and semi-structured. Our clients don't need to pay fee for undemanded subscription (SYSTEX Director)"
Resource managing mechanism	"In the cloud environment, the more important thing is that you should be able to take actions to deliver your services automatically. Accordingly, the automation of processes management plays a vital role. The interfaces for end users, subscribing for new sources and selling services are all considered to build up our platforms. Via our platforms, we can control resources needed and analyse information to get the feedback. Furthermore, we can trigger our flow and redeployment of our resources if there is necessity (Acer Manager)"

Value chain

Transforming form value chain to value architecture where various cloud computing resources from different levels (SaaS, PaaS, and IaaS) as modular services of the value architecture are integrated and offered to the customer. IT firms need to take advantage of alliances between different layers of service companies.

Value network

With the value architecture concept, value is co-created by a combination of players in the network, that is, more emphasis on the alliances between firms who offer complementary services which can form collective value co-creation networks. The more distinctive features of offering can attract more partners to compose it to be a part of their own company's value architecture.

Emerging Features of Cloud Service BM	Evidences from the Focus Group Studies
Scale out application	"Since we collect and process disclosed data from cloud, for most of businesses, they may feel the cloud is a stand-alone system. As the result, for them, cloud services are much easier to gain their acceptance. What is more, from the budget point of view, they own their own internal data via our services. They can also enjoy our cloud services including external intelligence information directly (Italian Deputy)"
Ecosystem based application	"We do provide our service via Hinet, hi-cloud ICE platforms. There are some SAS applications on these platforms. We are cooperation with Institute for Information Industry (III). By means of III's IDSC technology transfer to our company, we can provide our educational application services via these interactive platforms (Chairman, LEOSYS)."
Community-based application	"Regarding "health clouds" part, we are mainly in cooperation with the hospitals or with some communities through our cloud health information to help those who come to do some analysis of physiological information. As most of communities are less likely to operate with computers, we not only provide health cloud services but also provide kiosk built for some communities (Manager, ISP)"
Resource redistribution center	"The terms of e-business or/and cloud service, the concept of "undemand" need to be considered more closely. What role we play in value chain? All of us need to find our own and right position in this market. Especially, in cloud era, it is important to share resources with our partners and clients. In addition, the issues of tech knowledge are too expensive to gain. We have to find a better way to share what we have with our partners and clients (Associate, ISP)"

Competitive strategy

The complementarity of innovative feature of offering to the other actors in value network defines the scale and position of the company in the

Emerging Features of Cloud Service BM	Evidences from the Focus Group Studies
Intelligence service system	"The technology becomes more complex if we like to develop a whole system, especially in cloud era. It is noted that we have to pay our attention on "know-how" and "business architecture". That is, we have to combine the requirements from business with the bottom of the entire IT system (IT Associate)"
Reframe Ecosystem and partner	"For information service industry, both HR and their mindsets are quite different especially when we prompt cloud service. We provide our service not only in Taiwan but also in mainland. We have some branches elsewhere. It seems impossible to build up our cloud service systems everywhere. We have a cloud center construction in China. However, we are looking to find partners. We don't plan to build up our own cloud center (General Manager, IT software)"
Agile reconfiguration and deployment	"For our clients, there are no installation issues because of our increasing our cloud services with much more functions, smooth processes. It is believed that all of our clients have already noted the adaptabilities of our cloud systems (Associate, IT software)"

value architecture. Ambidextrous scale-up and scale-out strategy to increase the scope of value architecture.

Target market

Company has less customized requirements but are leveraging cloud services for part of their computing needs.

Conclusion

The findings from the analysis suggested that six cloud-dominant logic categories are needed for IT firm business transformation in

Emerging Features of Cloud Service BM	Evidences from the Focus Group Studies
Composite Innovation Model	"It is necessary to combine science and technology with service endpoints, because we want to develop our innovative applications with services innovation. It is very true that the so-called systematic approach here is to be able to really drive the services of the future with the optimization model. Furthermore, it may go further then be able to put forward a so-called application service (IT professional)"
Scale-up/down/out	"From my point of view, I do think that cloud service may provide services for SMEs. For SMEs, they don't need too complex IT systems. Therefore, we do a subtraction in the IT system. We rather provide more added services. For example, we certainly learned the information security management. Accordingly, we provide personal information applications for our clients. Hopefully, what we provide service solutions for our clients (Solutions Associate)"

Emerging Features of Cloud Service BM	Evidences from the Focus Group Studies
Replicative	"Based on the concept of EIP, we launch our cloud plan as the replica. For SMEs, EIP seems easy to copy and actually encountered the similar problems. The biggest issue for EIP is scale, as enterprise varies greatly in size. Every business process is not the same. Accordingly, the issue of customized is of to concern. (Deputy General Manager)"
	"For our business, we provide "Homogeneity Community Services". That is, we provide chain of catering services via our cloud service. We provide services to help our clients to make ordering, and accelerate the speed of service if it is possible. Our business model is sort of B2B2C. (General Manager)"

(Continued)

Table (*Continued*)

Emerging Features of Cloud Service BM	Evidences from the Focus Group Studies
Proactive and dynamic resource deployment	"For our business, we are much more care of the issue of skill–ability, the software and process skill–abilities. From my point of view, the game industry may fit the cloud business. Since the characteristics of game industry are quite unique. Their skill–abilities elasticity should be very good to offer 4–20 scenes at the same time. In the future, software industry should move in this direction (Software General Manager)"
Redefine Target Customer	"Cloud services for us are rather new markets, as our customer base is not our existing clients and we are not familiar with our original customers. We do conducting some research. We find that we should focus on small and medium enterprises. SMEs are always activeness and full of energy, creative, and innovative. However, SMEs' resources are limited. What the SMEs needed probably are more IT investments. For SMEs, investing in computer systems, hiring IT staffs may be over their budgets. Our company start from 2009. We focus on SAS and target SMEs. Via our service, SMEs just only need to pay attention to their know-how. We take care of their IT systems. What we provide is total solution. SMEs can operate their business via our cloud service (HU vice president, ISP)"
Redefine Target Customer	We are used to servicing our customers who are all big businesses. Accordingly, the entire import process relatively long. Therefore, we try to open up a new line for a new business regarding personal information issues. Personal information issues are received attention increasing in Taiwan. In comparison with our past DRM or security-related services, the applications of our new services are for SME (small and medium enterprises) with fewer competitors (Solutions Associate) .

cloud era positing that they can help scholars and managers analyze, design, and implement breakthrough advances in resource use and allocation decisions.

Business Model Parameter	Emerging Features of Cloud Service BM
	Requested as required
Value Proposition	Embedded IT services
	Customer self-service
	Service logic
Revenue Mechanisms	Undemand Data Model
	Resource managing mechanism
	Scale out application
Value Chain	Ecosystem-based application
	Community-based application
	Resource redistribution center
	Intelligence service system
Value Network	Reframe Ecosystem and partner
	Agile reconfiguration and deployment
Competitive Strategy	Composite Innovation Model
	Scale-up/down/out
	Replicative
Target Market	Proactive and dynamic resource deployment
	Redefine Target Customer

References

AI-Debei, M. M. and Avision, D. 2010. "Developing a Unified Framework of the Business Model Concept," *European Journal of Information Systems*, 19, 359–376.

Armbrust, M., Fox, A., Griffith, R., Joseph, A. D., Katz, R., Konwinski, A., Lee, G., Patterson, D., Rabkin, A., Stoica, I., and Zaharia, M. 2010. "A View of Cloud Computing," *Communications of the ACM*, 53(4), 50–58.

Byers, P. Y. and Wilcox, J. R. 1991. "Focus Groups: A Qualitative Opportunity for Researchers," *The Journal of Business Communication*, 28(1), 63–78.

Cao, H. 2014. "Innovation Strategy Analysis of Enterprise Economic Management in New Situation," *Market Modernization*, 1, 93–94.

Casadesus-Masanell, R. and Zhu, F. 2013. "Business Model Innovation and Competitive Imitation: The Case of Sponsor-based Business Models," *Strategic Management Journal*, 34, 464–482.

Chesbrough, H. 2007. "Business Model Innovation: It's Not Just About Technology Anymore," *Strategy and leadership*, 35(6), 12–17.

Choudhary, V. 2007. "Comparison of Software Quality under Perpetual Licensing and Software as a Service," *Journal of Management Information Systems*, 24(2),141–165.

Choudhary, V. and Vithayathil, J. 2013. "The Impact of Cloud Computing: Should the IT Department be Organized as a Cost Center or a Profit Center?" *Journal of Management Information Systems*, 30(2), 67–100.

Frith, H. 2000. "Focusing on Sex: Using Focus Groups in Sex Research," *Sexualities*, 3(3), 275–297.

Johnson, M. W., Christensen, C. M., and Kagermann, H. 2008. "Reinventing Your Business Model," *Harvard Business Review*, 50–59.

Lampel, J. and Shamsie, J. 2000. "Probing the unobstrusive Link: Dominant Logic and the Design of Joint Ventures at General Electric," *Strategic Management Journal*, 21, 593–602.

Madhavaiah, C., Bashir, I., and Shafi, S. I. 2012. "Defining Clouding Computing in Business Perspective: A Review of Research," *Vision*, 16(3), 163–173.

Morgan, D. L. 1996. "Focus Groups," *Annual Review of Sociology*, 22, 129–152.

O'hEocha, C., Wang, X., and Conboy, K. 2012. "The Use of Focus Groups in Complex and Pressurised IS Studies and Evaluation Using Klein & Myers Principles for Interpretive Research," *Information Systems Journal*, 22, 235–256.

Överlien, C., Aronsson, K., and Hydén, M. 2005. "The focus Group Interview as an In-depth Method? Young women talking about Sexuality," *Internal Journal of Social Research Method*, 8(4), 331–344.

Prahalad C. K. and Bettis R. A. 1986. "The Dominant Logic: A New Linkage between Diversity and Performance." *Strategic Management Journal* 7(6), 485–501.

Prior, S., Waller, A., and Kroll, T. 2013. "Focus Groups as a Requirements Gathers Method with Adults with Severe Speech and Physical Impairments," *Behaviour & Information Technology*, 32(8), 752–760.

Puchta, C., & Potter, J. 2002. "Manufacturing Individual Opinions: Market Research Focus Groups and the Discursive Psychology of Evaluation," *British Journal of Social Psychology*, 41(3), 345–365.

Rosemann, M. and Vessey, I. 2008. "Toward Improving the Relevance of Information Systems Research to Practice: The Role of Applicability Check," *MIS Quarterly*, 32(1), 1–22.

Schneider, S. and Spieth, P. 2013. "Business Model Innovation: Towards an Integrated Future Research Agenda," *International Journal of Innovation Management*, 17(1), 1–34.

Strauss, A., and Corbin, J. M. 1990. *"Basics of Qualitative Research: Grounded Theory Procedures and Techniques,"* Thousand Oaks, CA, Sage Publications.

Strickland, C. J. 1999. "Conducting Focus Groups Cross-culturally: Experiences with Pacific Northwest Indian perople," *Public Health Nursing*, 16(3), 190–197.

Teece, D. J. (2010). Business Models, Business Strategy and Innovation. *Long Range Planning*, 43(2/3), 172–194.

Tremblay, M. C., Hevner, A. R., and Berndt, D. J. 2010. "Focus Groups for Artifact Refinement and Evaluation in Design Research," *Communications of the Association for Information Systems*, 26, 599–618.

Chapter 13

Towards Commercialization of University Research Outcomes: Comparative Theories

Tamrin Amboala

School of Business IT and Logistics, RMIT University
Melbourne, Australia
s3518372@student.rmit.edu.au

Joan Richardson

School of Business IT and Logistics, RMIT University
Melbourne, Australia
joan.richardson@rmit.edu.au

John Lenarcic

School of Business IT and Logistics, RMIT University
Melbourne, Australia
john.lenarcic@rmit.edu.au

Abstract

The commercialization of research by academic scientists is recognized as an important driving force for technology transfer and wealth creation. Due to the complexity of the process involved, the success of

217

commercialization of inventions (innovations) from universities to industry is questionable. There is a paucity of general agreed commercialization in terms of execution processes to support inventions of prototypes and products moving from laboratories to the right market. This research aims to investigate the commercialization of research outcomes for IT products from the research centers to facilitate the commercialization objective. The analysis is carried out based on the comparative analysis based on different theories that underpinned technology commercialization. The analysis is expected to offer a research commercialization model and practical contribution for successful commercialization and licensing among academics.

Keywords: Incubation program, Academic entrepreneurs, Research commercialization.

Introduction

Entrepreneurship is described as the ability to associate all activities in order to gain profit and wealth from labor, land and capital (Nielsen, 2015; Sahlan *et al.*, 2015; Lourenco *et al.*, 2013; Rasmussen *et al.*, 2011) and recently from knowledge and technology (Gedeon, 2010, pp. 18–21). The entrepreneurial qualities of academia could be a driving force towards economic development through job creations and new ventures (Täks *et al.*, 2015). However, there is currently no consistent mechanism for tracking the impact of commercialization although there is a significant flow of scientific knowledge sharing between universities and academia (Rubin *et al.*, 2015). The personal attributes of entrepreneurs include autonomy and independence, creativity, moderate and calculated risk taking, drive and determination towards success (Ajagbe *et al.*, 2015). What is common among all references listed above is the association of risk or the ability of the entrepreneurs to take risk by exploiting those resources (Ajagbe *et al.*, 2015; Gedeon 2010, pp. 18–21; Täks *et al.*, 2015). The rewards for risk taking can be traced way back in the 20th century Risk Theory (Gedeon, 2010). This research addresses the importance of entrepreneurship qualities such as risk taking and capabilities in managing the resources coupled with the scientific knowledge to commercialize the innovations successfully.

The definition of entrepreneurship has evolved into other disciplines and has been widely applied to academics who are actively engaged both in research and commercialization of their innovations (inventions) (Mowery and Shane, 2002; Siegel *et al.*, 2004; Wright *et al.*, 2004). Academic entrepreneurship can be defined as the leadership process of creating value through acts of organizational creation, renewal or innovation that occurs within or outside the university that results in research and technology commercialization (Mowery and Shane, 2002) based on case studies at MIT University.

The research and commercialization occurs at the level of individuals or groups of individuals acting independently or as part of faculty or university systems that result and create new organizations, or initiate innovation within the university (Swamidass, 2013; Zhao, 2004; Este, 2008; Minguillo and Thelwall, 2015). Value from academic entrepreneurship is achieved through the integration of scientific activities, academic activities, and commercialization activities (Siegel *et al.*, 2004; Yusof *et al.*, 2009).

This Chapter investigates how HE institutions develop potential Intellectual Properties (IPs) for commercialization and spin-offs. As the number of patents granted do not reflect economic return (Henry *et al.*, 2005), the inabilities of IPs to generate economic return give an impression that universities are able to increase the number of IP. The evidence suggests that there is no direct relationship between IP and commercialization. Hence, further research is significant to investigate surrounding issues in the process in order to close this gulf by facilitating HE research commercialization. With regard to the commercialization of IPs in the university, academics play their role to ensure that innovations succeed, which will complement the paucity in the literature (Gedeon, 2010). The integrative review provides a guideline model for technology commercialization implementation in universities.

Literature review

Rubin *et al.* (2015) who conducted studies and research on commercialization of technological business incubator program in both Australia and Israel proposed a model that comprise the inter-relationships among three main stakeholders that included the: (1) Technological Knowledge Bearer (inventors, universities, etc.); (2) Market Knowledge Bearer; (3) Financial Knowledge Bearer (Porter, 2008). The interaction, communications, and collaborations of stakeholders drive the knowledge flow in technological business incubators. The research hypothesized that knowledge flow becomes a catalyst for the commercialization of universities' innovations (Rubin *et al.*, 2015).

However, despite the fact that there is evidence of significant knowledge flow between stakeholders (Rubin *et al.*, 2015), the ineffective and inefficient commercialization program might not be actively contributing to university technology transfer but rather the universities' resources. Rubin *et al.* (2015) estimate that 75% of university inventions and patents are not licensed at all. This poses a greater challenge for the inventors and innovators for commercialization of the Higher Education (HE) products as this drags the journey towards commercialization long and fraught with problems (Markman *et al.*, 2005).

Moreover, as stated by Markman *et al.* (2005), the relationship between universities (via the technology transfer office) with new venture creations and the commercialization program (science park) is poorly understood. More research is needed to understand the challenges of the entrepreneurs particularly on their ability to carry out the invention (knowledge transfer) from the university and their ability to sell off their inventions farther beyond the proof of concepts and prototype phase.

There is no evidence that university patenting licensing is profitable although a small number of them do succeed in attracting substantial additional revenues (Geuna and Nesta, 2006; Swamidass, 2013). Geuna conducted (Geuna and Nesta, 2006; Swamidass, 2013) a comparative IP research in selected universities in five European countries in Germany, Finland, Belgium, France, and Italy. Unlike U.S., the findings show that scientific discoveries are too pre mature for commercialization. The findings are generalized across all disciplines and in different technology fields. In other words, there is a huge gap between scientific discoveries and actual commercialization initiatives. In addition, outcomes of research commercialisation do not reach the same audience in Europe as in U.S. This finding raises challenges to fill the gap to improve the communication between the academia and the industry.

Siegel *et al.* map the process of commercialization which begins from scientific discovery towards negotiations and licensing. The process flow presented by Siegel *et al.* (2004) is quite comprehensive and has simililarities with the generic process (see Figure 1 below) suggested by Commonwealth Scientific and Industrial Research Organization (CSIRO) — the largest Australia national research agency (Upstill and Symington, 2002). The commercializing issue highlighted the importance of networking in determining the commercializing success. The commercializing issues of CSIRO is an evidence that incorporating market capabilities and expertise into the technology, thorough enggagement and collaboration with external entity are crucial components that need to be addressed for successful research commercialization (Upstill and Symington, 2002; Thorburn, 2000).

Entrepreneurship theory

Entrepreneurship in this context is very much related to the innovation produced by the academia as individuals and the institutions (universities) where they work (Yusof *et al.*, 2009). Joseph Schumpeter's innovation theory of entrepreneurship holds that an entrepreneurs have three major

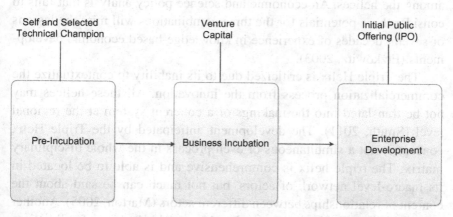

Figure 1. Generic Process Proposed By CSIRO for New Venture Capital (Upstill and Symington, 2002)

characteristics; innovation, foresight, and creativity (Scherer, 1986; Schumpeter, 1934). Schumpeter's innovation theory of entrepreneurship has advantages as it is applicable to investigate technology innovation. However, this theory requires new paradigm with regard to the academic entrepreneur's risk-taking ability and organizational skills, and application of the characteristics pertaining to innovation in the universities. Schumpeter's theory began in the late 19th century in agricultural innovation system and is applicable to large-scale businesses, however innovation in the universities must address institutional consideration (Bruton *et al.*, 2010) such as R&D in faculty, academic orientation research, and innovations as in the HE as well as individual aspect of individual academic entrepreneurs.

Triple helix

Another theory that is relevant to product commercialization is advocated by Etzkowitz (2003) based on the Triple Helix of university–industry–government relationship view. From the Triple Helix point of view, three dynamics can be distinguished: (1) the economic dynamics of the market (industry); (2) the internal dynamics of knowledge production (represented by universities); (3) and governance of the interface at different levels (represented by the government) (Etzkowitz, 2003). This theory put great emphasis on the holistic point of view by recombination of elements among the helices. An economic and science policy analysis that fails to consider these potentials for the three combinations will miss the lessons of several decades of experience in knowledge-based economic developments (Etzkowitz, 2003).

The Triple Helix is criticized due to its inability to contextualize the commercialization process from the innovation. All these helices may not be translated into the makings of a coherent system at the regional level (Smith, 2011). The development anticipated by the Triple Helix concept is not a simultaneous or even process in the whole disciplinary matrix. The triple helix is comprehensive and is able to be located in its macro-level network of actors, but not much can be said about the content of relationships between different actors (Marton, 2005). Another critique (Shinn, 2002) comments that the model is lacking of solid micro foundation furthermore, the vagueness of the model makes the connection between theory and empirical data problematic in some way (Shinn, 2002).

With regard to commercialization in HE, this research aims to investigate the commercialization of research outcomes from research centres to facilitate the research commercialization objectives. Understanding the characteristics of roles and functions of research centers with regard to successful commercialization of IT products require investigations of research questions from micro-level perspectives. For example, the 3rd helix pertains to how the government can influence or direct the commercialization of potential research outcomes in the university. This question requires much in-depth analysis on how the university governs the research project and aims for commercialization objectives. Furthermore how far are these objectives are translated into actual research allocation for wealth generation? In-depth analysis involve to understand the relationships involved among actors and stakeholders (academics, entrepreneurs, firms, etc.) with regard to commercialization success (Minguillo and Thelwall, 2015).

Etzkowitz (2003) highlights the importance of networking and incubators to formalize the commercialization. In certain cases, incubator becomes "club" linking groups of alumni firms with potential partners. Etzkowitz (2003) recommends the establishment of start-up firms from technology transfer, incubation and venture capital within and among organizations (HE). Incubator provides more facilities to support commercialization to become additional modes of dissemination of knowledge through commercial as well as academic channels which are described as the third mission apart from teaching and research (Etzkowitz, 2003). Although the linear model from university to industry is a fruitful and indeed inevitable feature to many academics, industries and governments, unconventional reverse linearity, starting from commercial needs, are increasingly commonplace.

Understanding the user requirements based on the actual appealing demand as early as possible even before the prototype development and continues iteratively (Nuseibeh and Easterbrook, 2000) This chapter seeks to provide explanation from the Triple Helix point of view with greater emphasis on industry engagement and incubation to resolve unmatched market requirements (Maine and Garnsey, 2006). Incorporating

industry into research commercialization to resolve issues of user requirements to answer why many patents and great potential commercialized
research have failed (Freeman, 1982; Maine and Garnsey, 2006).

Resource-based view (RBV)

Another theory that applies to university product commercialization is
Resource-based View (RBV). This theory emphasizes that the survival of
firms are very much dependent on resources available — both tangible
and intangible resources. Furthermore, this theory explains how those
resources must be exploited effectively to gain a competitive advantage
(Grant, 1991; Kakati, 2003). Both resources consist of spectrums that vary
in the context where the theory applies. For example, Jeremy (2005)
conducted research among 56 managers in Australia and concluded that
important resources that are crucial to entrepreneurship include capabilities, knowledge, and skills of firms. Although these intangible resources
hardly measure, they must be integrated and should blend together with
other resources (tangible) for a firms success.

Applying the RBV into HE context might reveal different results as
the orientation of success in the firms determines the survival in the competing industry, but on the other hand, commercialization success is driven
by academic research orientation.

In Table 1, both intangible assets (resources) and tangible assets are
divided in to different rows. Jeremy RBV intangible resources are listed
down and mapped with the proposed model in the Adapted RBV column.
Faculty and commercialization programs are categorized as intangible
assets based on the tacit nature of these assets. On the other hand, venture
capitalist/firms will be measured based on their commercialization collaboration in the commercialization program within the same category
(intangible).

The tangible resources which consist of physical assets and financial
resources will be mapped in the same way as below:

- Incubator Infrastructure (building, facilities, etc.)
- Funding/Grants/Investment (for commercialization)
- Human Resource (HR) staff involved in the technology transfer office

Table 1. Mapping Resource-based View with the RBV

	Jeremy Firms RBT	Adapted RBT on HE
Intangible Resources/ Intangible Assets	• Capabilities • Organization • Reputation • IP	• Faculty/Research Programs • Commercialization Programs • VC/Firms collaboration & capabilities
Tangible Assets	• Infrastructure/Building • Financial Capital • Financial Investment	• Incubator Infrastructure • Funding/Grants/Investment (for commercialization)

In addition, the result of this research emulated from the resource based theory will provide a confirmation based on the notion that the firms' dynamic capabilities (Eisenhardt and Martin, 2000) (know-how, skills, and expertise) are the most prominent factors in determining the firms' success based in the HE case context. The research questions can be derived from Table 1 on how the HE utilized the tangible resources and maneuvers the intangible resources from the research expertise. Maneuvering the intangible resources is more challenging as these resources are scattered throughout the different faculties and the capabilities of individual researchers and commercialization programs. Furthermore, the research commercialization has expanded beyond the universities with external entity (VC/firms) collaborations.

It is interesting to shed light on RBV with regard to commercialization of innovations and inventions in HEs. Universities as organizations comprised expertise in their own particular field. This expertise is dispersed in faculties and resides on individuals as intangible assets. Traditionally, the university resources (tangible assets) are channeled towards R&D as the university reputations are highly determined by the quality of the research discoveries and research findings (Grant, 1991; Jeremy, 2005; Kakati, 2003).

This research is concerned with the possible consequence and implication if both intangible and tangible resources are deliberately channeled into incubation programs under commercialization initiatives. RBV can be utilized as a tool to investigate whether significant and remarkable commercialization success can be achieved if orchestrating effort and resources are in place. However, incorporating the RBV into the university commercialization efforts requires slight adaptation of definitions of intangible resources to suit the HEs differing context as suggested by Fernández *et al.* (2000) and Hall (1993). For example, intangible assets as classified by Hall (1993) in the university have a very vague and broad meaning. It encompasses a wide range of knowledge, information, skills, judgment and wisdom, expertise, technology, and IPs both informally and formally shared among the academics (Gorman, 2002).

Further, for the sake of measuring the commercialization success, the concentration is given into the commercialization initiatives in the incubation program or any incubator-like programs such as technology and Science Park for commercialization of the R&D output. Focusing there on incubation and related programs is necessary as these serve as a platform for the knowledge sharing and a forefront entity to penetrate the market.

In addition, the commercialization initiatives should also incorporate the involvement of CV/firms for and all the available capabilities as intangible assets (and tangible assets) in the success of the university–industry ventures. As a new venture, the academic entrepreneurs are dependent on resources available in the incubation ecosystem; however, the resources alone are not sufficient to achieve commercialization objectives without formulating those resources in achieving the capability (Kakati, 2003). Therefore, it appears that the development of HE inventions (innovations) do not guarantee commercial success for the VC/firms without diverse technical skills and capabilities coupled with business and market capabilities which have been described as proof of market by Wright *et al.* (2004).

Expected implications

This research will contribute a theoretical model for successful commercialization and commercialization programs and describe the complex relationship between resources (finance, funding, and investment) and knowledge both tangible and intangible capabilities (Jeremy, 2005). Hence, it can provide an insight to enhance our understanding of the relationships between university and firms in the industry in terms of research commercialization (Minguillo and Thelwall, 2015). Understanding the characteristics, roles, and functions that comprise the technology research commercialization and those resources involved is deemed necessary. The outcomes provide a model on how to channel the universities' inventions (innovations) to the industry effectively (Siegel *et al.*, 2004; Wright *et al.*, 2004; Yusof *et al.*, 2009). Thus, the model offers best practice and guidelines for academics research commercialisations (Siegel *et al.*, 2004).

The outcomes are also expected to produce practical implications and serve as guidelines and best practices for university and research-based innovations developed in research centers or incubators (Wu *et al.*, 2015). The university–industry commercialization framework (Ambos *et al.*, 2007) provides a valuable insight for academic technology entrepreneurship. There are many lessons learnt from the research commercialization program such as the following:

- Higher commercialization rate of IPs leads to high economic returns through licensing agreements (Sahlan *et al.*, 2015; Markman *et al.*, 2005; D'Este and Perkmann, 2011). This quest benefits both academia entrepreneurs and the venture capitalist/firms.
- University incubation programs increase the quantity as well as quality of entrepreneurial activities at universities (Becker and Gassmann, 2006). Potential IPs often fail to penetrate the market as academics are not well versed to venture in the inventions (innovations) (Rubin *et al.*, 2015; Borg, 2001; Sahlan *et al.*, 2015) and access potential funding due to the absence of VC/firms partnerships.

Conclusion

Based on the discussion above, this research offers an insight of commercialization of IT/IS products and artefacts developed from the HE. More importantly, the research defines the relationships between university research and industry engagement and collaboration via science and technology parks and incubation programs. The commercialization venture which begins with formalizing the academic research to share the challenges at an early stage contributes to the commercialization performance (Wright *et al.*, 2004).

With regard to the characteristics of roles and functions of incubation programs (in science and technology park), the results will explain that technological expertise and market skills and knowledge work in tandem in determining the research outcomes and products success. The engagement of academics and industry in the incubation platform provides a solution defined by early researchers (Freeman, 1982; Maine and Garnsey, 2006).This research suggested that the successful are determined by the technology capabilities (Albert and Gaynor, 2006; Bergek and Norrman, 2008; Mian, 1997) and the abilities of those academic scientist to associate the inventions (innovations) with marketing capabilities (Albert and Gaynor, 2006; Borg, 2001; Mian, 1997) through research commercialization.

Furthermore, locating the HE incubation program accessible to venture capitalist/firms will benefit both parties mutually in terms of commercialization of research (Bergek and Norrman, 2008). Providing the infrastructure within multi-faceted milieu of research institutions benefited hugely from the close proximity of personnel, knowledge, and training resources which they offer and which could be harnessed (Albert and Gaynor, 2006; Borg, 2001; Mian, 1997).

The next research question pertaining to venture capitalist/firms engagement in HE in the commercializing IT/IS products must also be described based on both the technology expertise (Albert and Gaynor, 2006; Bergek, and Norrman, 2008; Mian, 1997) and marketing capabilities (Albert and Gaynor, 2006; Borg, 2001; Mian, 1997). This research suggests that being an industry player, the venture capitalist/firms have a better position to exploit the artifacts more than the academics and researchers.

Further research shall investigate in-depth pertaining to characteristics of individual academic scientists (D'Este and Patel, 2007; Perkmann and Walsh, 2007; Wu *et al.*, 2015) involved in the commercialization of IT/IS products. This research proves that the academics who catalyze research commercialization have high entrepreneurship characteristics (D'Este and Patel, 2007; Perkmann and Walsh, 2007).

References

Ajagbe, M. A., Isiavwe, D. T., Ogbari, E. M., and Sholanke, A. B. 2015. "Financing Early Staged Technology Based Firms in Malaysia," *Research Journal of Finance and Accounting,* 6(4), 210–221.

Albert, P. and Gaynor, L. 2006. "Technology Business Incubation Management: Lessons of Experience," *High-Tech Entrepreneurship: Managing Innovation, Variety and Uncertainty.* Routledge, London, pp. 131–143. Available at: http://journals.sagepub.com/doi/abs/10.5367/ijei.2012.0096.

Ambos, T., Makela, K., Birkingshaw, J., and D'Este, P. 2007. "When Does University Research Get Commercialised," In *Institutional and individual level predictors of commercial outputs from research-council funded projects, DRUID Summer Conference,* 18–20.

Becker, B. and Gassmann, O. 2006. "Corporate Incubators: Industrial R&D and What Universities Can Learn from Them," *The Journal of Technology Transfer,* 31(4), 469–483.

Bergek, A. and Norrman, C. 2008. "Incubator Best Practice: A Framework," *Technovation,* 28(1), 20–28.

Borg, E. A. 2001. "Knowledge, Information and Intellectual Property: Implications for Marketing Relationships," *Technovation,* 21(8), 515–524.

Bruton, G. D., Ahlstrom, D., and Li, H. L. 2010. "Institutional Theory and Entrepreneurship: Where Are We Now and Where Do We Need to Move in the Future?," *Entrepreneurship Theory and Practice,* 34(3), 421–440.

D'Este, P. and Patel, P. 2007. "University–Industry Linkages in the UK: What Are the Factors Underlying the Variety of Interactions with Industry?" *Research Policy,* 36(9), 1295–1313.

D'Este, P., and Perkmann, M. 2011. "Why do Academics Engage with Industry? The Entrepreneurial University and Individual Motivations," *The Journal of Technology Transfer,* 36(3), 316–339.

Eisenhardt, K. M. and Martin, J. A. 2000. "Dynamic Capabilities: What Are They?," *Strategic Management Journal,* 21(10–11), 1105–1121.

Etzkowitz, H. 2003. "Innovation in Innovation: The Triple Helix of University–Industry–Government Relations," *Social Science Information,* 42(3), 293–337.

Fernández, E., Montes, J. M., and Vázquez, C. J. 2000. "Typology and Strategic Analysis of Intangible Resources: A Resource-Based Approach," *Technovation,* 20(2), 81–92.

Freeman, C. 1982. *"The Economics of Industrial Innovation."* Frances Pinter, London.

Gedeon, S. 2010. "What Is Entrepreneurship?," *Entrepreneurial Practice Review,* 1(3), 16–36.

Geuna, A. and Nesta, L. J. 2006. "University Patenting and Its Effects on Academic Research: The Emerging European Evidence," *Research Policy,* 35(6), 790–807.

Gorman, M. E. 2002. "Types of Knowledge and Their Roles in Technology Transfer," *The Journal of Technology Transfer,* 27(3), 219–231.

Grant, R. M. 1991. "The Resource-Based Theory of Competitive Advantage: Implications for Strategy Formulation," *Knowledge and Strategy,* 33(3), 3–23.

Hall, R. 1993. "A Framework Linking Intangible Resources and Capabilities to Sustainable Competitive Advantage," *Strategic Management Journal,* 14(8), 607–618.

Jeremy, G. 2005. "Which Resources Matter the Most to Firm Success," *An Exploratory Study of Resource-Based Theory,* 25(9), 979–987.

Kakati, M. 2003. "Success Criteria in High-Tech New Ventures," *Technovation,* 23(5), 447–457.

Laudon, K. C., and Laudon, J. P. 1996. "*Management Information Systems: Organization and Technology-4/E.*" Prentice Hall, Upper Saddle River, New Jersey.

Lourenco, F., Taylor, T. G., and Taylor, D. W. 2013. "Integrating 'Education for Entrepreneurship' in Multiple Faculties in 'Half-the-Time' to Enhance Graduate Entrepreneurship," *Journal of Small Business and Enterprise Development,* 20(3), 503–525.

Maine, E. and Garnsey, E. 2006. "*Commercializing Generic Technology*: The Case of Advanced Materials Ventures," *Research Policy,* 35(3), 375–393.

Markman, G. D., Phan, P. H., Balkin, D. B., and Gianiodis, P. T. 2005. "Entrepreneurship and University-Based Technology Transfer," *Journal of Business Venturing,* 20(2), 241–263.

Marton, S. 2005. "Implementing the Triple Helix: The Academic Response to Changing University–Industry–Government Relations in Sweden," In *Reform and Change in Higher Education,* Springer, New York, pp. 325–342.

Mian, S. A. 1997. "Assessing and Managing the University Technology Business Incubator: An Integrative Framework," *Journal of Business Venturing,* 12(4), 251–285.

Minguillo, D. and Thelwall, M. 2015. "Which Are the Best Innovation Support Infrastructures for Universities? Evidence from R&D Output and Commercial Activities," *Scientometrics,* 102(1), 1057–1081.

Mowery, D. C. and Shane, S. 2002. "Introduction to the Special Issue on University Entrepreneurship and Technology Transfer," *Management Science*, 48(1), v–ix.

Nielsen, K. 2015. "Human Capital and New Venture Performance: The Industry Choice and Performance of Academic Entrepreneurs," *Journal of Technology Transfer*, 40, 453–474.

Nuseibeh, B. and Easterbrook, S., 2000, "Requirements Engineering: A Roadmap." *Proceedings of the Conference on the Future of Software Engineering*, ACM, (pp. 35–46).

Perkmann, M. and Walsh, K. 2007. "University–Industry Relationships and Open Innovation: Towards a Research Agenda," *International Journal of Management Reviews*, 9(4), 259–280.

Porter, M. E. 2008. *"Competitive Advantage: Creating and Sustaining Superior Performance."* Simon and Schuster, New York.

Rasmussen, E., Mosey, S., and Wright, M. 2011. "The Evolution of Entrepreneurial Competencies: A Longitudinal Study of University Spin-Off Venture Emergence," *Journal of Management Studies*, 48(6), 1314–1345.

Rubin, T. H., Aas, T. H., and Stead, A. 2015. "Knowledge Flow in Technological Business Incubators: Evidence from Australia and Israel," *Technovation*, 41–42, 11–24.

Sahlan, S. A. B., Rahman, N., and Amin, S. B. M. 2015. "Commercialization Behavior Among Academicians: Personal, Environmental and Entrepreneurial Self-Efficacy," *Australian Journal of Business and Economic Studies*, 1(1), 74–86.

Scherer, F. M. 1986. *"Innovation and Growth: Schumpeterian Perspectives,"* MIT Press Books (1).

Schumpeter, J. A. 1934. *"The Theory of Economic Development: An Inquiry into Profits, Capital, Credit, Interest, and the Business Cycle."* Transaction Publishers, Piscataway, New Jersey.

Shinn, T. 2002. "The Triple Helix and New Production of Knowledge Prepackaged Thinking on Science and Technology," *Social studies of science*, 32(4), 599–614.

Siegel, D. S., Waldman, D. A., Atwater, L. E., and Link, A. N. 2004. "Toward a Model of the Effective Transfer of Scientific Knowledge from Academicians to Practitioners: Qualitative Evidence from the Commercialization of University Technologies," *Journal of Engineering and Technology Management*, 21(1), 115–142.

Smith, L. H. 2011. "Triple Helix and Regional Development: A Perspective from Oxfordshire in the Uk," *Development and Learning in Organizations*, 25(2), 805–818.

Swamidass, P. M. 2013. "University Startups as a Commercialization Alternative: Lessons from Three Contrasting Case Studies," *The Journal of Technology Transfer,* 38(6), 788–808.

Täks, M., Tynjälä, P., and Kukemelk, H. 2015. "Engineering Students' Conceptions of Entrepreneurial Learning as Part of Their Education," *European Journal of Engineering Education,* 41(1), 53–69. Available at: http://www.tandfonline.com/doi/full/10.1080/03043797.2015.1012708.

Thorburn, L. 2000. "Knowledge Management, Research Spinoffs and Commercialization of R&D in Australia," *Asia Pacific Journal of Management,* 17(2), 257–275.

Upstill, G., and Symington, D. 2002. "Technology Transfer and the Creation of Companies: The CSIRO Experience," *R&D Management,* 32(3), 233–239.

Wright, M., Vohora, A., and Lockett, A. 2004. "The Formation of High-Tech University Spinouts: The Role of Joint Ventures and Venture Capital Investors," *The Journal of Technology Transfer,* 29(3–4), 287–310.

Wu, Y., Welch, E. W., and Huang, W.-L. 2015. "Commercialization of University Inventions: Individual and Institutional Factors Affecting Licensing of University Patents," *Technovation,* 36, 12–25.

Yusof, M., Siddiq, M. S., and Nor, L. M. 2009. "An Integrated Model of a University's Entrepreneurial Ecosystem," *Journal of Asia Entrepreneurship and Sustainability,* 5(1), 57.

Chapter 14

Blockchain Brings a New IT Capability: A Case Study of HNA Group

Wenchi Ying

School of Economics & Management, Beihang University
Beijing, 100191, China
yingwenchi@buaa.edu.cn

Suling Jia

School of Economics & Management, Beihang University
Beijing, 100191, China

Abstract

IT capability directly impacts organizational performance as well as internal and external cooperation, especially in the field of e-business. Blockchain, as an emerging information technology, has led to a significant trend involving IT-based transformation in recent years. However, despite fruitful research on IT capability and IT-based business innovation, the understanding on the applications of Blockchain technology remains unclear. Our study investigates the applications of this new Information Technology by examining a case study of HNA Group (formerly Hainan Airline), one of the Fortune 500 Companies. The findings of this case show that Blockchain brings a new IT capability — hybrid capability. This case highlights how to leverage

233

Blockchain and its capability to create a new IT application and business model, which contribute to the cooperation between different types of business units in a distributed network. Accordingly, this case shows a new IT-based innovative direction.

Keywords: Blockchain, HNA Group, IT Capability, Hybrid, Contradictory, Complementary.

Introduction

Blockchain is a new information technology (Swan, 2015), and this case study considers the IT capability brought by Blockchain to implement business innovation. Blockchain originates from Bitcoin, a peer-to-peer electronic cash system (Nakamoto, 2008). However, Bitcoin is only one case for decentralized payment transfer using the *Blockchain technology*, which is essentially a reliable matter to maintain a database of daily records using cryptography in a multi-party environment without the need of a trusted intermediary.

Traditionally, there is always a database behind a system such as the AliPay in China, which records the account balance and transactional data of users. The database likes a massive ledger, and we can consider the update of a database as bookkeeping. Generally, the authority of bookkeeping belongs to the system's owner, not the users, and the risks of database being tampered, destroyed, or exposed remain in this centralized model. However, Blockchain can solve the traditional problem and allow every user to take part in bookkeeping and to manage it together. Blockchain is like a massive ledger that involves every user in the bookkeeping process. At a certain period of time, the fastest and most qualified user will be selected to update the account. The user records the change on a Block, and distributes the copies to all the users as backup. Every Block of data is cryptographically chained together (i.e. hashing-plus-timestamping attestation functionality, Swan, 2015), and we call it *Blockchain* or *Distributed Ledger*. Thus, all the nodes have a copy of the most updated ledger to verify the next transactional authenticity by the plurality rule with identity-based encryption and transactional transparency throughout the ledger. Because of no centralized intermediary and Blockchain's technical characteristics, there is no specific bookkeeper, private identity information has no risk of exposure, transaction is transparent, and any node tampered or destroyed will not affect business operation, so that transaction and account management will be more safe, stable, effective, and low-cost.

Blockchain can be used in not only the finance industry but also other industries. However, discussions about the technology have remained at the conceptual level or the totally virtual situation such as Bitcoin, and have lacked empirical evidences. There are more challenges in the real world, especially involving the transaction between different types of business units. But it is imperative to investigate what capability of Blockchain could contribute to the real-world business situation, and how to leverage it to transform traditionally centralized business model.

Therefore, this case study examines the new IT capability brought by Blockchain contributions to business innovation. Following a case study approach (Pan and Tan, 2011), we conducted a qualitative study of HNA Group, China, one of the *Fortune 500 Companies*, to investigate the practices involving Blockchain-based business applications. The findings of this study reveal one kind of hybrid capability brought by Blockchain (Battilana and Lee, 2014; Pilkington, 2016), accompanied with a valuably successful experience about leveraging it. With an accurate understanding on its application, organizations could make good use of Blockchain in their business innovation, and discover a new IT-based innovative direction of contradictory-to-complementary (Wareham *et al.*, 2014).

Case background

HNA Group, founded in 1993 as a traditional airline in Hainan province, China, has created a business miracle by successfully transforming into a multi-national conglomerate. Nowadays, HNA Group's business fields have extended to airlines, airports, tourism, hotels, logistics, real estate, technical services, and finance. In 2016, HNA Group reaps revenues of over USD 29 billion, ranking 353rd on the *2016 Fortune 500 Companies*.

By 2015, HNA Group has nearly 400 subsidiaries, and 180,000 employees, thus corporate benefit planning becomes one of the most significant planning for Human Resource Management in this corporate. Traditionally, HNA's subsidiaries adopted different benefit schemes for employees, and the benefit items of each company were too simple or less optional, such as cash, gift cards, or a few kinds of goods. All of these led to the lack of benefit items and less customized experiences for employees and increasing costs for companies. To address these inherent problems, as most of the *Fortune 500 Companies* have done, HNA Group initiated a unified Flexible-Benefit Plans (FBP, for short) in order to allow employees to choose the benefits they want or need from a package of items offered by HNA. To enrich the benefit items, HNA Group planned to mobilize its suppliers to participate in FBP to provide abundant goods. Because of nearly 15,000 suppliers and 180,000 employees owned, HNA Group has enough bargaining power to achieve the diversity and discount of goods with high quality. Therefore, the Purchasing Administration department of HNA Group (HNA-PA, for short), who are managing these suppliers, would be responsible for developing and operating the unified FBP Platform to support the benefit transaction and delivery.

To achieve the benefit transaction and delivery, sharing information between HNA Group and suppliers is inevitable, and ensuring transactional safety and stability is vital for the FBP Platform. The traditional solution is to share the information of customers' identities and accounts, either with each other, or with a third party as the intermediary. If information was not shared, they could not trust each other. However, the data of 180,000 employees is a precious resource, i.e. potential customer resource. Traditional solution cannot ensure the secrecy and safety of HNA's core resource, cannot remove the transactional risk of hacker's attack or centralized server's downtime, and leads to higher technical cost.

Thus, HNA Group built the FBP Platform by introducing the emerging Blockchain technology to address these tensions, including three key points: (1) how to ensure the secrecy and safety of employees' data (i.e. HNA's core resources) and to share the data with the suppliers at the same time (necessity for transactions); (2) how to protect data from being tampered or destroyed and to verify the authenticity of transactions; (3) how to achieve the cooperation between different business units in the form of non-interference on the conditions above, especially in interconnecting the FBP Platform with several external e-business platforms.

The application of blockchain in building the FBP platform

We will examine how HNA Group successfully built the FBP Platform by leveraging the capability of Blockchain and describe this case in the following three sections.

Creating user's account and transactional block

HNA Group established a "Benefit Point Accumulation (BPA, for short)" system in the Platform to unify the digital cash form for FBP. Obviously, HNA Group first created the digital account for each employee or supplier to collect and pay BPAs in the Platform. HNA Group could deposit the money for benefits into a real bank account, and the FBP Platform would convert the money into the equal number of BPAs, which would be delivered into the digital account of each employee, respectively. Employees could spend the BPAs to buy the goods. Meanwhile, both employees and suppliers could deposit and withdraw BPAs by themselves.

In the platform, each account is encrypted by a unique couple of keys (public key & private key), which hides private identity of each employee. When someone initiates a payment action, the information system collecting the new data will establish a new Block, which records the data of accounts, transactional items, timestamp, and Hash number (identification of the block based on 256-bit Secure Hash Algorithm) involving this transaction. As Mr. Wang, the project manager for the HNA-B Platform described:

> The couple of keys displayed as a string of codes not only hides the real identity of the user but also ensures the authenticity of user accounts, while the transactional BPAs are open and transparent to the public. The Block combining both the encrypted and unencrypted data lays the foundation of transactional verification.

Managing ledger and verifying transaction

Each Block has its own timestamp, which proves that the data must have existed at the time. All of the Blocks form a chain by linking the current

Block's Hash number with the previous Block's Hash number according to the timestamps. This chain is Blockchain, which is a Ledger consisting of all the existed transactions' history. HNA Group deploys Blockchain's copies on a certain amount of computing servers (i.e. nodes) by broadcasting each transaction. Each server owning the whole Ledger database could calculate the BPAs' balance of each anonymous account according to all the records of transactions stored in the Blockchain. These nodes containing processing programs are allocated at several Data Centers of HNA, and form a distributed network. As Mr. Liu, the technical manager of HNA-PA, described:

> This database pattern of distributed integration contributes to the following verification. Meanwhile, with several computing servers with enterprise-class security policy, instead of every user's personal computer acting as a miner like in the Bitcoin system, we can ensure the processes of verification more safe and efficient.

HNA Group introduces the form of "check-voting with plurality rule" to simplify and improve the processes of verification. In the FBP Platform's distributed network, no matter where the new transaction occurs, e.g., an employee submits a payment request to a supplier; the server processing this transaction broadcasts it to all nodes. The nodes will collect the new transactional data into a Block and verify if the transaction is valid (e.g. not be tampered) and not already spent. Then, each node broadcast the results of verification again. Nodes accept the Block only if plurality of all nodes confirms the transactional authenticity in the form of voting, and this Block will be added into the chain, i.e. this payment will be accepted, and the corresponding BPAs will be transferred from the employee's account to supplier' account. Thus, an order will be generated by the supplier, who is going to deliver goods to the employee according to the order. Although the order contains the information of recipients, the information is incomplete and discrete, and totally different from the valuable information of employees.

Extending Blockchain's capabilities to external e-business platforms

Furthermore, in order to enrich the benefit items and extend the delivery channels, HNA Group not only mobilized more suppliers to participate into the FBP Platform, but also leveraged the Blockchain's capabilities mentioned above to interconnect the Platform with other external e-business platforms, e.g. JD.COM (an ecommerce giant in China). The FBP Platform, via a kind of standard interfaces, integrated the items of goods provided by JD.COM. HNA's employees could choose what they want on the website and submit the payment requests through the functionality in "My Shopping Bag". Since JD.COM had registered in the HNA's FBP, the Blockchain system behind the FBP Platform could create JD.COM's digital account by assigning a new couple of keys to JD.COM's platform. Simultaneously, HNA Group deployed Blockchain's copies on several servers located at JD.COM's Data Center, i.e. these servers had acted as verifying nodes to join the HNA's distributed network.

In the interconnection situation, HNA Group offers JD.COM huge customer traffic, while JD.COM provides HNA's employees with more items and discounts of goods. Obviously, blockchain technology enables HNA Group and JD.COM to cooperate seamlessly without mutual interference, thus, both companies are able to introduce customers of JD.COM into HNA's e-business platform without issue. As Mr. Qin, the deputy general manager of HNA-PA, described:

Because of ensuring the secrecy of core resources respectively, both of HNA Group and JD.COM can keep their own business operations independent. At the same time, because of sharing the Ledger database safely, both of them achieve an interdependent cooperation as well.

Moreover, this Blockchain-based solution contributes to a few upgrades on the existing information system instead of developing a new intermediary system. As Mr. Liu, the technical manager of HNA-PA, added:

The Blockchain-based application is a lightweight class of distributed information systems, which contribute to reducing the technical costs for both HNA Group and JD.COM.

So far, over 200 subsidiaries of HNA participate in the FBP. The FBP Platform had been running online since May 2015 and had been upgraded to connect with JD.COM which provided over 50,000 types of goods since January 2016. Especially in the promotion during the Spring Festival of China, the FBP Platform contributed to 130 million RMB sales within 7 days, and the fruits from Hainan province provided by JD.COM were widely praised. During this period, the FBP Platform had been running safely, stably, and efficiently due to the use of the Blockchain.

Lessons learned

In general, common sense suggests that "private-secrecy" and "public-sharing", "distributed" and "integrated", "independent", and "interdependent" are contradictory tensions. We always just utilize a combination of complementary technology characteristics, instead of contradictory ones, to achieve business innovation. But, this case shows that the Blockchain, as an emerging information technology, brings a kind of hybrid capability to balance these contradictory tensions in IT applications and to transform these tensions into the complements. Thus, when how to leverage the Blockchain technology for business innovation receives wide attention, this case provides the practitioners with some implications discussed as follows.

Firstly, this case informs that it is priority to make clear what data needs to be protected or shared during the process of transactions. For instance, HNA Group insists that the employee's identity is the secret data (i.e. HNA's core resource) in the form of a digital account within the Platform, while the transactional records such as BPAs balance should be publicly shared with suppliers in order to make sure each real account's credit can be calculated. Obviously the data need to be protected and can be encrypted and its authenticity can be ensured, by a couple of unique keys (public key and private key). Then, on this basis, the private data and the public data can be aggregated into the Block by the Hash algorithm. In our case, the "private-secrecy" and the "public-sharing" of transactional data are no longer a contradictory tension but are hybridized to be the complementary ones by the Blockchain technology.

Secondly, in order to ensure stable and safe transaction, this case demonstrates that it is vital to mobilize their IT resources as verifying nodes for managing the Ledger database (i.e. Blockchain) together. While the Ledger database integrates all the Blocks with the complete check-voting programs, its copies are distributed on all the nodes for verification, instead of an intermediary. Furthermore, HNA Group deploys the Ledger on a certain amount of nodes which are specially selected (e.g., several enterprise-class servers located at HNA) to improve the verifying efficiency and reliability, instead of relying on all the servers or all personal computers as the miners. In our case, the Blockchain technology hybridizes the "distributed" pattern with the "integrated" pattern to complement each other.

Thirdly, this case further illustrates that the application above, without interfering, can inter-operate with external e-business platforms. JD.com shares the items of goods with HNA Group via a kind of standard interfaces, while HNA Group shares the anonymous accounts and transactional BPAs balance with JD.COM by the distributed Ledger, and deploys several verifying nodes in JD.COM. Besides this, there are few updates on their own platforms and business model, and the technical cost is also low. In this case, the Blockchain technology hybridizes "interdependence" with "independence" to contribute to the win–win outcomes, where HNA Group and JD.COM not only cooperate interdependently but also keep their own business operations independent.

Last but not least, it shows that the Blockchain technology brings a hybrid capability for IT application and business innovation. This capability to innovate will direct practitioners to implement a new Blue Ocean Strategy from the technical contradictory-to-complementary perspective.

Conclusion

Despite the obvious significance of IT capability to enable organizations to innovate, the new capability brought by emerging Blockchain technology remains elusive to many companies and their managers. Findings from this case study highlighted Blockchain's hybrid capability and Blockchain-based application and business model. Our study illustrates the critical value of Blockchain to CIOs and CEOs and explains how to leverage it to create a new IT application and business model. We hope the findings will provide organizations with a new IT-based innovative perspective. Future research could focus on organizations from other business fields to extend our understanding on the Blockchain-based applications and the accordingly hybrid capability.

References

Battilana, J., and Lee, M. 2014. "Advancing Research on Hybrid Organizing–Insights from the Study of Social Enterprises," *The Academy of Management Annals,* 8(1), 397–441.

Nakamoto, S. 2008. "Bitcoin: A Peer-to-Peer Electronic Cash System".

Pan, S. L., and Tan, B. 2011. "Demystifying Case Research: A Structured–Pragmatic–Situational (SPS) Approach to Conducting Case Studies," *Information and Organization,* 21(3), 161–176.

Pilkington M. 2016. "Blockchain Technology: Principles and Applications. Research Handbook on Digital Transformations," F. Xavier Olleros and Majlinda Zhegu (eds.), Edward Elgar, Cheltenham.

Swan, M. 2015. *"Blockchain: Blueprint for a New Economy,"* O'Reilly Media, Inc., Sebastopol, California.

Wareham, J., Fox, P. B., and Cano Giner, J. L. 2014. "Technology Ecosystem Governance," *Organization Science,* 25(4), 1195–1215.

Appendix A

Table A. List of Interviewees

Position		Rank
1	Operating President, HNA Group, overseeing the entire HNA Group operation	Top manager (TM)
2	Deputy general manager, HNA-PA, responsible for introduction of Blockchain technology, and overseeing the entire projects of Blockchain applications	TM
3	Assistant President, HNA Institute of Economist, responsible for strategic planning of HNA	TM
4	Senior manager, HNA Business Service Co. Ltd., responsible for operation of HNA FBP	Middle manager (MM)
5	Senior manager, HNA-PA, responsible for purchasing management	MM
6	Junior Staff A, HNA-PA, responsible for implementation of HNA FBP	Junior Staff (JS)
7	Junior Staff B, HNA-PA, responsible for implementation of the Wallet System of HNA Benefit Platform	JS
8	Junior Staff C, HNA-PA, responsible for IT building involving purchasing management information system	JS
9	Junior Staff D, HNA-PA, responsible for institutional improvement of purchasing management	JS
10	Director of Institute of Technology, EcoTech Group of HNA Group (HNA-ET-IT), responsible for overseeing the entire technology innovation	MM
11	Operating manager, HNA-ET-IT, responsible for technology innovation management	MM
12	Junior F, HNA-ET-IT, responsible for IT implementation	JS
13	CTO, the HNA's Partner providing Blockchain technology, responsible for technical supporting	Technology Partner
14	CIO, the HNA's Partner providing Blockchain technology, responsible for technical supporting	Technology Partner
15	Supplier A, one of the suppliers of HNA	Supplier
16	Supplier B, one of the suppliers of HNA	Supplier
17	Supplier C, one of the suppliers of HNA	Supplier
18	Supplier D, one of the suppliers of HNA	Supplier

Chapter 15

The Role of Disruptive Innovation in Building a Shared Economic Platform: A Case Study of Sheke Net (SKN), China

Haibo Hu

School of Business Administration at the Jiangxi University
of Finance and Economics, China

Tao Huang

Center for Industrial Production
Aalborg University
Aalborg, Denmark
15270990295@163.com

Yang Cheng

Center for Industrial Production
Aalborg University
Aalborg, Denmark

Abstract

Disruptive innovation is a powerful means of broadening and developing new markets and providing new functionality, especially one that involves building a shared economic platform. However, despite Disruptive Innovation Theory has created a significant impact on management practices and aroused plenty of rich debate within academia, it is still not clearly understood how one might successfully achieve business model innovation by building a shared economic platform. Thus, this Chapter the adopts the case study methodology and analyses the process of disruptive innovation, aiming to disambiguate this black box by examining the case study of Sheke Net (SKN), a network platform of architectural design, China. The findings of this chapter highlight the significant role played by disruptive innovation in achieving a shared economic model. The findings of this chapter contribute to the research both on disruptive innovation and shared economic platform.

Keywords: Disruptive innovation, Shared economic platform, Business model; Architectural design, Sheke Net.

Introduction

Disruptive Innovation Theory has created a significant impact on management practices and aroused plenty of rich debate within academia. Disruptive Innovation Theory, advanced by Christensen (Christensen, 1997, 2006; Christensen and Bower, 1996; Christensen and Raynor, 2003), was built up based on a series of previous technological innovation studies. It proposes that companies could attract more people into the new value network with more convenient and cheaper disruptive innovation, and then disrupt the entire industry (Christensen, 1997). In the process of disruptive innovation, companies should offer new proposition through new technology, and integrate both internal and external resources and establish the sustainable business model to support the value proposition (Hwang and Christensen, 2008).

When the new technology is diffused to customers, companies shall establish disruptive channels (Christensen and Raynor, 2003), so as to promote the technology along with other entities in the value chain. Christensen and Raynor (2003) assumed two types of customers with regard to disruptive innovation: entirely new non-consumers in markets outside of existing markets, and overshot customers in existing markets.

Disruptive innovation happens in a process. On the basis of the concept of value network, Christensen and Raynor (2003) put forward disruptive innovation analysis framework, including three dimensions: time, performance, and the new value network (Figure 1). In general,

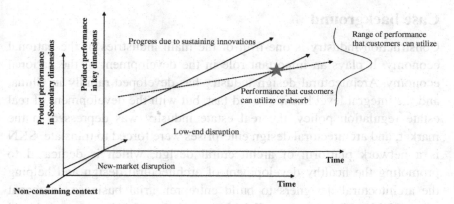

Figure 1. The Disruptive Innovation Model
Source: Christensen, C., and Raynor, M.

a disruptive innovation is enabled from four various angles such as internal vs. external, and marketing vs. technology (Yu and Hang, 2010). From the internal perspective, many scholars explore disruptive innovation from the value system which consists of the four essential factors of business model: Value Source, Value Creation, Value Delivery, and Value Capture (Rayna and Striukova, 2014). Against such a backdrop, we have conducted a qualitative study of SKN, China to investigate the role of disruptive innovation in the process of building a shared economic platform.

Based on these arguments, Christensen *et al.* (2001) further pointed out that the previously discussed disruptive innovation only occurred at the low-end market of the developed countries and the low-income groups of developing countries were excluded from the disruption process. This case analysis considers the role of disruptive innovation in building shared economic platform. The main purpose of our study is to shed light into the evolution process of a shared economic platform. Shared economy as a form of business model is gradually subverting the traditional business model.

As exploratory research (Pan and Tan, 2011), the case study methodology is the most appropriate strategy to address the "how" question in this chapter (Eisenhardt, 1989; Yin, 2009). This case study reveals that disruptive innovation helps to enhance the firm's ability to deal with various problems encountered in building a shared economic platform.

Case background

Construction industry is one-fifth of the main industries of the national economy. It plays an important role in the development of the national economy. Architectural design industry has developed rapidly in China, and the integral level has improved fast, but with the development of real estate regulation policy, the real estate industry was depressed in the market, and architectural design enterprises were forced to translate. SKN is a network platform of architectural design, which is dedicated to promoting the healthy development of architectural design and helping the architectural designers to build entrepreneurial business. In recent years, SKN has been setting off the beaten track and trying to use a shared economic model to integrate industrial resources and remold the industrial status. As specimens, its process is full of ups and downs, which has quite typical meaning for Internet companies.

Shared economy is a gradually emerging research topic in the field of the business model innovation research. This case, based on the clue of how SKN Net builds a shared economic model from aspects of the construction, operation of network platform, and the building of the industrial ecosystem, illustrates how the flexural process would be with the leadership of SKN CEO Huangbiao Xu. Therefore, it leads to the discussion between academia and business circle, that is, for the traditional industries, can this emerging shared economy business model create sustainable competitive advantage and achieve success?

The disruptive innovation journey at SKN

The background of SKN's birth

With the trend of "Internet+" emerging, the industrial structure in China has started translating units into multiple units and its comprehensive national strength also has become increasingly strong. Besides, industry I and industry II have achieved a great development. As the important symbol of national innovation capability and industrial competitiveness, the real estate industry has also been significantly improved. Architectural design also follows the pace of the trend of rapid development of the real estate industry. But at the same time, the architectural design industry is facing the integration of huge, urgent, and authoritative resource. According to the relevant statistics, by the end of 2013, the number of registered national engineering design personnel was 2.44 million, and in 2014 was 3.8 million. Besides, there is still a large number of registered survey and design industry practitioners, the per capita annual output of survey design industry is 30,000 per person. It is expected that the number of national engineering design staff will reach about 6 million in 2015. The growth rate will be maintained at 15~20% every year.

The growth of the engineering design personnel directly has led to the vigorous development of architectural design. It not only greatly improved the overall image of the architecture field, but also promoted the sales and development of the real estate and enhanced the domestic architecture field's core competitiveness in the international market. Architectural design has developed from the traditional mode of department and fixed design to the mode which focused on personalized and free design. Designers are also not only pursuing the wages, but also designing inspiration and free space.

Due to the poor collocation of projects with designers in the building design industry, idle resources of designers appear frequently, overcapacity has turned up in the industry, and majority of small and medium-sized design institutes are facing the crisis of bankruptcy or reorganization. The traditional design institute Director Huangbiao Xu, who has the spirit of innovation and entrepreneurship, established SKN (Figure 2), whose aim

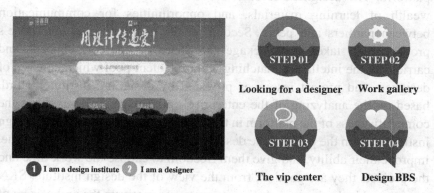

Figure 2. The Official Website Interface of SKN

Source: Based on the case study.

is to integrate the resource of the architecture design enterprises, and eventually become an integrated platform based on capital sharing, project collaboration, and data shared.

The process of SKN's establishment

In recent years, the problem of overcapacity in the construction industry has become increasingly prominent. How to adjust the structure of the industry has aroused the concern of all parties. The medium and small designing institutes are facing two major difficulties. First, due to the geographical constraints and other reasons, there are not enough outstanding designers working for the designing institute, as a result, the design projects cannot achieve the state of optimal resource allocation. Second, a part of designers have limited number of projects, which directly leads to the wastage of designers resources.

Based on the present situation, SKN has independently researched and developed the architectural design industry platform website — SKN. They commit to building a shared platform for designers, design institutes, and developers, which make it possible for them to carry out information communication, business interaction, and coordination of design.

The establishment of SKN has experienced four stages. First, at the research of enterprise's project background, SKN seizes the designers' demands for starting a business, committed to building a resource service platform. The designers of SKN can obtain a stable source of project, wealth of learning materials, and opportunities for communication between partners and peers. Second, at the positioning of enterprise's product, SKN takes the "Package and Share" as the core concept, and carries out the intelligent matching with the talent pool which consists of designers and project resources provided by designing institute. Third, based on the analyzing of the enterprise's advantage, SKN explores the competitiveness of the platform in two dimensions of designers and design institutes, from the point of the designer, SKN may increase their revenue, improve their ability, and give them freedom to choose the work time and the projects they are good at; from the view of the design institute, SKN can expand its business, reducing its costs and motivate the enthusiasm of

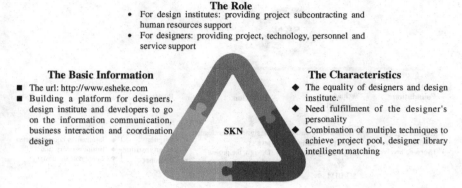

The Role
- For design institutes: providing project subcontracting and human resources support
- For designers: providing project, technology, personnel and service support

The Basic Information
- The url: http://www.esheke.com
- Building a platform for designers, design institute and developers to go on the information communication, business interaction and coordination design

SKN

The Characteristics
- The equality of designers and design institute.
- Need fulfillment of the designer's personality
- Combination of multiple techniques to achieve project pool, designer library intelligent matching

Figure 3.   Three Major Advantages of SKN

Source: Based on the case study.

the staff. Fourth, at the planning of enterprise's strategy, SKN develops strategies in the perspective of the market layout and product planning. In the layout of the market, SKN chose Beijing as the center, and Nanchang as the pilot, then gradually spread to first-tier and second-tier cities.

SKN's platform mainly includes two dimensions: design institute and designer (Figure 3). By making use of the trait that idle resources of designers cannot match well with design project, SKN is committed to build the shared platform of architectural design industry.

The operation of SKN

Resource redistribution based on network platform

SKN is committed to building a platform sharing the full area of resources (Figure 4) by establishing the information communication, business inter-action and design coordination between designer, design institute, and the developer. From the point of the designing institute, they will upload the design manuscripts and plan drawings for the site, at the same time, they will send the information of staff requirements, design specifications, and data to the site. From the view of the designer, the design personnel can register by sending their qualifications, design features, and design background to the site. On the platform, designers can not only seek

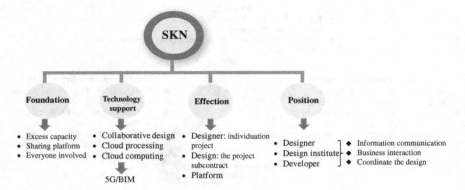

Figure 4.   Characteristics of Shared Economic Platform — SKN

Source: Based on the case study.

project alone, but also can accept projects provided by platform with the technology of intelligent matching. Based on the network platform, SKN can reallocate resources and provide projects, technology, personnel, and service support for the designers to start up business. What's more, it can also provide the designing institute with the support of the project and human resources. SKN provides a vast amount of technical information and a technical exchange platform online, and provides accurate technical training to designers according to their needs offline. The platform is able to help designers to grow at the highest speed.

The subcontract of projects based on information technology

According to the present situation of architectural design industry, SKN uses different information technologies according to the different periods (Figure 5), the platform is mainly focusing on the application of collaborative design technology, cloud processing, and cloud computing etc. to break the technology barriers of designers' remote communication and build technical docking platform between designers, then finish the project design process in the cloud at the same time. SKN links the project process through BIM Technology, taking the relevant information and data of the construction project as a model, then simulates the real information of building with the use of the digital information simulation, which leads to the architectural design industry achieving the connectivity

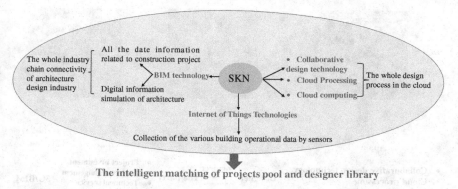

Figure 5.   The Auxiliary Technology of SKN

Source: Based on the case study.

of the whole industry chain. Meanwhile, the network technology will collect all kinds of construction operation data through the sensor, thus they will be reflected to the Internet in real time.

The three-step strategy

SKN is committed to network platform building to stimulate the designer's enthusiasm. SKN has developed a future development planning — "three-step" strategy (Figure 6), namely translating the stage from sharing economic model of professional service platform to incorporate designers and contracting party resources open cooperation, and finally to industrial docking interface (5G/BIM), then a industry ecosystem will be formed. In the stage of professional service, the technical barriers of the designers' remote communication will be solved by the application of collaborative design technology, cloud processing, and cloud computing, etc. The designers can work on the platform so that design projects are not just in a designing team, but also can be carried out easily and conveniently in the whole country. What's more, the application of BIM Technology will lead to the architectural design industry achieving the connectivity of the whole industry chain.

In the future, efforts will be devoted to expand the relevant project of the architectural design, thus SKN will derive more services in related area such as investment in the project, project management, technical services,

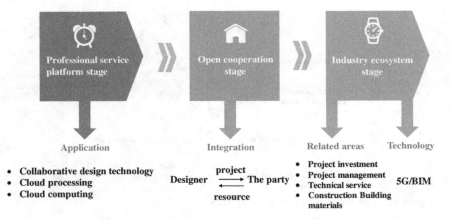

Figure 6.   The Three Steps Strategy of SKN

Source: Based on the case study.

construction and building materials, etc. and a multi-dimensional service platform will be established to promote the development of Industry 4.0 ecosystem.

Lessons learned

Based on the above analysis, this chapter argues that disruptive innovation comes from the source of one or several aspects of major reversal in the value system, which includes Value Source, Value Creation, Value Delivery, and Value Capture. Our case study demonstrated how disruptive innovation played a crucial role in building a shared economic platform, aimed at business model innovation. Based on the innovation of value system, further discussion about the internal logic of disruptive innovation has been done, and a new theoretical analysis framework of disruptive innovation has been proposed (Figure 7), which will help us understand the role of disruptive innovation in the shared economy model better. The lessons learned in our case study are discussed as follows.

Value source: Technology

Technology is the source of the disruptive innovation. Christensen pointed out that "technology" is a process in which a mechanism shifts labor,

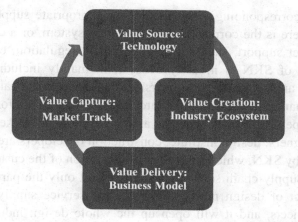

Figure 7.   Theoretical Analysis Framework of Disruptive Innovation
Source: Based on the related literature and the case study.

capital, raw materials, and information into more valuable products and services. "Innovation" is the change that has happened in one or more of these techniques (Christensen, 1997). As previously noted, the basic assumptions of the theory of disruptive innovation is that the development of the technology improvement is faster than the market demand. So if there is no technical change, disruptive innovation would not happen. This case shows that the value source of disruptive innovation lies in the combination of collaborative design, cloud processing, cloud computing, and the application of 5G/BIM.

Value creation: Industry ecosystem

Ecosystem is the carrier of disruptive innovation to create value. Ecosystem is able to expand the network of the value, refers to the economic union on the basis of the interaction of organizations or individuals, which consists of customers, suppliers, major manufacturers and other related entities, and those entities can provide market business solutions by cooperating with each other (Moore, 1993, 1996). Disruptive innovation success depends not only on the characteristics of technology and the recognition of the characteristics in market (Henderson and Clark, 1990; Christensen, 1996), but also on the compatibility between it and its technology ecosystem (Adner and Kapoor, 2010), for example, if there is a corresponding infrastructure, or appropriate supplier system, whether there is the corresponding marketing system, or a complementary product support, standard or government regulation, etc. Another subversion of SKN is industry ecosystem, mainly including channel subversion and supply chain subversion. In the aspect of channel subversion, the market of the traditional architectural design platform is building developers, and sales channels assume traditional marketing model, while designers, design institute, construction developers are effectively integrated by SKN, which achieves the integration of the customer. In the aspect of supply chain subversion, SKN is not only the party awarding the contract of design projects but also the service supply partner of design projects, and it will open up the whole design industry supply chain effectively.

Value delivery: Business model

The business model is an organization system for the business and stakeholders who can deliver customer value to obtain a sustainable income (Osterwalder *et al.*, 2005). A technology in itself does not necessarily generate disruptive impact, only the disruptive technologies and new business models combined can produce disruptive impact (Hwang and Christensen, 2008). Hart and Christensen (2002) pointed out that the reason of disruptive innovation's failure in a mature enterprise is that the enterprise's business model has been unable to support the development of disruptive technologies. For example, when entering the low-income groups developing markets, companies need the business model innovation to improve the flexibility of payment method in order to resolve the group's affordability problem (Mendoza and Thelen, 2008). Combined with this case, in terms of value delivery, the business model innovation of SKN mainly reflects in its shared economic model of architectural design platform. Specifically, SKN builds a transparent resource shared platform for design institute, designers, and construction developers.

As a platform, SKN will arouse the designers' inner passion by entrepreneurship, and connect them with the design institute by information communication, business interaction, and coordination. What's more, it can provide excellent designers for design institute to perfect the talent support system, achieving the integration of the resource from the architecture design industry, and eventually becomes an integrated platform based on capital shared, project collaboration, and data shared.

Value capture: Market track

Market track is the terminal of disruptive innovation, when disruptive innovation is received by a market or a value network, its economic value will be ultimately achieved. As mentioned earlier, the market penetration of disruptive innovation is a gradual process. Market track refers to the market evolution path of innovative products. If innovative products go along the existing homogenous market, which has been the type of products being sold in the market, even if the scale, but not to the new market, thus the innovation only goes along existing rail market; if the innovation meets the new requirements and a new non-traditional market is opened, a new market track will emerge. Based on the above analysis, this case shows that SKN broke the mode of the traditional market operation of architectural design, achieved the conversion of the market track from offline to online, and set up a good communication mechanism between small and medium-sized design institute, designers and construction developers, what's more, it made up for the deficiency of the existing architectural design industry and activated the vitality of the architectural design market.

Conclusion

Despite the significance of disruptive innovation, the process of developing a shared economic platform remains elusive to many firms. We hope that our findings from the case study will provide some practical implications for more firms to better manage the development of a shared economic platform, which is a critical step toward successfully building a industry ecosystem. We learned that it is especially significant for traditional factories to achieve business model innovation. Future research should focus on firms from other industries to extend our understanding of how business model innovation could be achieved through disruptive innovation functionalities.

Acknowledgments

This chapter was supported in part by National Social Science Foundation of China under Grants 15BGL033 and the scholarship under the State Scholarship Fund awarded by the China Scholarship Council (CSC).

References

Adner R., and Kapoor, R. 2010. "Value Creation in Innovation Ecosystems: How the Structure of Technological Interdependence Affects Firm Performance in New Technology Generations," *Strategic Management Journal*, 31(3), 306–333.

Christensen, C. M., and Bower, J. L. 1996. "Customer Power, Strategic Investment, and the Failure of Leading Firms," *Strategic Management Journal*, 17(3), 197–218.

Christensen, C. M. 1997. "The Innovator's Dilemma: When New Technologies Cause Great Firms to Fail," Harvard Business School Press, Boston, MA.

Christensen, C. M., Craig, T., and Hart, S. 2001. "The Great Disruption," *Foreign Affairs*, 80(2), 80–95.

Christensen, C., and Raynor, M. 2003. *"The Innovator's Solution: Creating and Sustaining Successful Growth"*. Harvard Business School Press, Boston, MA.

Christensen, C. M. 2006. "The Ongoing Process of Building a Theory of Disruption," *Journal of Product Innovation Management*, 23, (39–55).

Eisenhardt, K. M. 1989. "Building Theories from Case Study Research". *The Academy of Management Review*, 14(4), 532–550.

Hart, S. L, and Christensen, C. M. 2002. "The Great Leap-driving Innovation from the Base of the Pyramid," *Mit Sloan Management Review*, 44(1), 51–56.

Henderson, R. M., and Clark, K. B. 1990. "Architectural Innovation: The Reconfiguration of Existing Product Technologies and the Failure of Established Firms," *Administrative Science Quarterly*, 35(1), 9–30.

Hwang, J., and Christensen, C. 2008. "Disruptive Innovation in Health Care Delivery: A Framework for Business — Model Innovation," *Health Affairs*, 27(5), 1329.

Mendoza, R. U., and Thelen, N. 2008. "Innovations to Make Markets More Inclusive for the Poor," *Development Policy Review*, 26(4), 427–458.

Moore, J. F. 1993. "Predators and Prey: A New Ecology of Competition," *Harvard Business Review*, 71, 75–86.

Moore, J. F. 1996. "The Death of Competition: Leadership and Strategy in the Age of Business Ecosystems," Harper Collins, New York.

Osterwalder, A., Pigneur, Y., and Tucci, C. L. 2005. "Clarifying Business Models: Origins, Present, and Future of the Concept," *Communications of the association for Information Systems*, 16(1), 1–25.

Pan, S. L., and Tan, B. C. C. 2011. "Demystifying Case Research: A Structured–Pragmatic–Situational (SPS) Approach to Conducting Case Research," *Information and Organization*, 21, 161–176.

Rayna, T., and Striukova, L. 2014. "The Impact of 3D Printing Technologies on Business Model Innovation," Springer International Publishing, pp. 119–132.

Yin, R. K. 2009. *"Case Study Research: Design and Method,"* 4th edn., Thousand Oaks, CA, Sage Publications.

Yu, D. and Hang, C. C. 2010. "A Reflective Review of Disruptive Innovation 3 Theory," *International Journal of Management Reviews*, 12(4), 435–452. http://onlinelibrary.wiley.com/doi/10.1111/j.1468-2370.2009.00272.x/full.

Chapter 16

Developing Capabilities for the IT-enabled Organizational Transformation: A Case of Traditional Manufacturing Enterprise in China

Delin Zeng

School of Economics and Management, Beihang University
zengdelin007@hotmail.com

Zhengyan Cui

School of Economics and Management, Beihang University
4363401@163.com

Taohua Ouyang

School of Economics and Management, Beihang University
taohuaouyang@hotmail.com

Zhenya Tan

School of Economics and Management, Beihang University
tanzhy@buaa.edu.cn

Abstract

As business environments become more volatile and digitized due to the development of digital technology, IT-enabled organizational transformation (ITOT) remains one of the signature issues for information systems research. Because of the complex and uncertain nature of ITOT, researchers pay attention to the development of dynamic capabilities that enable company response more effectively. However, the process of how organizations develop capabilities to achieve the ITOT still needs to be explored. Using dynamic capability as a theoretical lens, the case study inductively derived a process framework that identifies six key capabilities by adopting a dual-level analysis (strategic and operational levels) and offered clear guideposts on how these capabilities may be developed to realize ITOT. Our study benefits both academics and practitioners by contributing to cumulative theoretical developments and by providing practical insights.

Keywords: IT-enabled organizational transformation, Dynamic capabilities, Dual-level Analysis, Process model, Case study.

Introduction

As business environments become more dynamic and digitized, i.e., driven by Information Technology (IT) (Pavlou and El Sawy, 2010), organizational transformation has become more imperative for survival and prosperity for contemporary organizations (Besson and Rowe, 2012). IT is also often regarded as a powerful tool to enable transformation in organization (Venkatraman, 1994). Prior research suggests that IT provides firms with extensive functionalities to reshape business strategies and enhance operational efficiency to achieve transformation (Tan *et al.*, 2010; Gregory *et al.*, 2015). However, the failure rate of IT-enabled organizational transformation (ITOT) remains considerably high (Liang *et al.*, 2007) for two reasons. First, complex and turbulent nature of ITOT makes it difficult for firms to adjust to changing conditions without appropriate management (Daniel and Wilson, 2003). Second, firms may lack specific instructions to develop the organizational capabilities through suitable actions (Huang *et al.*, 2014). As a matter of fact, whether a firm is able to attain business transformation depends on the organizational capabilities and how capabilities evolve at different transformation stages (Barney, 1991; Montealegre, 2002).

The increasing number of researchers and practitioners have to pay attention to the characteristics of how organizations leverage IT to achieve organizational transformation (Kim *et al.*, 2007; Gregory *et al.*, 2015), especially focus on the dynamic capabilities which reflect a firm's ability to respond to the volatile market change (Eisenhardt and Martin, 2000). However, despite the growing knowledge about the relationship between dynamic capabilities and ITOT, the process of how organizations develop their capabilities to facilitate the overall process of ITOT still needs to be explored.

To address the knowledge gap, this Chapter employs a case study of the capability development experience of manufacturing enterprise to analyze how firms may develop their capabilities through appropriate actions for ITOT. The manufacturing enterprise is Xi'an Aero-Engine PLC (XAEP), one of the major aircraft engine designers and manufacturers with more than 50 years of history in China. We inductively derived a process framework that identifies six capabilities and offered clear guideposts on how these capabilities may be developed to improve ITOT in a dynamic and volatile environment.

The chapter is structured as follows. First, we explore the theoretical background for our framework, then describe the data collection and analysis methods. Second, we provide a case description to analyze capability development in the ITOT. Finally, we discuss the contributions of our study for both research and practice, as well as directions for future research.

Theoretical Background

Organizational transformation in IS research

ITOT is regarded as a significant mechanism to derive business value from strategic IT investments (Venkatraman, 1994). With the rapid development of IT, ITOT has attracted much attention recently (Kim *et al.*, 2007; Gregory *et al.*, 2015). The extant literature relevant to ITOT can be divided into two key areas: (1) some papers are factor-oriented which identify a wide range of fundamental factors that will influence ITOT that includes organizational inertia (Hannan *et al.*, 2002); (2) the others are stage-oriented which focus on the process of ITOT (Teoh and Chen, 2013; Pan *et al.*, 2015).

Studies of the former category emphasize that organizational inertia makes organizational transformation an important theoretical and practical problem due to the essential paradox of organizing (Besson and Rowe, 2012). Existing literatures also point out that the kinds of organizational inertia should be considered primarily depending on the different analytic levels, e.g., individual, sector, or organization (Besson and Rowe, 2012). The latter category develop discourse concerning the process of organizational transformation before and after. One of the most prominent three-phase models is "Unfreeze–Transition–Refreeze" presented by Lewin (1951). Existing literatures argue that certain issues (e.g., type of managerial actions and organizational capabilities) should be required to exert their effects, depending on the phase considered (Pan *et al.*, 2015). In recent years, some scholars even proposed that IS research should describe and conceptualize the process of transformation when studying such a phenomenon (Besson and Rowe, 2012).

Although many meaningful research findings were generated from the previous studies, there are still several gaps in the literature. First, there are insufficient papers to shed some light on the process of how to enact an effective ITOT. Second, the fundamental role of organizational capabilities and IT have already been acknowledged in the process of transformation. However, how to develop organizational capabilities through appropriate actions for the ITOT is not answered by prior studies. To fill these gaps in the literature, we adopt the dynamic capabilities perspective to discuss how firms develop capabilities to respond to changes in volatile business environments.

Dynamic capabilities in IS research

Dynamic capability is defined as the ability to acquire competitive advantage by creating new technological, organizational, and managerial resources to obtain congruence with the changing environment (Teece *et al.*, 1997; Eisenhardt and Martin, 2000). It emphasizes capabilities and resources evolve over time as organizations learn and adapt to change (Calvin *et al.*, 2011).The evolution consists of three stages (Helfat and Peteraf, 2003), which begin with the founding stage, followed by the development stage, before reaching the maturity stage, in which capabilities become more embedded within organizational routines (Kim *et al.*, 2007). Dynamic capability concept has also increasingly been incorporated into the study of organizational transformation (Klievink and Janssen, 2009; Dixon *et al.*, 2010) because the firms require different types of capabilities to deal with the turbulence caused by transformation, which in turn contributes to the organizational transformation.

Actually, we have witnessed increasing research interest in dynamic capabilities in the IS area recently (Pan *et al.*, 2015). Sambamurthy *et al.* (2003) argue that a firm's IS capability in conjunction with inter-functional and inter-organizational coordination mechanisms can enable organizations to sense the external and internal changes, as well as conceive appropriate actions to seize market opportunities. Yet, notwithstanding the academic and practical contributions of the growing research in this area, our understanding of the links between the mobilization of resources/capabilities and ITOT remains limited. Hence, we provide the process model of capability development in the context of ITOT from two levels: strategic level and operational level. Because we believe that the dual-level analysis would provide a more complete view of the capability development process, which retains the strategic perspective of organizational actions, while allowing the operational perspective of departmental actions (Pan *et al.*, 2006). In a word, by understanding the central role of appropriate capabilities from dual-level perspective, firms can better adjust themselves to facilitate transformation.

Research methodology

Method and case selection

The case research methodology is particularly appropriate for this study for two reasons. First, the research question is a "how" question that is appropriate to explore through case studies (Walsham, 1995). Second, both dynamic capabilities and ITOT are complicated and multi-dimensional phenomenon is embedded in the organizational context (Teece *et al.*, 1997; Besson and Rowe, 2012), which makes it more appropriate to research the phenomenon through interpretations of relevant stakeholders (Klein and Myers, 1999) rather than a quantitative approach.

XAEP is selected as a suitable case organization based on the following two criteria: (1) the case organization is a traditional company that launched its ITOT and must face great amount of internal and external challenges that necessitate appropriate organizational capabilities; (2) the case organization should ideally have developed diverse proper organizational capabilities to overcome these challenges facing ITOT processes, which, in turn, enacted for the effective ITOT at organizational and operational levels. XAEP's organizational transformation meets these criteria.

Data collection

Data were primarily collected from the following three sources: (1) semi-structured interviews conducted in June 2014; (2) internal archival materials, such as meeting minutes, from different departments; and (3) public sources, including books, news, and publications written about XAEP. The reasons for collecting data from multiple sources was to establish a unique perspective incorporating both organizational insiders' and outsiders' points of view (Evered and Louis, 1981) and to triangulate the themes and conclusions (Miles and Huberman, 1984).

Access to the case site was granted in February 2014. In order to accurately identify and conceptualize the phenomenon (Pan and Tan, 2011), we spent 2 months scanning archival materials before the onsite data collection. Thus, an initial set of pertinent themes, constructs, and arguments were pre-identified by analyzing the archival data and literature, which was used as a "sensitizing device" (Klein and Myers, 1999) to guide the following on-site data collection and analysis (Eisenhardt and Graebner, 2007).

On-site data collection was then conducted at XAEP's headquarters in June 2014. Extensive interviews and analyses were conducted during our visit to XAEP. In total, 21 informants, who were primarily from senior management, middle management, and their subordinates, including the senior vice president, CIO, and department directors, participated in our interview sessions.

Data analysis

Data analysis was performed at the same time as data collection to take advantage of the flexibility offered by the case study method (Eisenhardt, 1989). We conducted three independent steps to understand the primary data while eliminating preliminary biases.

First, the similar data were highlighted and arranged into themes until a final set of themes was developed. This method was conducted to eliminate unrelated data within the value of comments collected and its potential for variance (Corbin and Strauss, 2014). Second, we performed a detailed analysis. The final set of themes was organized and codified without preliminary analytic biases. Third, we aligned empirical data with our theoretical lens and research model (Kirsch, 2004). An overview of the overall research strategy as well as the measures we conducted to ensure the reliability and validity of our conclusions are presented in Table 1.

The case study

Case background

The case firm we selected is XAEP, which is principally engaged in manufacture and distribution of aircraft engines and affiliated with AVIC Xi'an Aircraft Industry (group) Company Ltd. (AVIC XAC) founded in 1958. XAEP is the top-ranked manufacturer and service provider of aircraft engines and derivative products in China, selling a wide range of products in both domestic and overseas markets.

Despite its substantial success in the past, there are two primary challenges towards which XAEP also has to take serious attitudes from a dynamic external and internal organizational environment. The first challenge stems from the National Informatization Development Strategy (NIDS) launched by the Chinese government in 2007, which is an essential reason for XAEP to implement IT-enabled transformation. The other challenge comes from the sustained and rapid business growth, which makes the existing information system not enough to support the companies' business development. However, as a traditional manufacturing enterprise with more than 50 years of history, effective systems integration for the organizational transformation was contended with a

Table 1. An Overview of the Overall Research Strategy

	Preliminary Data Collection	Onsite Data Collection
Data Collection	◇ Searched secondary data from multiple sources ◇ Gathered internal archival data	◇ Interviewed TMT, IT departments, and business units ◇ Group discussions with other researchers were conducted
	Preliminary Data Analysis	Offsite Data Collection
Data Analysis	◇ Created chronological timeline of XAEP's ITOT ◇ Reviewed extensive literature on ITOT and dynamic capabilities	◇ Searched and selected evidences that supported the theoretical constructs and processes ◇ Ensured data-theory-model alignment via internal group discussions
Time	February 2014–May 2014	June 2014–September 2014
	Mechanisms to Establish Reliability	Mechanisms to Establish Validity
	◇ Prepared semi-structured interview guides with open-ended and relevant questions (Ferlie *et al.* 2005) ◇ Collected data from multiple sources to enable triangulation and cross-validation (Klein and Myers, 1999) ◇ All of the interviews were taped and transcribed to ensure the accuracy and completeness of data (Yin, 2003)	◇ Set up an interview panel of five researchers to enable the validation of interpretations and observations (Yin,2003) ◇ Theoretical constructs were repeatedly confirmed with informants to ensure data-model alignment (Pan and Tan, 2011) ◇ Ensured emergent process models and final conclusions were supported by the literature (Eisenhardt,1989)

myriad of challenges, such as organizational inertia, rigid structure, and even the improper culture, etc.

Despite the various difficulties encountered, XAEP's constant endeavors guaranteed the successful implementation of ITOT. Starting from 2008, the company has integrated its fragmented information systems and achieved the alignment of IT and business processes to create an innovative information system platform successfully within 8 years.

The attainments are chiefly attributed to the development of capabilities at strategic and operational levels during the various phases of the transformation process. The process of XAEP's ITOT can be viewed as three phases, namely, the unfreeze phase, transition phase, and refreeze phase. Data collected are presented according to the sequence of these phases in the following subsections.

Unfreeze phase

In 2008, although XAEP announced the launch of ITOT, there were still contrasting points of view from Top Management Team (TMT) to the ordinary employees. Some executives considered that ITOT was not worth an investment of much time and effort because IT was just an auxiliary tool. Consequently, a working group was established and tasked with the execution of ITOT, which was directly helmed by a vice president and comprised senior executives and department heads. The most crucial things for the group were to dissociate TMT from the existing belief and create a shared vision. Several meetings were held within the group, in which the importance and essential nature of ITOT for XAEP's future development were extensively discussed. In particular, the group established a common vision — an awareness and objective for implementing organizational transformation that was shared throughout the organization.

Apart from addressing the strategic level challenges above, XAEP also needed to tackle the operational level challenges which were mainly from ordinary employees in the business unit. Originally, some business units were suspicious of the usefulness of ITOT due to past experience, which inclined them to resist change. To overcome the challenges, XAEP initially sought to adopt the good advice from the staffs and launch extensive awareness campaigns in order to dissociate employees from the existing practice. Subsequently, the working group then established special Key Performance Indicators (KPIs) to assure the continuity of ITOT. These KPIs were decomposed into unit-specific KPIs which became mandatory targets and were tied to financial incentives for every business unit. XAEP also developed a performance management IT system to make the performance more transparent and visible, which motivated the business units towards the enactment of ITOT. The corroborating evidence is presented in Table 2.

Transition phase

Once the motivation for ITOT was created in the unfreeze phase, XAEP soon realized that the next biggest challenge was to harmonize the business process and integrate the multiple information systems. Without further delay, the company took effective measures at the strategic and operational levels.

At the strategic level, two initiatives were pursued. The first initiative was to build mutual understanding with external vendors. As XAEP's IT department lacked relevant experience, it sourced an external vendor who had prior experience in developing new IT infrastructure to meet XAEP's specific needs. In order to quickly familiarize the vendor with XAEP's requirements, many interventions were undertaken by the firm. Such close interaction was beneficial to the development of ITOT as it facilitated better communication and mutual understanding. The second initiative was to cultivate an inter-departmental culture. Before the transformation, various departments at XAEP only focused on their own business which can pose an enormous obstacle to form the common information platform for ITOT.

Additionally, the firm needed to coordinate the knowledge resource at operational level for the ITOT. Therefore, the first thing at the operational level was to conduct the business process reengineering (BPR) for integration among the operational departments. With the help of external vendors, IT department worked very closely with operational departments to analyze current business processes by understanding the needs of every

Table 2. Unfreeze Phase: Capability Development at Strategic and Operational Levels

Strategic Level	**Deconstruction of Strategic Inertia**	
	Dissociating TMT from the existing belief	"Our mindset (with regard to ITOT) changed…After several discussions, we realized that it was difficult to cope with the future business, fast requirements without the ITOT…we can balance the productive task and ITOT if reasonable management measures a taken" — Senior Executive of production department
	Creating shared vision	"The company conducted many internal discussions through a variety of channels…now everyone(TMT members) began to realize that XAEP should obtain the competitive advantage of the future through the ITOT" — the Senior executive of IT department
Operational Level	**Deconstruction of operational inertia**	
	Dissociating employee from the existing practice	"We (the staff of the business units) felt that ITOT was different from past practice, because the company started to pay attention to our real requirements… We knew we should take a more active part in this organizational transformation as the functional units." — the staff, production department
	Creating a new reward system	"At the beginning of transformation, XAEP invented many new KPIs for us…we will gain some rewards if we make a contribution to ITOT, so everyone is inclined to participate more actively than ever before. No doubt, it is a good thing for the smoother ITOT" — the staff, IT department

unit and identifying the interfaces of key activities within and between the functions, which facilitated the systems integration.

Besides conducting the BPR for integration, XAEP also developed the localized IT versions for particular operation within the department. Hence, the company mandated the IT department and related production departments to align new technological solutions with XAEP's business processes for developing local versions of the software which provided tailored support for the XAEP. The supporting evidence of the above content is presented in Table 3.

Refreeze phase

The cumulative experience of the first two phases had led to significant changes across the organization. How to stabilize the changes for continuous improvement of ITOT was an essential objective at the refreeze phase. At the strategic level, XAEP firstly identified the responsible collaborators who were dependable and useful to the ITOT in order to assign the suitable department or employee to the right task. For instance, as the IT department was largely credited for their technical expertise in the previous phases of ITOT, it was institutionalized as an IT Information Center by the TMT which expanded its role in directing future development of IT. The company, moreover, established the formal collaborative arrangement with the stakeholders to secure their sustained commitment for the ITOT.

In addition, XAEP pursued two initiatives at the operational level for stabilizing the changes. On the one hand, the company supported an open learning environment to share employees' experiences. On the other hand, XAEP needs to routinize the cost-effective IT operations in organizational business processes. Then, the company built a knowledge system to record the detailed processes specific to the industry, which was imperative for knowledge retention, especially regarding the tacit knowledge possessed by employees.

In essence, in the refreeze phase, XAEP took some actions to support capability development to stabilize the changes of ITOT. Table 4 contains references to such actions.

Table 3. Transition Phase: Capability Development at Strategic and Operational Levels

		Coordination of social resource
Strategic Level	Building mutual understanding with external vendors	"We established and maintained the collaborative relationship with our vendors through close communication and interaction." — Senior executive of IT department
	Cultivating an inter-departmental culture	"How to facilitate the close cooperation among different sectors was a key of ITOT…We should develop a culture of partnership characterized by deep trust." — the Vice President
		Coordination of knowledge resource
Operational Level	Conducting the BPR for integration among the operational departments	"We (the staff of operational departments) started to understand the nature of business process and got a holistic picture of the organizational operations through sorting out the various links of the work process."-the staff, Production Department
	Enhancing the expert knowledge communication for alignment between IT and operational departments	"In a word, the staff of IT and operational departments solved the difficulties together based on the intimate knowledge of business and technical optimization perspective respectively." — the staff, IT department

Table 4. Refreeze Phase: Capability Development at Strategic and Operational Levels

Institutionalization of Role Structure

Strategic Level	Identifying the responsible collaborators	"After the completion of the first two phases, we already identified some imperative issues and the collaborators that could be responsible for them… Assigning the right persons to the right roles can foster sustainable commitment from stakeholders for the ITOT." — the vice president
	Formalizing the collaborative arrangement	"We signed a formal contract to make SAP become our long-term cooperating partner in order to keep effective collaborations with us for the ITOT." — the Senior executive of IT department

Institutionalization of Process Structure

	Sharing employees' experiences	"We (the staff of various units) often shared individual experiences to gain an up-to-date view of the organization's operations by lots of event meetings." — the staff, Production department
Operational Level	Routinizing the cost-effective IT operations	"To facilitate the dissemination of knowledge about the cost-effective IT operations among all employees, every department was committed to updating relevant industry-specific information in the system" — the staff, IT department

Discussion

By integrating the different activities that were enacted by XAEP across the three phases, a process model of capability development in achieving ITOT (refer to Table 5) can be inductively derived.

Unfreeze phase: Deconstruction of inertia

Prior literature has suggested that how the organizational inertia can be overcome is an important issue in an organizational transformation initiative (Besson and Rowe, 2012). From our findings, to create the motivation for change, a firm must possess deconstruction capability at strategic and operational levels which can overcome organizational inertia and reduce conflicts (Pan *et al.*, 2006) in the unfreeze phase.

Strategic inertia refers to the habitual reliance on a previous organizational formula (Hodgkinson and Wright, 2002), which was an obstacle to the company's transformation among senior executives. Just as some XAEP's executives believed that the current situation was still working and the company is unnecessary to carry out the ITOT. Therefore, the deconstruction of strategic inertia is remarkably important for the organizational transformation (Kelly and Amburgey, 1991). The case of XAEP also reveals the deconstruction capability at strategic level was developed through two actions: dissociating TMT from the existing belief and creating shared vision.

Operational inertia is defined as the inability to enact internal change in organizational operations in the face of significant external change. (Miller and Friesen, 1980; Chen *et al.*, 2014). The staffs tend to resist the changes or respond slowly to threats and opportunities due to the operational inertia. As XAEP's frontline workers doubt the usefulness of ITOT and refused to make a commitment to change at the initial phase of ITOT, how to develop the capability for the deconstruction of operational inertia is an important thing at operational level. In the case of XAEP, two actions were pursued: dissociating employee from the existing practice and creating a new reward system.

Table 5. A Process Framework of Capabilities Development at Strategic and Operational Levels for ITOT

Phases	Unfreeze	Transition	Refreeze
Strategic Level	Key Capabilities Developed at Each Phase:		
	Deconstruction of Strategic Inertia	Coordination of Social Resource	Institutionalization of Role Structure
	Key Actions that Support these Capabilities:		
	1. Dissociating TMT from the existing belief	1. Building mutual understanding with external vendors	1. Identifying the responsible collaborators
	2. Creating shared vision	2. Cultivating an inter-departmental culture	2. Formalizing the collaborative arrangement
Operational Level	Key Capabilities Developed at Each Phase:		
	Deconstruction of Operational Inertia	Coordination of Knowledge Resource	Institutionalization of Process Structure
	Key Actions that Support these Capabilities:		
	1. Dissociating employee from the existing practice	1. Conducting the BPR for integration among the operational departments	1. Sharing employees' experiences
	2. Creating a new reward system	2. Enhancing the expert knowledge communication for alignment between IT and operational departments	2. Routinizing the cost-effective IT operations
Outcome	Implementing ITOT successfully		

Transition phase: Coordination of resource

After the motivation for change was created, the company should develop the capability for taking effective transformative measures. To build the organizational capabilities, firm-specific resources must be adequately integrated with key activities (Teece *et al.*, 1997). At XAEP, two pertinent generic types of resources were coordinated at the transition phase, namely social resource (e.g., culture, trust, stakeholder relationship, and commitment) and knowledge resource (e.g., declarative knowledge/ know-what, transactive memory/ know-who, and procedure knowledge/ know-how) (Calvin *et al.*, 2011). Our process model suggests coordination of resources enables the various departments to make a contribution to ITOT based on their intimate knowledge, respectively.

At the strategic level, coordination of social resource is the focal capability which should be developed in the transition phase. Previous literature points out that a key reason of ITOT failure is the inappropriate management of social and relational issues (Kim *et al.*, 2007; Cui and Pan, 2015). In this case, two key actions that support coordination of social resource were pursued. The first action was to build mutual understanding with external vendors due to XAEP needed to create new IT infrastructure to meet XAEP's specific needs, the relevant experience of which XAEP's IT department lacked. The second action was to cultivate an inter-departmental culture that ensured the success of organizational transformation (Tan *et al.*, 2015).

Our findings also suggest that the focal capability which should be developed is coordination of knowledge resource at the operational level. The enactment of knowledge resource is a primary capability for organizational transformation (Calvin *et al.*, 2011). In our case study, XAEP took two actions to support the capability. On the one hand, the company conducted the BPR which was conducive to integrate different areas of knowledge among the operational departments. On the other hand, the firm enhanced the expert knowledge communication for alignment between IT and operational departments. The misalignment between information system and distinctive business process leads to the inefficiency of enterprise and even the failure of ITOT (Sia and Soh, 2007). Thus, IT and operational departments in XAEP were encouraged to communicate with each other by exchanging their respective knowledge.

Refreeze phase: Institutionalization of structure

As the ITOT proceeded into the refreeze phase, stabilizing the changes became an important task for the organization (Lewin, 1951). Hence, institutionalization of structure is the focal capability which should be developed at this stage. Our model suggests two key capabilities were fostered by some supportive actions at strategic and operational levels respectively, namely institutionalization of role structure (Crawford and Lepine, 2013) and institutionalization of process structure (Vanhatalo *et al.*, 2009).

At the strategic level, institutionalization of role structure ensures the different divisions have greater clarity on the scope, function, and limits of their roles, and for what tasks and outcomes they are held responsible after the previous phase. At XAEP, two key actions were pursued to support institutionalization of role structure. The first action was to identify the responsible collaborators for the ITOT. A prime example is the IT department was institutionalized as an IT Information Center which had more influence over the future development of information systems as the TMT recognized their excellent technical expertise. Following this, formalizing the collaborative arrangement was the second action. For example, to maintain effective cooperation with external vendors, XAEP signed a formal contract with SAP and made the two firms to become the long-term mutually cooperating partners.

At the operational level, our model suggests that institutionalization of process structure is the focal capability which should be developed. Process structure is a framework of identifiable and measurable process elements (steps, activities, tasks, procedures) that defines process boundaries within which every element is interconnected to other elements (Müller *et al.*, 2008). Institutionalization of process structure is the guarantee that the process of ITOT can be performed more effectively. Therefore, XAEP took two actions to support the capability. Firstly, employees' experiences garnered from previous phases in terms of technical and process know-how were encouraged to share during daily meetings of various functional divisions. Secondly, routinizing the cost-effective IT operations was an essential action for institutionalization of process structure. As has been noted in the literature, knowledge codification is an important step that ultimately results in capability development (Zollo and Winter, 2002).

In our case, XAEP developed dedicated systems to optimize the daily IT operations, in which efficient processes specific to company as well as task standards and operation criterions were recorded.

Conclusion

Theoretical and practical contributions

This case study highlights implications for researchers and practitioners. For researchers, firstly, it complements the existing literature by unraveling the black box of the ITOT in the complex and transitional environment in China. Organizational transformation is still a new frontier for IS research (Besson and Rowe, 2012), especially in a developing country with a dynamic business environment such as China. Through the study that unfolded over the ITOT at XAEP, a traditional manufacturing enterprise, we look forward to generating interest and insights into Information Communication Technology (ICT) practices and research in China. Second, our study provides an empirically grounded ITOT process framework based on the dynamic capabilities perspective. By identifying six key capabilities and offering the related key actions during various stages of ITOT from a dual-level analysis, namely strategic and operational levels, we believe researchers can have a more holistic vision of the capability development process in the context of ITOT (Pan *et al.*, 2015).

This study also provides practical implications. First, our research identified the key capabilities which are crucial for practitioners to develop at each phase of ITOT. It helps the managers to ascertain the capability that is pertinent in various stages of ITOT and adapt their plans accordingly. Second, the process model provides insights into how to develop capabilities by taking appropriate actions. We believe practitioners could use the process model as a detailed roadmap to leverage their resources to develop capabilities for implementing ITOT successfully in the contemporary business environment.

Limitation

Although this Chapter is based on the single case study method which is a "typical and legitimate endeavor" (Lee and Baskerville, 2003) in qualitative research, it is associated with the problem of generalizability and external validity (Walsham, 2006). While we acknowledge that statistical generalization is impossible from a single case, we nevertheless contend that our research is generalizable beyond its singular context as the derived model is not only grounded in the empirical reality of our case study, but it is also corroborated by the established literature. Hence, this study invokes the principles of "analytic generalization" (Yin, 2003). Future research could validate propositions of this study statistically, so that the boundary conditions of our findings can be better refined.

Acknowledgments

The authors would like to thank the National Natural Science Foundation of China (71632003, 71529001, 71472012, 71172176), the Ministry of Education of Humanities and Social Science project (14YJA630045), the Project of Beijing Philosophy and Social Sciences (15JGB119), and the Aviation Science Fund (2014ZG51073) for supporting this work.

References

Barney, J. 1991. "Firm Resources and Sustained Competitive Advantage," *Journal of Management*, 17(1), 99–120.

Besson, P., and Rowe, F. 2012. "Strategizing Information Systems-enabled Organizational Transformation: A Transdisciplinary Review and New Directions," *Journal of Strategic Information Systems*, 21(2), 103–124.

Calvin, C. M., Hackney, R., Pan, S. L., and Chou, T. C. 2011. "Managing e-Government System Implementation: A Resource Enactment Perspective," *European Journal of Information Systems*, 20(5), 529–541.

Chen, J. E., Pan, S. L., and Ouyang, T. H. 2014. "Routine Reconfiguration in Traditional Companies' e-commerce Strategy Implementation: A Trajectory Perspective," *Information & Management*, 51(2), 270–282.

Corbin, J., and Strauss, A. 2014. "*Basics of Qualitative Research: Techniques and Procedures for Developing Grounded Theory*," Thousand Oaks, CA, Sage Publications.

Crawford, E. R., and Lepine, J. A. 2013. "A Configural Theory of Team Processes: Accounting for the Structure of Taskwork and Teamwork," *Academy of Management Review*, 38(1), 32–48.

Cui, M., and Pan, S. L. 2015. "Developing Focal Capabilities for e-commerce Adoption: A Resource Orchestration Perspective," *Information & Management*, 52(2), 200–209.

Daniel, E. M., and Wilson, H. N. 2003. "The Role of Dynamic Capabilities in e-Business Transformation," *European Journal of Information Systems*, 12(4), 282–296.

Dixon, S. E., Meyer, K. E., and Day, M. 2010. "Stages of Organizational Transformation in Transition Economies: A Dynamic Capabilities Approach," *Journal of Management Studies*, 47(3), 416–436.

Eisenhardt, K. M. 1989. "Building Theories from Case Study Research," *Academy of Management Review*, 14(4), 532–550.

Eisenhardt, K. M., and Graebner, M. E. 2007. "Theory Building from Cases: Opportunities and Challenges," *Academy of Management Journal*, 50(1), 25.

Eisenhardt, K. M., and Martin, J. A. 2000. "Dynamic Capabilities: What are They?" *Strategic Management Journal*, 21(10–11), 1105–1121.

Evered, R., and Louis, M. R. 1981. "Alternative Perspectives in the Organizational Sciences: 'inquiry from the inside' and 'inquiry from the outside,'" *Academy of Management Review*, 6(3), 385–395.

Ferlie, E., Fitzgerald, L., Wood, M., and Hawkins, C. 2005. "The Nonspread of Innovations: The Mediating Role of Professionals," *Academy of Management Journal*, 48(1), 117–134.

Gregory, R. W., Keil, M., Muntermann, J., and Mähring, M. 2015. "Paradoxes and the Nature of Ambidexterity in IT Transformation Programs," *Information Systems Research*, 26(1), 57–80.

Hannan, M. T., Laszlo, P., and Carroll, G. R. 2002. "Structural Inertia and Organizational Change Revisited III: The Evolution of Organizational Inertia," *Research Papers Series*, 29. https://pdfs.semanticscholar.org/735c/4ca808277eca670a666523ef39deca44bebe.pdf.

Helfat, C. E., and Peteraf, M. A. 2003. "The Dynamic Resource Based View: Capability Lifecycles," *Strategic Management Journal*, 24(10), 997–1010.

Hodgkinson, G. P., and Wright, G. 2002. "Confronting Strategic Inertia in a Top Management Team: Learning from Failure," *Organization Studies*, 23(6), 949–977.

Huang, P. Y., Pan, S. L., and Ouyang, T. H. 2014. "Developing Information Processing Capability for Operational Agility: Implications from a Chinese Manufacturer," *European Journal of Information Systems*, 23(4), 462–480.

Kelly, D., and Amburgey, T. L. 1991. "Organizational Inertia and Momentum: A Dynamic Model of Strategic Change," *Academy of Management Journal*, 34(3), 591–612.

Kim, H. J., Pan, G., and Pan, S. L. 2007. "Managing IT-enabled Transformation in the Public Sector: A Case Study on e-Government in South Korea," *Government Information Quarterly*, 24(2), 338–352.

Kirsch, L. J. 2004. "Deploying Common Systems Globally: The Dynamics of Control," *Information Systems Research*, 15(4), 374–395.

Klein, H. K., and Myers, M. D. 1999. "A set of Principles for Conducting and Evaluating Interpretive Field Studies in Information Systems," *MIS Quarterly*, 23(1), 67–94.

Klievink, B., and Janssen, M. 2009. "Realizing Joined-up Government — Dynamic Capabilities and Stage Models for Transformation," *Government Information Quarterly*, 26(2), 275–284.

Lee, A. S., and Baskerville, R. L. 2003. "Generalizing Generalizability in Information Systems Research," *Information Systems Research*, 14(3), 221–243.

Lewin, K. (1951). "Field Theory in Social Science: Selected Theoretical Papers," ed. Dorwin Cartwright. Oxford, England, Harpers. http://psycnet.apa.org/record/1951-06769-000.

Liang, H., Saraf, N., Hu, Q., and Xue, Y. 2007. "Assimilation of Enterprise Systems: The Effect of Institutional Pressures and the Mediating Role of Top Management," *MIS Quarterly*, 31(1), 59–87.

Miles, M. B., and Huberman, A. M. 1984. "*Qualitative Data Analysis: A Sourcebook of New Methods*," Thousand Oaks, CA, Sage Publications.

Miller, D., and Friesen, P. H. 1980. "Momentum and Revolution in Organizational Adaptation," *Academy of Management Journal*, 23(4), 591–614.

Montealegre, R. 2002. "A Process Model of Capability Development: Lessons from the Electronic Commerce Strategy at Bolsa de Valores de Guayaquil," *Organization Science*, 13(5), 514–531.

Müller, D., Reichert, M., and Herbst, J. 2008. "A New Paradigm for the Enactment and Dynamic Adaptation of Data-driven Process Structures," in *Advanced Information Systems Engineering*. Springer, Berlin Heidelberg.

Pan, S., Pan, G., and Hsieh, M. H. 2006. "A Duallevel Analysis of the Capability Development Process: A Case Study of TT&T," *Journal of the American Society for Information Science and Technology*, 57(13), 1814–1829.

Pan, S. L., and Tan, B. 2011. "Demystifying Case Research: A Structured–Pragmatic–Situational (Sps) Approach to Conducting Case Studies," *Information and Organization*, 21(3), 161–176.

Pan, G., Pan, S. L., and Lim, C. Y. 2015. "Examining How Firms Leverage IT to Achieve Firm Productivity: RBV and Dynamic Capabilities Perspectives," *Information & Management*, 52(4), 401–412.

Pavlou, P. A., and El Sawy, O. A. 2010. "The 'Third Hand': IT-enabled Competitive Advantage in Turbulence through Improvisational Capabilities," *Information Systems Research*, 21(3), 443–471.

Sambamurthy, V., Bharadwaj, A., and Grover, V. 2003. "Shaping Agility through Digital Options: Reconceptualizing the Role of Information Technology in Contemporary Firms," *MIS Quarterly*, 27(2), 237–263.

Sia, S. K., and Soh, C. 2007. "An Assessment of Package–Organisation Misalignment: Institutional and Ontological Structures," *European Journal of Information Systems*, 16(5), 568–583.

Tan, B. C., Pan, S. L., and Hackney, R. 2010. "The Strategic Implications of Web Technologies: A Process Model of How Web Technologies Enhance Organizational Performance," *IEEE Transactions on Engineering Management*, 57(2), 181–197.

Tan, B., Pan, S. L., and Zuo, M. 2015. "Harnessing Collective IT Resources for Sustainability: Insights from the Green Leadership Strategy of China Mobile," *Journal of the Association for Information Science and Technology*, 66(4), 818–838.

Teece, D. J., Pisano, G., and Shuen, A. 1997. "Dynamic Capabilities and Strategic Management," *Strategic Management Journal*, 18(7), 509–533.

Teoh, S. Y., and Chen, X. 2013. "Towards a Strategic Process Model of Governance for Agile IT Implementation: A Healthcare Information Technology Study in China," *Journal of Global Information Management*, (JGIM), 21(4), 17–37.

Vanhatalo, J., Völzer, H., and Koehler, J. 2009. "The Refined Process Structure Tree," *Data & Knowledge Engineering*, 68(9), 793–818.

Venkatraman, N. 1994. "IT-enabled Business Transformation: From Automation to Business Scope Redefinition," *Sloan Management Review*, 35(2), 73.

Walsham, G. 1995. "Interpretive Case Studies in IS Research: Nature and Method," *European Journal of Information Systems*, 4(2), 74–81.

Walsham, G. 2006. "Doing Interpretive Research," *European Journal of Information Systems*, 15(3), 320–330.

Yin, R. 2003. *"Case Study Research: Design and Methods,"* 2nd edn., Thousand Oaks, CA, Sage.

Zollo, M., and Winter, S. G. 2002. "Deliberate Learning and the Evolution of Dynamic Capabilities," *Organization Science*, 13(3), 339–351.

Chapter 17

Transaction Orientation vs. Relationship Orientation: Consumer Logic of Enterprise Digital Empowerment

Xin Dai

Huazhong University of Science and Technology, Wuhan, China
daixin@vip.163.com

Ying Zhou

Huazhong University of Science and Technology, Wuhan, China

Jingyuan Gong

Huazhong University of Science and Technology, Wuhan, China

Abstract

It is an important channel for traditional and Internet enterprises to improve the market competitiveness by employing digital technologies in order to realize consumer empowerment nowadays. However, few researches focus on consumer perspective which is based on the enterprise digital empowerment. Here we present a qualitative case study method to compare the differences in empowering consumers during digital empowerment between two house decoration companies by adopting three dimensions of empowerment process (structural, psychological, and resource empowerments). Two empowerment models are derived — the traditional

285

enterprise's vertical-empowerment model (building online Internet platform and offline store) and Internet enterprise's horizontal-empowerment model (only developing resource integration platforms) depicting the process of empowering the consumer. Based on these two models, we further illustrate the digital empowerment for consumer by introducing transaction and relationship marketing theory. This study complements the empowerment literature where it lacks theoretical basis and comparative studies. For instance, through uncovering the consumer perspective, traditional enterprises can have a better understanding of how to transform itself the digital way and also be insightful for Internet enterprises.

Keywords: Digital empowerment, Consumer logic, Transaction orientation, Relationship orientation, Case study.

Introduction

Consumer empowerment results from products, services, and practices that expand consumers' freedom and control over the choice and action to shape their consumption experiences (Jarret, 2003; Pitt *et al.*, 2002; Kaiser, 2002; Wathieu *et al.*, 2002). This is of particular note in shopping, which is not simply obtaining products but also an experience and enjoyment. Successful firms try hard to understand what consumers want and how to improve consumer satisfaction and empowerment by providing pleasant marketing environments and options, and relevant information. All enterprises want is to increase brand value and consumer loyalty, achieve their market position and long-term development (Sharp, 2006).

Consumer empowerment is a transformation process provided by enterprises, their first consideration is the choice of methods and tools. Frequently, they investigate the tools from experience of objective environment (Langeard, 1981; Newman and Patel, 2004), Product customization (Prahalad and Ramaswamy, 2003), Social media technologies (Pehlivan *et al.*, 2000; Deighton and Kornfeld 2009; Labrecque *et al.*, 2013), Multi-channel information exchange platform (Fenech and O'Cass, 2003; Peterson and Merino, 2003) and so on. In the tide of the Internet, most traditional businesses build a network platform to provide consumers with more convenient conditions, such as KFC opening the official website to facilitate consumer orders. As for Internet companies, with the improvement of the platform structure online, building excellent reputation and maintaining valid relationship with consumers could obtain long-term development. For example, LETV aims to build a complete closed-loop platform ecosystem, including content provider, platform supplier, terminal enterprise, and helper applications.

Despite the significance of findings from the stream of literature, research on this issue has been limited, merely focused on enterprise perspective: Management strategy adaptation (Smircich and Stubbart, 2008; Kumar, 2007), Dynamic capabilities (Catherine and Ahmed, 2007; Zahra *et al.*, 2009), and Collaborative Innovation (Jon Sundbo, 1997; Valente, 1996). Among these, collaborative innovation is related to customer empowerment, since customer empowerment and enjoyment is related to the collaboration and interaction. Although all the streams are relevant to activities about managing requirement changes, its enigmatic that adaptation may not work effectively if enterprises are not guided by the consumer empowerment perspective. Therefore, strategies may not take effect properly if their empowerment is not supported by market orientation.

As a result, we adopt the consumer empowerment as our theoretical lens, combining it with the enterprise market orientation to bridge the gap from enterprise and customer perspective. We introduce two new concepts of vertical empowerment (combing online Internet platform and offline store) and horizontal empowerment (developing Internet resource integration platforms). Above all, we derive our research question: how do traditional and Internet enterprises exploit digital tools in order to realize consumer empowerment? And why are they doing these according to enterprises' market orientation?

Literature review

Empowerment

The concept of empowerment emanates from the civil and feminist movements. Empowerment has been studied in diverse fields such as community psychology, management, political science, education, health, and sociology (Hur, 2006). Definition of empowerment is varied in different research areas. In management, empowerment is concerned with improving employee's self-efficacy and self-determination (Spreitzer, 1995; Thomas and Velthouse, 1990). From the perspective of consumers, many studies examine how to empower consumers with more information and choices (Pires *et al.*, 2006; Broniarczyk and Griffin, 2014).

Overall, empowerment theory emphasizes the importance of individual internal demands from a positive perspective to improve self-efficacy and self-determination and give respect to the rights of the individual. As for organizations, empowerment refers to giving chances for enterprises by using various tools and instruments, then stimulating social innovation and creating business opportunities.

Consumer empowerment

Based on the empowerment theory, researches find out that shopping is a process about empowerment and enjoyment for consumers (Martineau, 1958). Then Shankar (2006) pointed out that consumer empowerment was transferred from producers, which was equivalent to having their power of choice. Pires (2006) defined empowerment is essentially derived from consumers' knowledge and information obtained from network and other channels. This is mainly related to the core of consumer empowerment, as a process up to a change in the choice environment may lead to consumers "feeling" more empowered (Wathieu *et al.*, 2002; Schiffman and Kanuk, 2000).

Currently, companies take actions to realize consumer empowerment mainly from the following aspects. First, most work involves improving the effectiveness of marketing environments, enlarging the set of available options, and flexibility in defining one's choices (Newman and Patel, 2004). The second is studies about customized products, boosting perceived empowerment and enjoyment for consumers or improving their willingness to participate in future virtual new-product development projects (Ansari and Mela, 2003; Franke *et al.*, 2013). The third is about implications of using information and communication technologies (ICTs), such as giving consumer access to more information (Amichai, 2008), exploring effects of online brand community on customer's purchasing tendency (Pace and Cova, 2006; Pires, 2006).

Digital empowerment

Nowadays, digitalization has played an important role in economics and business practices in a large range of industries, which has fundamentally transformed consumer behaviors. The fundamental reason for the emergence of digital empowerment is the explosion of digital technologies in driving business activities and social innovation (Pires and Aisbett, 2003). Digital technology, particularly the Internet, has been described as an enabler of a global marketplace, characterized by "equal access for consumers to information about products, prices, and distribution" (Meissner and Strauss, 2008).

Earlier research on digital empowerment mainly centers on the following aspects: (1) using digital empowerment promotes economic development, such as providing a new tool to rural economic development (Leong *et al.*, 2016); (2) widely use in the fields of sociology, such as supervision to government; (3) among business and consumer research, increasing employee autonomy in decisions (Leonard-Barton, 1995), digital transformation (Agarwal *et al.*, 2010), customized products, and so on.

Three dimensions of empowerment

By using the existing knowledge of the empowerment perspective as the theoretical lens, we find three dimensions (structural, psychological, and, resource empowerments) of the empowerment process to anticipate the emergence of enterprises' empowerment process. Early work on empowerment developed out of two motivational frameworks: the job characteristics model (Hackman and Oldham, 1980) and Bandura's (1978) work on self-efficacy. They emphasized structural and psychological dimensions, respectively.

Structural empowerment builds upon job design and job characteristics' research, focuses on the transition of authority and responsibility from senior manager to employee (Kanter, 1979). Accordingly, structural empowerment is primarily concerned with resources (Conger and Kanungo, 1988; Siegall and Gardner, 2000), focusing on improving external conditions, increasing access to information channels, which can be characterized as basic foundations to build other dimensions (Spreitzer and Doneson, 2005).

With the rapid growth in ICT usage, consumers have the same power in channels and supply chain (Denegri *et al.*, 2006). e-business Model appears in the development of network technology as well. For instance, through the O2O (Online to Offline) mode, consumers can get convenience by disinterring mediation from supply chain integration through the channel reconstruction (Kim and Hahn, 2009). Take Groupon for example, which offers deeply discounted goods and services to millions of customers through geographically targeted daily email marketing campaigns, enhancing purchasing and bargaining power of consumers.

Psychological empowerment essentially acts as a mediating mechanism, tying the antecedent conditions with work-related outcomes (Maynard, 2012). Laschinger *et al.* (2001) provided evidence that psychological empowerment mediates the relationship between structural empowerment and individual satisfaction about the resource. Overall, the core of psychological empowerment is to maximize individual-level satisfaction and provide guidance to the process of behavior.

Based on literature, we found individual psychological empowerment that originated in areas within the organization defined as a process of enhancing feelings of self-efficacy. Skudiene *et al.* (2013) found front-line employee recognition and empowerment has a positive impact on customer's perceived value, giving the important interrelationships between employee and consumer's psychological empowerment. Consumer individuals get psychologically empowered by large choices on the Internet (Knott *et al.*, 2006). Internet has increased the customer value, reducing information asymmetry transactions, conversion costs, and enhancing transparency (Barrutia and Echebarria, 2005).

Resource empowerment forms a prerequisite for them. After research on relationship between resources and psychological dimensions, most literatures mention that individuals preferred useful control over a number of selected resource items, rather than the limited set (Bourdieu, 1984; Hui and Bateson, 1991). So the effect of resource availability on relationship between structural and psychological empowerment is huge (Logan and Ganster, 2007).

From a consumer perspective, empowerment is dependent on the enterprises. After consumers raised awareness of power, the first thing was to change the dispersed situation. For access to more information about market and larger choice sets due to the global reach of the Internet, by having ability to exchange news and opinion with peers, to change their perceptions and behavior in a rapid and largely unchecked manner, and to define brands on their own (Legris *et al.*, 2003; Morrissey, 2005).

Market orientation

Transaction marketing and relationship marketing are two largely different paradigms (see Table 1 below). Before the 80s, marketing paradigm was trade-oriented and product-centered, focusing on one single transaction's success, providing appropriate customer service and few commitments.

Transaction marketing, by definition, means that enterprises want to achieve organizational objectives that emphasize on product profitability. Marketing focuses on achieving profit maximization that revolves around the application of a firm's resource to markets, customers, and products in the most efficient and cost-effective manner.

The concept of **relationship marketing** was first proposed in 1983 by Berry, stressing long-term relationship with the consumer, taking the

Table 1. Difference between Transaction Marketing and Relationship Marketing

Aspects	Transaction Marketing	Relationship Marketing
Basic assumptions	Economic man, focus on product and results	Social man, focus on process, and results
Enterprise focus	Increasing the benefits	Sustainable competitive advantage
Enterprise supply	Emphasis on product based on 4Ps	Maintain relationships based on 4Ps
Price flexibility	High price sensitivity	Low price sensitivity
Product dimension	Adding more value to the core product	Offering product quality and supporting services
Customer satisfaction measurement	Market share and revenue	Market reputation and customer satisfaction
Resource	Levitt, (1983), Kotler, (1994)	Hunt and Morgan, (1994), Grönroos (1990), Berry *et al.* (1991)

relational approach, focusing on creating new value in the interaction and the relationship to build a sustainable competitive advantage. The core of relationship marketing is to build maintenance of relations between company and other participants in micro environment.

Methodology

We chose the case study as our research methodology for three reasons. (1) Research question is based on "how" and is thus better answered through inductive methods (Yin, 2003). This study focuses on exploring an enterprise and how to use digital measures to realize consumer empowerment, as well as the mechanisms behind their behavior, which is suited for a case study. (2) We recognized that there is no established theoretical model. The interpretive approach allows new, unexpected findings that are not identifiable with the outset of the inquiry to emerge from the data (Yin, 2003). (3) Since the study aims to break theoretical ground, a case study is more effective, because of its strength in exploring new conceptual arguments. To fill these gaps, we take a Structured–Pragmatic–Situational (SPS) approach to conduct case research (Pan and Tan, 2011) by addressing the same question in several settings, and using similar research procedures in each setting to highlight the design's institutional and methodological features.

Case selection

Case selection is an important segment to use cases to build the theory. We chose the theoretical sampling method, selecting GUOJJ.COM (formed by Grandland Decoration INC.) and Tubatu.com (formed by BINCENT INC.). At the same time, we use focusing and polarization principles posed by Eisenhardt (1989). The two companies are representatives of the research for one of them is an Internet platform enterprise and another is for comparison a traditional business, which is the opposite of a developed enterprise. By analyzing these two cases, we could find common and complementary characteristics to achieve replication and expansion, improving external validity of the study.

Data collection

It recommends that using a variety of data sources enables a more solid basis for inductive and field-based case studies. We collected data through interviews, observations, and secondary sources: (1) semi-structured interviews conducted from April 2015, including strategic planners, senior managers, human resource director, as well as the Internet platform manager and other interviewers. Most interviews were recorded, and photographs and additional notes were taken to provide more details; (2) participant observation conducted from the July 2015; we participated in the meeting about the strategic planning in Grandland and visited Tubatu city branches; (3) internal archival materials, such as the speeches of company executives, company website information, and so on; (4) public sources like media coverage, industry analysis reports, etc.

Case description

GUOJJ.COM

GUOJJ.COM is an Internet business which was opened up by the Shenzhen Grandland Decoration Group Inc (short for "Grandland") during business structure adjustment in 2015. Founded in 1995, Grandland is an integrated large public company specializing in design and construction of architectural decoration, research and development of green building materials, with a complete set of the highest industrial certifications. After 20 years of development, Grandland achieves remarkable success in customer resources, brand reputation, capital accumulation, etc. In January 2005, GUOJJ was formally launched, with designer, construction management, and suppliers as the base of the platform, including the combination of Internet technology, modern IT technology, and VR technology to build the scenario of an e-commerce platform.

Analysis of three empowerment dimensions of GUOJJ (Figure 1)

Structural empowerment (1) What You See Is What You Get (WYSIWYG). The online service of GUOJJ is very convenient, 10 minutes of waiting see

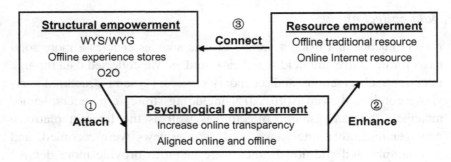

Figure 1. GUOJJ's Three Dimensions and Path to Consumer Empowerment

accomplished house decoration by the designer and 1 minute to see the quotation. Meanwhile, all the main materials, furniture, soft decorative assembly are all available buying, so that it can assure that for the decoration effect achieves "WYSIWYG" for customers; (2) Providing offline store design and experience. 20 minutes later after the online registration, an appointment will be made to invite the customer to chat in an offline shop. Currently, there are four "experience" shops in Nanshan, Longgang, Luohu, Longhua, cooperating with high-tech and interactive appliances; (3) Connecting online services and offline stores. User's APP, project manager's APP, supervisor's APP around, and background ERP all combine with each other. These APPs make it easy for users to obtain daily information about the process of construction, achieving information transparency, and providing convenience with full use of digital technologies.

Resource empowerment (1) **Holding experience resources offline.** Grandland has developed in decoration and construction field for more than 20 years. From production design to house decoration company, construction teams and decoration materials, Grandland always can implement professional service team for online propaganda; (2) **Developing thorough supply chain online by digital tools**. In the front end, GUOJJ provides consumer all-round experience with its website, WeChat store, App store, offline experience, etc. In the back end, it operates according to the fine management of manufacturing to achieve process, standardization, transparency of information, based on powerful supply chain system.

Psychological empowerment (1) Enhancing transparency and information resources online. GUOJJ used digitization to innovate a lot, like pioneering of nine unique technologies, the first SKU quotation system, independent DIY design, and so on. Taking "rendering the effect picture in ten seconds" as an example, a traditional house decoration company usually takes a week to provide an effective picture, but GUOJJ can provide 3D rendering on the spot in 10 seconds; (2) Showing standardized product — "Quality house" via VR technology. Effects of the scenes shown in offline experience venues entirely conform to its online description. This allows users to reduce the psychological burden about the significant issue of house decoration, psychologically empowering consumers through the structural mode of online and offline connection.

Tubatu.com

Tubatu.com was set up by Shenzhen Bin Xun Technology Co., Ltd. in July 2008, determined to become the leader in the field of house decoration in China and the most valuable Internet enterprise in China. It has greater than 100 city branch offices, 10 filiales and has served more than 6 million families, accumulated 60,000 regular companies and 600,000 interior decorators. Tubatu acts as a role of the third-party trading platform. It continuously improved platform service chain, enhancing the degree of satisfaction and Internet word-of-mouth. In 2009, Tubatu invited thousands of designers, now it has more than 100,000 certified designers, providing specialized and customized services.

Analysis of the three dimensions of empowerment of Tubatu (Figure 2)

Structural empowerment (1) Tubatu is a platform that makes trade matching. It collects various decoration companies, designers, construction units, and consumers and gets them to know each other through providing classified information and a large amount of reliable information, so that consumers can choose the most suitable decoration company by comparison;

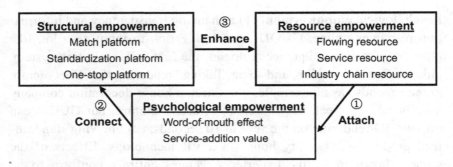

Figure 2. Tubatu Three Dimensions and Path to Consumer Empowerment

(2) Shifting to the standardization of house decoration platform, Tubatu cut its sales staff and controlled quality of house decoration company rationally. If a decoration company wants to enter the platform, it must pass the test, and the constructors must be trained in Tubatu; (3) Integrating upstream and downstream resources, it launched "cloud supervisor" in June 2016, which meant that Tubatu not only further optimized the industrial chain, but also met the needs of various crowds by upgrading and reducing channelization and standardization.

Resource empowerment (1) Using high-quality content to get network traffic. Tubatu encourages users to take initiatives to share decorating processes, such as broadcasting renovation sites progress, decoration diary, etc. What's more, Tubatu creates an unique evaluation system, with the principles of reality, including their contract, the photos of decorating site. Those online user resources not only form a word of mouth, but also attract more customers to participate; (2) Building in-depth transformation of the service chain. Tubatu supervises project progress to ensure the quality of the decoration by using "renovation warranty" service and launched the funds managed services to protect the security of users' money, which is similar to Alipay; (3) Integrating industry chain resources. With existing online resources, Tubatu began to expand the supply and service chains, such as "Tubatu Mall", which can offer first-line building materials to the owners at low price and high quality, creating a one-stop technology experience for consumers.

Psychological empowerment (1) Rich online business resources and good reputation. In the first phase, Tubatu mainly solves the asymmetric information of whole industry, providing users with information services and facilitating transactions. One can obtain free house design, free quotes audit, free geomantic guide, which gained wide reputation and user information; in second stage, Tubatu shifts to integration platform. Launching a series of warranty services, as well as strong control of supply chain and service chain, Tubatu gains confidence from its customers; (2) Improving online services to enhance consumer value. The transformation of Tubatu structure is based on the psychological needs of the user, such as "renovation warranty" and "cloud supervisor".

Comparison of GUOJJ and Tubatu

Comparison of three dimensions of empowerment (Table 3)

Vertical empowerment mode of GUOJJ. Grandland addresses the concerns of decoration defects by existing excellent decoration teams and well-trained designers. The business model of "Internet + House-decoration" aggregates a large amount of resources, which improves the shopping experience of customers. (1) Integrating external Internet resources. The continuously declining profit margin of traditional real-estate business has the influence on decorating the industry with the highest input but lower gross profit. For this reason, Grandland mainly focuses on three new businesses; customization home decoration, Internet platform, and smart house. The Internet house-decoration platform GUOJJ introduces talents from outside and develops the business actively; (2) Using digital tools. GUOJJ is combined with the Internet technology, modern IT technology, virtual reality, and virtual reinforcement technology to create scenario-based e-commerce platform, using the online platform for offline resources drainage to promote the transformation and upgrading of the enterprise.

The Horizontal empowerment mode of Tubatu. The development of businesses for information matching platform cannot guarantee the quality of Tubatu fundamentally. Effectively controlling its decoration companies to ensure construction quality and reputation is becoming the consumers' pain point. Therefore, Tubatu carries on the transformation as

Table 2. Three Elements of Empowerment of GUOJI and Tubatu

Enterprise	Environment at Characteristics	Three Dimensions of Empowerment	Enterprise Effect
GUOJI	1. A large number of Internet companies, traditional decoration companies and portfolio companies enter the Internet house decoration market, which brings revolution, transparency and disintermediation to the industry 2. Traditional house decoration business models are miscellaneous. Due to customer dispersion, business scale is always difficult to enlarge 3. Among all the platforms, arranging the overall process from design to decoration of the industry is really complex, so there is no real absolute leading enterprise	1. Structural empowerment: focusing on turning network traffic to offline service. Performance: Internet technology, modern IT technology, VR technology to enhance the combination online and offline 2. Resource empowerment: relying on the offline resources to improve the construction of Internet Performance: 20 years experience in the industry, experienced construction team, full range of after-sales service, financial support from Grandland 3. Psychological empowerment: online and offline integration to increase the user experience Performance: "Disinterring mediation", "full process service", "what you see is what you get", etc.	DUOJI currently has 16,129 existing owners, who apply for the decoration services, from registration to shop. The advisory rate is about 15–20%, the conversion rate on finally signing the bill is about 30%. The offline stores have gained 30–40 million profit since they opened. There are four "experience" which have stores opened in Shenzhen with large orders

Tubatu

1. House decoration has no standardized products, which leads to price opaqueness, budget trap, inferior materials in the market. Consumers usually cannot get guarantees and give negative feedback

2. Based on information match, most Internet house decoration platforms just provide information and services to users and suppliers at first, unable to control the quality of the decoration, providing inferior consumer experience

1. Structure empowerment: from the matchmaking platform to a one-stop platform, improvement platform
   Performance: "renovation warranty", "Tubatu mall", "cloud supervisor," etc.

2. Resource empowerment: relying on online resources to accelerate the integration of industrial chain.
   Performance: in cooperation with building materials enterprises, providing third-party supervisor

3. Psychological empowerment: converging word-of-mouth effect, increasing consumer added value .
   Performance: Transforming the service chain, user evaluation system, the third-party supervision model

Tubatu now has a total of more than 260 city branches, 10 filiales, gathered 70,000 formal decoration companies, 60 million interior designers, 400 million daily independent user visits. The average daily decoration request orders reached 4 million, and it offered service to 1,100 million households in China. It has the sole decoration knowledge online library in China

Table 3. Three-dimensional Empowerment Path of Two Enterprises

GUOJI

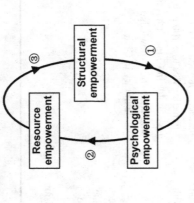

Transaction marketing orientation

Vertical empowerment model: by using traditional offline resources to seek Internet platform structure, providing consumers O2O integrated structure to complete psychological empowerment, ultimately integrating with enterprise's overall resources to form a closed loop

Based on **transaction marketing orientation**, the platform brings internet traffic for resource transformation to close a deal

Tubatu

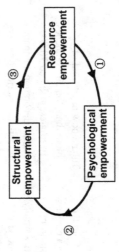

Relationship marketing orientation

Horizontal empowerment model: taking advantage of the Internet platform, improving the industrial resource supply chain, and ultimately providing a full range of integrated services resources to complete the psychological empowerment for consumers, making a more robust structure to form a closed loop

Based on **relationship orientation**, the platform provides more convenience for users to maintain good relationship follows: (1) Improving entering barriers of the platforms, eliminating non-standard business. In 2016, Tubatu begins to totally reorganize decoration companies on the platform, giving strict censorship for entering merchants. (2) Aiming at the solution of decoration companies' upgrading within the platform, requesting the money of decoration in platform can be completely supervised to constrain decoration companies. (3) Providing free objective third party supervision service. Accepting and making three parties enabled decoration companies to receive the payment of the corresponding node. Tubatu is slowly becoming a company which gathered owners, designers, industrial workers and excellent companies, and house building material manufacturers to build a one-stop service platform.

Transactional and relational marketing (Table 3)

Tubatu, whose mode is **horizontal empowerment**, belongs to **relationship Marketing.** (1) Taking advantage of word of mouth effect on the Internet. Tubatu builds a system of whole decoration industry chain that shares reputation, encouraging consumers to take the initiative to share Tubatu's work; (2) Emphasis on the service quality of the platform. Tubatu continuously improves the level of service and quality, strengthens the relationship with the customers through understanding consumers' demand and market trends; (3) Caring about long-term interactive communication. Tubatu provides third party supervision service and free on-site inspection for owners, applying LETV's VR products fully to offline stores to reduce the cost of consumers' decisions.

However, GUOJJ, whose mode is **vertical empowerment**, belongs to **transaction marketing.** (1) Paying attention to the offline sales and experience. GUOJJ's CEO Wang Li has said GUOJJ' mode could be divided into two parts: "Consulting Services in the front and removable manufacturing in the back". The main effect of the online platform is to attract people and transform consumers successfully and enhance turnover; (2) Providing standardized products. "Boutique house" is the GUOJJ's design team's alpha test for the potential customer in the Eleventh China (Shenzhen) International Cultural Industry Fair. It's a fully decorated standard house product for majority of young people in Shenzhen; (3) Caring about the product quality for a single user. Grandland is responsible to consumer on the processes of design, construction, installation, after-sales service, so that they can meet consumers' demand for high quality house decoration.

Research proves that we know that different environmental backgrounds and resources can influence the development of enterprise. (1) Internet business emphasizes on relationship marketing, while the traditional enterprises with rich offline resources focus on transaction marketing. Transaction marketing lies in the target customers. Tubatu, rising in the condition of Internet resources, gathered all the parties' resources to improve the platform; the other one is the traditional enterprise like GUOJJ; their traditional experience can provide consumers with "one-stop" service; (2) Industries with long-cycle products and high prices usually have transaction orientation. As a part of living expenditure, spending on house improvement is characterized as low frequency and high consumption. Housing and decoration is still an important part of the household expenditure budget. Among the traditional house improvement enterprises, most of them mainly focus on achieving the satisfaction of customers in single service; (3) Relationship marketing weighs more for customer retention and platform development. House decoration is a complex task, which covers a long and trivial process of design, construction, material selection, installation, and after-sales service. As research shows that almost 99% of people don't know how to decorate reasonably, they tend to choose a trustworthy house decoration company. Internet decoration platforms focus on offering information and service for the products.

Contributions, Limitations, and Conclusions

In the study we use "structural, psychological, resource" as of the three dimensions empowerment to analyse the traditional enterprise's "vertical empowerment" and Internet platform enterprise's "horizontal empowerment", and find the different marketing orientations behind their empowerment path. Different cycle processes are due to the different motivations of enterprises.

Our research offers two key **theoretical contributions**. (1) Study addresses the literature gap in consumer empowerment and digital empowerment by introducing three dimensions in the process of empowerment as structural, resource, and psychological. On the one hand, digital empowerment brings the Internet platform to the house decoration industry, improving transparency of information about the industry, in some way enhancing the consumer experience satisfaction, altering the growth pattern of the whole industry. On the other hand, the three dimensions forming the path for consumer empowerment provide support to the theory, where previous studies haven't formed a specific implementation of the empowerment path, so this study provides a more clear and effective idea to fill the gaps in the theoretical study; (2) Exploration enterprises' marketing orientation for consumer empowerment. The three dimensions form the path that could increase the consumer satisfaction; resource is the basis for promoting the integration of structural resources for consumers. Through the process of empowerment, relationship between consumers and businesses transforms into a consumer-centered co-creator of value. This view is the same as Heinonen *et al.* (2010) suggests that consistently thinking consumers will be the ultimate leaders in the supply chain; marketing research paradigm should be emphasized from the previous Goods Dominant Logic or Service Dominant logic to the Customer Dominant logic. Transaction marketing and relationship marketing complement each other. Their final purpose is to establish a good relationship with customers. Neither is appropriate or best on the level of consumer empowerment.

This study also generates **practical insights**. Our findings suggest the practical considerations of how to realize consumer empowerment. (1) Platform-based business should achieve "horizontal empowerment" based on the relationship marketing orientation. Setting the structure as a starting point to empower, when consumers proposed a new resource requirement, platform-based companies began to promote "light to heavy" changes, urging resources to improve the structure platform, eventually forming a closed complete consumer empowerment path under the orientation of relationship marketing. Thus, by continuous improvement of integration platform structure, psychological demands of consumer can be met. Tubatu achieves online "from light to heavy" and perfects the line of the supply chain process, continuing to build an integrated platform ecosystem; (2) Traditional business shift to "vertical empowerment" based on transaction-oriented marketing. Initially their traditional advantages in resources could meet the needs of consumers, but soon the Internet market is taking a large number of consumer resources. In the competitive condition, traditional enterprises embarked on the path of transformation on the Internet. Relying on resources to develop an online platform could enhance consumer psychology empowerment, and ultimately form a closed complete empowerment loop for consumers to achieve more transactions. Traditional businesses's shift to a vertical platform formed the structure of O2O connection in the sublimation process strengthening the online structure and offline resource in order to provide users with more personalized service and more complementary resources to form consumer psychological empowerment.

Our findings should be viewed in the context of this **limitations**. (1) We conducted this study in the context of the house decoration industry. Compared to other industries, decoration industries are characterized as having a high average of customer transaction and low consumption frequency. Therefore, in the future we may research different industries to explore the process for consumer empowerment. Nonetheless, we posit that our findings may serve as a basis for validation or further exploration in future research. (2) Our findings are based on a case study is between the traditional enterprise and the Internet platform enterprise. Future research could form different stages of development of enterprises, analyse consumer empowerment action with the corresponding marketing orientation. (3) In this study, we set the perspective of three dimensions forming consumer empowerment behind enterprise's action logic. Future research could further refine the character of three empowerment dimensions. Despite its limitations, we believe that our study will interest practitioners and researchers in the areas of consumer empowerment and marketing orientation.

References

Agarwal, R., *et al.* 2010. "Research Commentary — the Digital Transformation of Healthcare: Current Status and the Road Ahead," *Information Systems Research*, 21(4), 796–809.

Amichai-Hamburger, Y. 2008. "Internet Empowerment," *Computers in Human Behavior*, 24(5), 1773–1775.

Ansari, A., and Mela, C. F. 2003. "E-Customization," *Journal of Marketing Research*, 40(2), 131–145.

Bandura, A. 1978. "Social Learning Theory of Aggression," *Journal of Communication*, 28(3), 12–29.

Barrutia, J. M., and Echebarria, C. 2005. "The Internet and Consumer Power: The Case of Spanish Retail Banking," *Journal of Retailing & Consumer Services,* 12(12), 255–271.

Berry, L. L., Conant, J. S., and Parasuraman, A. 1991. "A Framework for Conducting a Services Marketing Audit," *Journal of the Academy of Marketing Science,* 19(3), 255–268.

Bourdieu, P. 1984. *"Distinction: A Social Critique of the Judgement of Taste."* Harvard University Press, Cambridge, Massachusetts.

Broniarczyk, Susan M., and Griffin, J. G. 2014. "Decision Difficulty in the Age of Consumer Empowerment," *Journal of Consumer Psychology,* 24(4), 608–625.

Catherine, L. Wang., and Ahmed, P. K. 2007. "Dynamic Capabilities: A Review and Research Agenda," *International Journal of Management Reviews,* 9(1), 31–51.

Conger, J. A., and Kanungo, R. N. 1988. "Behavioral Dimensions of Charismatic Leadership," In *Charismatic Leadership: The Elusive Factor in Organizational Effectiveness,* Conger, J. A., Kanungo, R. N. and Associates, eds., Jossey Bass, San Fransico, pp. 78–97.

Deighton, J., and Kornfeld, L. 2009. "Interactivity's Unanticipated Consequences for Marketers and Marketing," *Journal of Interactive Marketing,* 23(1), 4–10.

Denegri-Knott, J., Zwick, D., and Schroeder, J. E. 2006. "Mapping Consumer Power: An Integrative Framework for Marketing and Consumer Research," *European Journal of Marketing,* 40(9), 950–971.

Eisenhardt, K. M. 1989. "Making Fast Decisions in High-Velocity Environments," *Academy of Management Journal,* 32(3), 543–576.

Fenech, T., and O'Cass, A. 2003. "Web Retailing Adoption: Exploring the Nature of Internet users Web Retailing Behaviour," *Journal of Retailing & Consumer Services,* 10(2), 81–94.

Franke, N., Keinz, P., and Klausberger, K. 2013. "Does This Sound Like a Fair Deal?" Antecedents and Consequences of Fairness Expectations in the Individual's Decision to Participate in Firm Innovation," *Organization Science,* 24(5), 1495–1516.

Grönroos, C. 1990. "Relationship Approach to Marketing in Service Contexts: The Marketing and Organizational Behavior Interface," *Journal of Business Research,* 20(1), 3–11.

Hackman, J. R., and Oldham, G. R. 1980. *"Work Redesign."* Reading, MA: Addison Wesley.

Heinonen, K., Strandvik, T., Mickelsson, K., Edvardsson, B., Sundström, E., and Andersson, P. 2010. "A customer-dominant logic of service," *Journal of Service Management,* 21(4), 531–548.

Hui, M. K., and Bateson, J. E. G. 1991. "Perceived Control and the Effects of Crowding and Consumer Choice on the Service Experience," *Journal of Consumer Research*, 18(2), 174–84.

Hunt, S. D., and Morgan, R. M. 1994. "Organizational Commitment: One of Many Commitments or Key Mediating Construct?" *Academy of Management Journal*, 37(6), 1568–1587.

Hur, M. H. 2006. "Empowerment in Terms of Theoretical Perspectives: Exploring a Typology of the Process and Components Across Disciplines, *"Journal of Community Psychology*, 34(5), 523–540.

Jarrett, K. 2003. "Labour of Love An Archaeology of Affect as Power in E-Commerce," *Journal of Sociology*, 39(4), 335–351.

Jon Sundbo. 1997. "Management of Innovation in Services," *Service Industries Journal*, 17(3), 432–455.

Kaiser, T. 2002. "The Customer Shall Lead: E-Business Solutions for the New Insurance Industry," *Geneva Papers on Risk and Insurance — Issues and Practice*, 27(1), 134–145.

Kanter R. M. 1979. "Power Failure in Management Circuits," *Harvard Business Review*, 57(4), 65–75.

Kim, J., and Hahn, K. H. 2009. "The Effect of Offline Brand Trust and Perceived Internet Confidence on Online Shopping Intention in the Integrated Multi-Channel Context," *International Journal of Retail & Distribution Management*, 37(2), 126–141.

Kotler, P. 1994. *"Marketing Management: Analysis, Planning, Implementation, and Control."* Prentice-Hall International, Upper Saddle River, New Jersey.

Kumar, A. 2007. "From Mass Customization to Mass Personalization: A Strategic Transformation," *International Journal of Flexible Manufacturing Systems*, 19(19), 533–547.

Labrecque, L. I., *et al.*, 2013. "Consumer Power: Evolution in the Digital Age," *Journal of Interactive Marketing,* 27(4), 257–269.

Langeard, É. 1981. "Services Marketing: New Insights from Consumers and Managers," *Marketing Science Institute*, 81, 177–178.

Laschinger, H. K., Finegan, J., Shamian, J., and Wilk, P. 2001. "Impact of Structural and Psychological Empowerment on Job Strain in Nursing Work Settings: Expanding Kanter's Model," *Journal of Nursing Administration*, 31(5), 260–272.

Legris, P., Ingham, J., and Collerette, P. 2003. "Why Do People Use Information Technology? A Critical Review of the Technology Acceptance Model," *Information & Management*, 40(3), 191–204.

Leonard-Barton, D. 1995. "Wellsprings of Knowledge: Building and Sustaining the Sources of Innovation," *Social Science Electronic Publishing*, 17(1), 387–392.

Leong, C. M. L., Pan, S., Newell, S., and Cui, L. 2016. "The Emergence of Self-Organizing E-Commerce Ecosystems in Remote Villages of China: A Tale of Digital Empowerment for Rural Development," *MIS Quarterly*, 40(2), 475–484.

Levitt, T. 1983. "The Globalisation of Markets," *Harvard Business Review*, 61(3), 92–92.

Logan, M. S., and Ganster, D. C. 2007. "The Effects of Empowerment on Attitudes and Performance: The Role of Social Support and Empowerment Beliefs," *Journal of Management Studies*, 44(8), 1523–1550.

Martineau, P. 1958. "The Personality of the Retail Store," *Harvard Business Review*, 36(1), 47–55.

Maynard, Travis, M., Gilson, L. L., and Mathieu, J. E. 2012. "Empowerment — Fad or Fab? A Multilevel Review of the Past Two Decades of Research," *Journal of Management*, 38(4), 1231–1281.

Meissner, J., and Strauss, A. 2008. "Network Revenue Management with Inventory-Sensitive Bid Prices and Customer Choice," *European Journal of Operational Research*, 216(08), 459–468.

Morrissey, B. 2005. "Advertisers Fight Banner Blindness with News Feeds," *Adweek*, 46(36), 10–10.

Newman, A. J., and Patel, D. 2004. "The Marketing Directions of Two Fashion Retailers," *European Journal of Marketing*, 38(7), 770–789.

Pace, S., and Cova, B. 2006. "Brand Community of Convenience Products: New Forms of Customer Empowerment — the Case "My Nutella Community"," *European Journal of Marketing*, 40(10), 1087–1105.

Pan, S. L., and Tan, B. 2011. "Demystifying Case Research: A Structured–Pragmatic–Situational (SPS) Approach to Conducting Case Studies," *Information & Organization*, 21(3), 161–176.

Pehlivan, E., Sarican, F., and Berthon, P. 2011. "Mining Messages: Exploring Consumer Response to Consumer- vs. Firm-generated Ads," *Journal of Consumer Behaviour*, 10(10), 313–321.

Peterson, R. A., and Merino, M. C. 2003. "Consumer Information Search Behavior on the Internet," *Psychology & Marketing*, 20(2), 99–121.

Pires, G. D., and Aisbett, D. 2003. "The Relationship between Technology Adoption and Strategy in Business-to-Business Markets: The case of e-commerce," *Industrial Marketing Management*, 32(4), 291–300.

Pires, G. D., Stanton, J., and Rita, P. 2006. "The Internet, Consumer Empowerment and Marketing Strategies," *European Journal of Marketing*, 40(40), 936–949.

Pitt, L. F., *et al.*, 2002. "The Internet and the Birth of Real Consumer Power," *Business Horizons*, 45(4), 7–14.

Prahalad, C. K., and Ramaswamy, V. 2003. "The New Frontier of Experience Innovation," *Mit Sloan Management Review*, 44(4), 12–18.

Schiffman, L. G., and Kanuk, L. L. 2000. *"Consumer Behavior."* Prentice Hall, Upper Saddle River, New Jersey.

Siegall, M., and Gardner, S. 2000. "Contextual Factors of Psychological Empowerment," *Personnel Review*, 29(29), 703–722.

Škudienė, V., *et al.*, 2013. "Front-Line Employees' Recognition and Empowerment Effect on Retail Bank Customers' Perceived Value," *Journal of Service Science*, 6(1), 105–116.

Smircich, L., and Stubbart, C. 2008. "Strategic Management in an Enacted World," *Academy of Management Review*, 10(4), 724–736.

Spreitzer, G. M. 1995. "An Empirical Test of a Comprehensive Model of Intrapersonal Empowerment in the Workplace," *American Journal of Community Psychology*, 23(5), 601–29.

Spreitzer, G. M., and Doneson, D. 2005. "Musings on the Past and Future of Employee Empowerment." In T. Cummings ed. *Handbook of Organisational Development*, Thousand Oaks, CA, Sage.

Thomas, K.W., and Velthouse, B. A. 1990. "Cognitive Elements of Empowerment: An 'Interpretive' Model of Intrinsic Task Motivation," *Academy of Management Review*, 15(4), 666–681.

Valente, T. W. 1996. "Network Models of the Diffusion of Innovations," *Computational & Mathematical Organization Theory*, 2(2), 163–164.

Wathieu, L., *et al.*, 2002. "Consumer Control and Empowerment: A Primer," *Marketing Letters*, 13(3), 297–305.

Wilke, 2005. "Process Optimization and Characterization of Silicon Microneedles Fabricated by Wet Etch Technology," *Microelectronics Journal*, 36(7), 650–656.

Yin, R. K. 1989. *"Case Study Research: Design and Methods."* Thoudand Oaks, CA, Sage, pp. 206–207.

Yin, R. K. 2003. *"Case Study Research: Design and Methods."* Thousand Oaks, CA, Sage.

Zahra, S. A., Sapienza, H. J., and Davidsson, P. 2009. "Entrepreneurship and Dynamic Capabilities: A Review, Model and Research Agenda," *Journal of Management Studies*, 43(4), 917–955.

Chapter 18

How Do Scarcity Messages Lead to Impulsive Online Purchase? The Perspective of Arousal

Junpeng Guo

College of Management and Economics Tianjin University
Nankai District, Tianjin, China 300072
guojp@tju.edu.cn

Liwei Xin

College of Management and Economics Tianjin University
Nankai District, Tianjin, China 300072
lw_xin@tju.edu.cn

Yi Wu

College of Management and Economics Tianjin University
Nankai District, Tianjin, China 300072
yiwu@tju.edu.cn

Abstract

With the proliferation of e-commerce, online promotion strategy of limited quantity and limited time is widely used by online retailers to entice consumer purchases. However, few research works have investigated the exact effects of such a promotion strategy on consumers' impulsive online purchase. Based on the environmental psychology view, this proposal focuses on the mediating role of arousal in explaining the impacts of scarcity messages in aspects of limited quantity and limited time on impulsive purchase. To empirically verify the research model, we plan to conduct a lab-controlled experiment. Finally, both potential theoretical and practical contributions and future plans are elaborated in this proposal.

Keywords: Environmental psychology, Impulsive online purchase, Scarcity message, Arousal.

Introduction

Singles' Day — symbolized by its single-digit heavy date, 11/11 — began 7 years ago, when unattached college kids went online to hunt for bargains. Alibaba, China's largest e-commerce giant, started offering huge discounts to mark the day. Thereafter, this shopping event has grown exponentially, now being a shopping festival globally. For Singles' Day 2015, the company raked in $5 billion during the first 90 minutes of the sale, totaling $14.3 billion in just 24 hours largely through its online shopping platforms, Taobao.com and Tmall.com.[1] Singles' Day is a shopping carnival for online consumers, and online shops utilized promotion strategy of limited quantity and limited time, in which a limited amount of products are on sale within a given time period, to entice impulsive purchases. The scarcity messages about limited quantity and limited time provide an online shopping environment that might shape consumers' impulsive purchase decision-making.

Specifically, in a limited-quantity scarcity message (LQS), the promotional offer is made available for a predefined quantity of the product. In a limited-time scarcity message (LTS), the offer is available for a predefined period, after which the offer becomes unavailable. Scarcity seems to create a sense of urgency among buyers that results in increased quantities being purchased, shorter searches, and greater satisfaction with the purchased products, the accompanying impulsive buying. Prior research has shown

---

[1] http://www.businessinsider.com/how-alibaba-made-143-billion-on-singles-day-2015-11. Accessed on May 8, 2016.

that purchase restrictions are used as informational cues by customers to evaluate promotion strategies (Gabler and Reynolds, 2013). Although ample studies have emphasized the influences of scarcity messages on impulsive purchases in the offline contexts, scant research has been devoted to the online shopping environment.

Compared to the offline shopping environment, the two types of scarcity messages are more visible and are updated in a timely manner. Online consumers are able to view the timely changes of decreasing supply amount and feel the time pressure by counting down the available shopping time. Patterns of manifestation of scarcity messages are different in online vs. offline environment. IT could easily be designed to manipulate perceptions of scarcity that could be potentially more difficult to manipulate offline. Scarcity messages create a sense of urgency and constitute the dominant stimuli in online environment. Scarcity messages manipulated by IT provide an online shopping environment that might shape consumers' impulsive purchase decision making. Therefore, to bridge the gap, this study aims to elaborate how limited-quantity information and limited-time information to online shopping environment influence the consumers' impulsive purchase.

Consumers often act impulsively when making online purchase decisions, triggered by easy access to products, easy purchasing (e.g., 1-Click ordering), lack of social pressures, and absence of delivery efforts (Jeffrey and Hodge, 2007). The marketing and IS literatures show that impulsive purchase can be studied from the state of mind created by the online shopping environment (Koo and Ju, 2010). Prior literature has demonstrated the irrationality of impulsive purchase decision making from the online shopping environment perspective. Verhagen and van Dolen (2011) suggested that the irrational decision making of online impulsive purchase occurs without a thoughtful consideration of why and for what reason one needs the product. Specifically, there are two core elements characterizing this irrational impulsive buying decision making. First, the process is unplanned and lacks cognitive deliberation. Second, emotions dominate the impulsive buying process (Verhagen and van Dolen, 2011). Therefore, this study draws on the environmental psychology view and posits that arousal stimulated by online shopping environment (i.e., LQS, LTS) affects consumers' impulsive purchase.

To fill the above research gaps, this study aims to address the following research questions:

(1) What are the impacts of LQS and LTS on online consumer arousal toward impulsive purchase?
(2) How does consumer arousal lead to impulsive online purchase?

By answering these research questions, this study provides the following theoretical contributions. First, this proposal examines the mechanism through which online scarcity messages influence impulsive consumer responses and investigates the impacts of scarcity messages on impulsive online purchase. Second, this study enriches the irrational decision-making literature of impulsive purchase from the perspective of arousal. In addition, this study is with its practical contributions. On one hand, it provides design guidelines on the successful use of limited-quantity and limited-time promotion strategy. On the other hand, this proposal also suggests that online consumers should pay close attention to their emotional responses toward the online promotion strategy.

Theoretical foundations

Impulsive purchase

Impulsive purchase is defined as "a purchase that is unplanned, the result of an exposure to a stimulus, and decided on the spot" (Piron, 1991). The stimulus in the definition can be an actual product, service, or the extrinsic attributes of the product, such as the shopping environment or atmosphere. On one hand, when exposed to a stimulus, an individual experiences a sudden, spontaneous urge or desire to buy the stimulus, regardless of the impetus (e.g., individual trait or environmental cue) (Rook, 1987). On other hand, the impulsive purchase occurs only after the individual first experiences the urge to purchase impulsively (Rook, 1987).

Impulsive purchase is distinguished from unplanned purchase. Unplanned purchase is "the purchase of a product that was not planned prior to entering the store" (Park *et al.*, 1989). The term "impulsive buying" refers to a narrower and more specific range of phenomena than "unplanned purchasing" does. More importantly, it identifies a psychologically distinctive type of behavior that differs dramatically from contemplative modes of consumer choice. (Rook, 1987). This study focuses on impulsive buying, which occurs when a consumer experiences a sudden, often powerful and persistent urge to buy something immediately.

The urge to buy impulsively (UBI) is defined as "the state of desire that is experienced upon encountering an object in the environment" (Beatty and Ferrell, 1998); it is a qualified and reasonable proxy for actual impulsive purchase (Parboteeah *et al.*, 2009; Wells *et al.*, 2011; Xiang *et al.*, 2016). Therefore, this study adopts UBI as an appropriate and effective proxy for impulsive purchase behavior.

Ample studies have investigated the role of environmental cues on online impulsive purchase, mainly from the perspective of website quality characteristics (e.g., Adelaar *et al.*, 2003; Floh and Madlberger, 2013; Parboteeah *et al.*, 2009; Verhagen and van Dolen, 2011; Wells *et al.*, 2011; Wu *et al.*, 2016). With the advances of e-commerce, a new type of promotion strategy, i.e., limited-quantity and limited-time offer, is widely used by online retailers to entice consumers' impulsive purchases. For instance, Alibaba, China's largest e-commerce giant, holds sale events to utilize this limited-quantity and limited-time offer on Singles' Day. The success of the limited-quantity and limited-time offer relies on e-commerce websites' capabilities in timely updation of the information on quantity and time for online consumers. The information an limited-quantity offer and information on limited-time offer are viewed as scarcity messages (Cialdini, 2009), and these two types of information constitute the online informational environment for consumers.

The environmental psychology view of online scarcity message

The environmental psychology view proposes that environmental stimuli are linked to behavioral responses by the primary emotional responses of arousal, pleasure, and dominance (Mehrabian and Russell, 1974). Environmental psychology has been used when investigating impulsive online purchase, which extends our knowledge of online environment and impulsive purchase (Adelaar *et al.*, 2003). Environment factors (e.g., scarcity messages) influence people's affective responses to the environment, which in turn induce people to approach or avoid the environment (Mehrabian and Russell, 1974). Emotion of affective response can be classified based on three independent and bipolar dimensions: pleasantness, arousal, and dominance (Russell and Mehrabian, 1977). Subsequent research has found that pleasantness and arousal explain most of the variance in affect and behavior, and arousal is the most critical type of emotional state (Donovan and Rossiter, 1982; Russell and Pratt, 1980). However, few research works have confirmed the connection between scarcity messages and pleasantness. Literature has also presented that there is no significant difference in pleasantness among individuals in response to scarcity condition (Zhu and Ratner, 2015). Therefore, this study focuses on arousal as the consumers' emotional state from the online informational environment.

Arousal is defined as the neurophysiological basis underlying all processes in the human organism, ranging from sleep to excitement with intermediate states of drowsiness to alertness (Russell and Mehrabian, 1977). It is the basis of emotions, motivation, information processing, and behavioral reactions (Bagozzi *et al.*, 1999; Kroeber-Riel, 1979). Donovan and Rossiter (1982) showed that arousal–non-arousal dimension taps the degree to which a person feels alert, excited, stimulated, or active in the situation. In particular, there are two types of arousals: excited arousal and competitive arousal. On one hand, excited arousal is the feeling of excitement reflecting high levels of arousal combined with high levels of pleasure and joy, where environmental cues (e.g., warm color, fast music tempo, scent) would activate excited arousal (Mattila and Wirtz, 2001; Wu *et al.*, 2008). On the other hand, competitive arousal is an adrenaline-laden emotional state that can arise during competitive interactions (Malhotra, 2010), where arousal based on rivalry, time pressure, and audience effects can trigger the desire to win (Ku *et al.*, 2005).

Prior research has theorized potential theoretical connections between scarcity messages and arousal (Cialdini, 2009; Pribram and McGuinness, 1975). Research on activation and attention explicates that arousal is typically produced by input changes to which an organism is unaccustomed, particularly when the input is scarce, surprising, and novel (Pribram and McGuinness, 1975). According to Cialdini (2009), when something that people like is less available, they become physically agitated, such that their focus narrows, emotions rise, and cognitive processes are often suppressed by "brain-clouding arousal". Zhu and Ratner (2015) examined that the underlying mechanisms of scarcity polarize preferences, demonstrating that the effect of scarcity salience on choices is mediated by consumers' perceived arousal.

Research model and hypothesis development

Figure 1 shows the research model.

Effects of scarcity messages on arousal

An LQS offer is restricted to a set number of units. Units are limited, often administered on a first-come, first-served basis, and run until they are sold out. This creates a sense of time pressure and uncertainty for an LQS deal. Combining for the retail auctions, consumers under time pressure are believed to elicit an excited arousal (Adam *et al.*, 2015) and research has shown that time pressure increases arousal (Maule *et al.*, 2000).

Furthermore, consumers compete for the advantageous inequity that accrues to the recipient of promotions (Barone and Roy, 2010). The promotion of LQS, accompanying time pressure and rivalry, makes a consumer feel that he or she in direct competition with other consumers. Such a situation will stimulate the consumer and result in competitive arousal. Prior studies show that time pressure, rivalry, and audience effects increase competitive arousal that a consumer experiences (Ku *et al.*, 2005). In a similar situation in the auctions, the object is limited and being bid for under time pressure with rivals, which significantly stimulates competitive

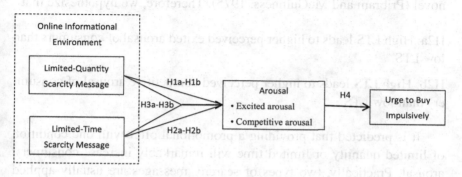

Figure 1. Research Model

arousal and affects the consequences (Adam *et al.*, 2015; Malhotra, 2010). Therefore, we propose that

H1a: High LQS leads to higher perceived exited arousal of consumers than low LQS.

H1b: High LQS leads to higher perceived competitive arousal of consumers than low LQS.

In the case of LTS, consumers can buy the product at any moment within a period of time, and the supply is abundant but time is scarce. Consumers only have to complete the deals before the deadline. Even though the consumers know the existence of many others, there is no conflict of interest between each other and competitive arousal in consumers. However, obtaining a bargain becomes more like "winning" a bargain, where the bargain provides both utilitarian as well as hedonic fulfillment (Garretson and Burton, 2003). Scarce products on sale open a gate to obtain the bargain and stimulate the emotion; consumers feel excited or joyous because of the utilitarian satisfaction. In addition, a festival's program content can affect both attendees' emotions and hedonism (Grappi and Montanari, 2011). LTS is the core feature of the online promotion strategy and motivates consumers' purchase intention as attending the event is outside the daily routine. Furthermore, scarcity appeal plays an important strategic role to create an excitement around promotions (Aggarwal *et al.*, 2011). Research on activation and attention explicates that arousal is typically produced by input changes to which an organism is unaccustomed, particularly when the input is scarce, surprising, and novel (Pribram and McGuinness, 1975). Therefore, we hypothesize that

H2a: High LTS leads to higher perceived exited arousal of consumers than low LTS.

H2b: High LTS leads to higher perceived competitive arousal of consumers than low LTS.

It is predicted that providing a promotional offer with one condition of limited quantity or limited time will remarkably increase consumers' arousal. Practically, two types of scarcity messages are usually applied synchronously in the promotion strategy. We believe that presence of an online promotion offer under both scarcity conditions will accelerate the effect of different degrees for consumer's responses.

The interaction between LOS and LTS should increase tension of perceived competitive arousal. Research has shown that time pressure increases arousal (Maule *et al.*, 2000) and Finucane *et al.* (2000) found that when human decision makers face time pressure, they have a general tendency to rely on affect, which in turn is accompanied by increased arousal levels. In the condition of low LOS, the perceived competitive arousal is increased by the effects of LTS. In the condition of high LQS, however, the perceptibly increased competitive arousal caused by LTS is unapparent with the existing high competitive arousal from high LQS. Therefore, we hypothesize that

H3a: There is an interaction effect between LQS and LTS on perceived competitive arousal, i.e. in the high LQS condition, the effect of LTS in term of increasing competitive arousal is less prominent than that in the low LQS condition.

In comparison to fixed-price and traditional offers, online promotion strategy has the potential to provide an exciting shopping experience. The excited arousal is generated by the websites and the advertisement campaigns of internet platforms. Time pressure produced by LTS fuels the perceived excited arousal in the activities. In the condition of LTS, increasing the degree of scarcity in terms of quantity means it is more difficult to get products, which affects the competitive arousal but has no effect on excited arousal. Therefore, we propose that

H3b: There is no interaction effect between LQS and LTS on perceived excited arousal, i.e. in the high LQS condition, the effect of LTS in terms of increasing excited arousal is not significantly different from that in the low LQS condition.

Effects of arousal on urge to buy impulsively

The affective reactions to the environment will determine an individual's response, e.g., UBI (Mehrabian and Russell, 1974). In a traditional shopping context, a positive relationship has been found between positive affective reactions (i.e. enjoyment) and UBI (Beatty and Ferrell, 1998). In the online context, perceived enjoyment will have a positive effect on the impulsive urge to buy (Chang *et al.*, 2014; Parboteeah *et al.*, 2009). Moreover, we focus specifically on time pressure and the inherent social competition under online promotion strategy, as these factors are considered to be the main drivers for so-called competitive arousal. In auctions, such competitive arousal may ultimately lead to auction fever (Ku *et al.*, 2005; Malhotra, 2010). With respect to auction fever, competitive arousal theory suggests that arousal can impair the bidders' decision making, and push them to bid past their limits (Ku *et al.*, 2005). Adam *et al.*, (2015) showed that affective processes have a definite influence on human decision making when bidders compete with human opponents. In addition, excitement has a positive effect on desire to stay at the mall and increases patronage intentions (Baker and Wakefield, 2011; Wakefield and Baker, 1998). Therefore, we posit that

H4: Arousal is positively related to consumers' UBI.

Proposed research methodology

Experimental design

A laboratory-controlled experiment with 2 (i.e. LQS: high vs. low) × 2 (i.e. LTS: high vs. low) factorial design will be conducted to test the proposed hypotheses. The LQS and LTS will be shown on a fake online retailer webpage by manipulating the number of restricted products and time of discounts. We selected mobile cases as our product category due to their popularity among Chinese college students and product affordability. Particularly, all products are on sale and discount settled according to the actual situation of Tmall.com on Singles' Day.

Sample and experimental procedures

Subjects in this experiment will be students at a large public university. Prior to the experiment, subjects will be asked to provide information about demographics and online shopping experience. At least 160 subjects will be recruited to take part in the experiment. Subjects will be randomly assigned to four experimental conditions. The random assignment will be performed once for every subject. They will be presented with an experimental website with different experimental treatments in which they can browse the product information. Subjects will be told to imagine that the scenario is real and browse the website carefully. Afterwards, subjects will be instructed to complete a questionnaire that contained measurement items of the research variables (shown in Table 1). The measures will

Table 1. Variable Measurements

Construct	Items	Source
UBI	As I browsed the products, I had the urge to purchase items other than or in addition to my specific shopping goal	Parboteeah *et al.* (2009)
	Browsing the information on products, I had a desire to buy items that did not pertain to my specific shopping goal	
	While browsing the products, I had the inclination to purchase items outside my specific shopping goal	
Excited arousal	As I browsed the products, I felt excited	Chang *et al.* (2012)
	As I browsed the products, I felt enthusiastic	
	While browsing information of the products, I felt happy	
	While browsing information of the products, I felt inspired	
Competitive arousal	I thought I might lose the opportunity to purchase the product if others bought it first	Aggarwal *et al.* (2011); Ku *et al.* (2005)
	I felt there is a lot of competition from other buyers to purchase the limited product	
	In order to get the limited deal, I thought I have to make the purchase before others do	
	I felt the heightened feelings of rivalry and time pressure	
	I felt the higher adrenaline-laden emotional state	

utilize a 7-point Likert-type scale anchored by 1 (Strongly Disagree) and 7 (Strongly Agree). Finally, subjects will be debriefed and thanked.

Concluding remarks

Potential contributions

Drawing on the impulsive online buying literature and the environmental psychology theory, this study proposes a theoretical model to explain the effect of online scarcity messages. Regardless of the website characteristics, this study suggests that context of website plays an important role in the impulsive purchase process. Promotional discounts are effective and LQS and LTS extremely fuel the enthusiasm for the products, which lead to the special emotion: arousal. The study intends to explain the relative effectiveness of LQS and LTS appeals, and expects to find that different types of scarcity messages may have differential effects on consumer's excited arousal and competitive arousal.

In addition, this study is with practical contributions. First, for product managers interested in creating excitement and competition around their promotions, scarcity appeal has played a considerable strategic role. Managers can draw on LQS (e.g., releasing a new brand) and LTS (e.g., expanding sales) for generating buyer enthusiasm. Secondly, there is one noteworthy emotion for consumers. Arousal unconsciously manipulated by the retailers using the scarcity messages aims at promoting consumption. Being careful controlling arousal for in consumers is an effective way to avoid impulsive buying.

Future plan

As a research-in-progress work, the first future step is to complete our experiment and empirically test our research model. Next, the design and context of this study examiner the effects of LQS and LTS; the magnitude of price discount was kept constant. Given that scarcity messages are frequently in conjunction with discount, it should be interesting to examine whether varying the amount of discount influences or moderates any degree of emotion.

Product category is another significant factor influencing impulsive purchase. Both academic and practical evidences show that differences exist regarding consumers' impulsive purchase behaviors, regarding distinct products, even within the same online shopping environment. Floh and Madlberger (2013) has called for future research attention on clarifying the roles of consumers' product involvement to gain a better understanding of the characteristics of online consumers. In this regard, this study is interested in and plans to adopt the concept of product involvement, which refers to the extent to which a consumer perceives a product to be important (Zaichkowsky, 1985), to examine the contextual effects of product category on the mechanisms between scarcity messages and impulsive purchase from the individual consumer perspective.

This study enriches the irrational decision-making literature of impulsive purchase from the perspective of arousal; however, studies have also showed the rational decision-making process of impulsive online purchase (Jiang *et al.*, 2010; Park *et al.*, 2012). For example, when interacting with online e-commerce websites, consumers process product-related information (e.g., variety of selection, price attribute) using their cognitive reactions (e.g., browsing) (Song *et al.*, 2015), and these are thus posited as an important component of the impulsive buying process. According to the feelings-as-information theory, these affect-congruent judgments reflect that consumers use their current feelings as a source of information in evaluating target objects, essentially asking themselves, "How do I feel about this?" (Schwarz and Clore, 1983). Therefore, one of the future theoretical directions is to incorporate the rational decision-making process between online scarcity messages and impulsive purchase in this study.

References

Adam, M. T. P., Krämer, J., and Müller, M. B. 2015. "Auction Fever! How Time Pressure and Social Competition Affect Bidders' Arousal and Bids in Retail Auctions," *Journal of Retailing*, 91(3), 468–485.

Adelaar, T., Chang, S., Lancendorfer, K. M., Lee, B., and Morimoto, M. 2003. "Effects of Media Formats on Emotions and Impulse Buying Intent," *Journal of Information Technology*, 18(4), 247–266.

Aggarwal, P., Jun, S. Y., and Huh, J. H. 2011. "Scarcity Messages," *Journal of Advertising*, 40(3), 19–30.

Bagozzi, R. P., Gopinath, M., and Nyer, P. U. 1999. "The Role of Emotions in Marketing," *Journal of the Academy of Marketing Science*, 27(2), 184–206.

Baker, J., and Wakefield, K. L. 2011. "How Consumer Shopping Orientation Influences Perceived Crowding, Excitement, and Stress at the Mall," *Journal of the Academy of Marketing Science*, 40(6), 791–806.

Barone, M. J., and Roy, T. 2010. "Does Exclusivity Always Pay Off? Exclusive Price Promotions and Consumer Response," *Journal of Marketing*, 74(2), 121–132.

Beatty, S. E., and Ferrell, M. E. 1998. "Impulse Buying: Modeling Its Precursors," *Journal of Retailing*, 74(2), 169–191.

Chang, H.-J., Yan, R.-N., and Eckman, M. 2014. "Moderating Effects of Situational Characteristics on Impulse Buying," *International Journal of Retail & Distribution Management*, 42(4), 298–314.

Chang, Y. K., Labban, J. D., Gapin, J. I., and Etnier, J. L. 2012. "The Effects of Acute Exercise on Cognitive Performance: A Meta-Analysis," *Brain Research*, 1453(0), 87–101.

Cialdini, R. B. 2009. "*Influence: Science and Practice*." Pearson Education Boston.

Donovan, R. J., and Rossiter, J. R. 1982. "Store Atmosphere: An Environmental Psychology Approach," *Journal of Retailing*, 58(1), 34–57.

Finucane, M. L., Alhakami, A., Slovic, P., and Johnson, S. M. 2000. "The Affect Heuristic in Judgments of Risks and Benefits," *Journal of Behavioral Decision Making*, 13(1), 1.

Floh, A., and Madlberger, M. 2013. "The Role of Atmospheric Cues in Online Impulse-Buying Behavior," *Electronic Commerce Research and Applications*, 12(6), 425–439.

Gabler, C. B., and Reynolds, K. E. 2013. "Buy Now or Buy Later: The Effects of Scarcity and Discounts on Purchase Decisions," *The Journal of Marketing Theory and Practice*, 21(4), 441–456.

Garretson, J. A., and Burton, S. 2003. "Highly Coupon and Sale Prone Consumers: Benefits Beyond Price Savings," *Journal of Advertising Research*, 43(02), 162–172.

Grappi, S., and Montanari, F. 2011. "The Role of Social Identification and Hedonism in Affecting Tourist Re-Patronizing Behaviours: The Case of an Italian Festival," *Tourism Management*, 32(5), 1128–1140.

Jeffrey, S. A., and Hodge, R. 2007. "Factors Influencing Impulse Buying During an Online Purchase," *Electronic Commerce Research*, 7(3–4), 367–379.

Jiang, Z., Chan, J., Tan, B. C. Y., and Chua, W. S. 2010. "Effects of Interactivity on Website Involvement and Purchase Intention," *Journal of the Association for Information Systems*, 11(1), 34–59.

Koo, D.-M., and Ju, S.-H. 2010. "The Interactional Effects of Atmospherics and Perceptual Curiosity on Emotions and Online Shopping Intention," *Computers in Human Behavior*, 26(3), 377–388.

Kroeber-Riel, W. 1979. "Activation Research: Psychobiological Approaches in Consumer Research," *Journal of Consumer Research*, 5(4), 240–250.

Ku, G., Malhotra, D., and Murnighan, J. K. 2005. "Towards a Competitive Arousal Model of Decision-Making: A Study of Auction Fever in Live and Internet Auctions," *Organizational Behavior and Human Decision Processes*, 96(2), 89–103.

Malhotra, D. 2010. "The Desire to Win: The Effects of Competitive Arousal on Motivation and Behavior," *Organizational Behavior and Human Decision Processes*, 111(2), 139–146.

Mattila, A. S., and Wirtz, J. 2001. "Congruency of Scent and Music as a Driver of in-Store Evaluations and Behavior," *Journal of Retailing*, 77(2), 273–289.

Maule, A. J., Hockey, G. R. J., and Bdzola, L. 2000. "Effects of Time-Pressure on Decision-Making under Uncertainty, Changes in Affective State and Information Prexessing Strategy. Pdf," 104(3), 283–301.

Mehrabian, A., and Russell, J. A. 1974. "*An Approach to Environmental Psychology*." The MIT Press, Cambridge, Massachusetts.

Parboteeah, D. V., Valacich, J. S., and Wells, J. D. 2009. "The Influence of Website Characteristics on a Consumer's Urge to Buy Impulsively," *Information Systems Research*, 20(1), 60–78.

Park, C. W., Iyer, E. S., and Smith, D. C. 1989. "The Effects of Situational Factors on in-Store Grocery Shopping Behavior: The Role of Store Environment and Time Available for Shopping," *Journal of Consumer Research*, 15(4), 422–433.

Park, E. J., Kim, E. Y., Funches, V. M., and Foxx, W. 2012. "Apparel Product Attributes, Web Browsing, and E-Impulse Buying on Shopping Websites," *Journal of Business Research*, 65(11), 1583–1589.

Piron, F. 1991. "Defining Impulse Purchasing," *Advances in Consumer Research*, 18, 509–514.

Pribram, K. H., and McGuinness, D. 1975. "Arousal, Activation, and Effort in the Control of Attention," *Psychological Review,* 82(2), 116.

Rook, D. W. 1987. "The Buying Impulse," *Journal of Consumer Research*, 14(2), 189–199.

Russell, J. A., and Mehrabian, A. 1977. "Evidence for a Three-Factor Theory of Emotions," *Journal of Research in Personality*, 11(3), 273–294.

Russell, J. A., and Pratt, G. 1980. "A Description of the Affective Quality Attributed to Environments," *Journal of Personality and Social Psychology*, 38(2), 311.

Schwarz, N., and Clore, G. L. 1983. "Mood, Misattribution, and Judgments of Well-Being: Informative and Directive Functions of Affective States," *Journal of Personality and Social Psychology*, 45(3), 513–523.

Song, H. G., Chung, N., and Koo, C. 2015. "Impulsive Buying Behavior of Restaurant Products in Social Commerce: A Role of Serendipity and Scarcity Message," In *Proceedings from PACIS 2015: The 19th Pacific Asia Conference on Information Systems*, Singapore.

Verhagen, T., and van Dolen, W. 2011. "The Influence of Online Store Beliefs on Consumer Online Impulse Buying: A Model and Empirical Application," *Information & Management*, 48(8), 320–327.

Wakefield, K. L., and Baker, J. 1998. "Excitement at the Mall: Determinants and Effects on Shopping Response," *Journal of Retailing*, 74(4), 515–539.

Wells, J. D., Parboteeah, V., and Valacich, J. S. 2011. "Online Impulse Buying Understanding the Interplay between Consumer Impulsiveness and Website Quality," *Journal of the Association for Information Systems*, 12(1), 32–56.

Wu, C.-S., Cheng, F.-F., and Yen, D. C. 2008. "The Atmospheric Factors of Online Storefront Environment Design: An Empirical Experiment in Taiwan," *Information & Management*, 45(7), 493–498.

Wu, I.-L., Chen, K.-W., and Chiu, M.-L. 2016. "Defining Key Drivers of Online Impulse Purchasing: A Perspective of Both Impulse Shoppers and System Users," *International Journal of Information Management*, 36(3), 284–296.

Xiang, L., Zheng, X., Lee, M. K. O., and Zhao, D. 2016. "Exploring Consumers' Impulse Buying Behavior on Social Commerce Platform: The Role of Parasocial Interaction," *International Journal of Information Management*, 36(3), 333–347.

Zaichkowsky, J. L. 1985. "Measuring the Involvement Construct," *Journal of Consumer Research*, 12(3), 341–352.

Zhu, M., and Ratner, R. K. 2015. "Scarcity Polarizes Preferences: The Impact on Choice among Multiple Items in a Product Class," *Journal of Marketing Research*, 52(1), 13–26.

Chapter 19

The Perspective of Manufacturing Enterprise Innovation Ecosystem Evolution Based on Technology Affordance: Transformation Path of the Bright Moon Company

Bo Hu, Baozhou Lu, and Zhibin Liu

Abstract

Qingdao Bright Moon Group (BMG) a high-tech enterprise which uses kelp as raw material, is the world's largest seaweed biological product enterprise. This chapter mainly describes BMG's two important transformation stages through the modes of technological innovation and Internet + innovation, realizing the upstream and downstream industry chain extensions.

Keywords: Industrial chain extension, Transformation, Technology affordance.

Introduction

Represented by "Internet +" digital technology in the manufacturing enterprise, how should the process of the transformation of science and technology be implemented to give constraints? Represented by "Internet +" digital technology innovation in manufacturing enterprises, how should one play a role in the formation of ecosystem? Both these problems help explore the problems in this Chapter. Using technology to create an innovation ecosystem, so as to promote manufacturing enterprise transformation, is a big challenge for managers. Figure 1 shows the relationship of questions and theory.

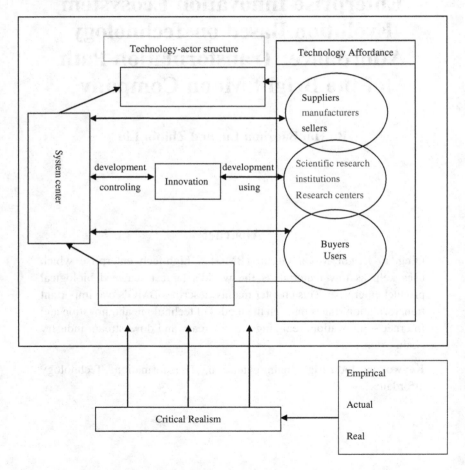

Figure 1. Relationship of Technology Affordance and Innovation Ecology System

In the ecological system of innovation, enterprises in the center of the system develop and control the innovation platform, and technology research and development and product applications interact with each other. The new platform can help in the convenient management of the enterprise itself, and also can attract more enterprises, which are doing technology research and development and product application to join the innovation ecosystem. Technology research and development of relevant institutions can cooperate with enterprises located in the center of the system innovation platform and innovation, so that we can put both parties in sync to develop together. We explore the case of Qingdao Bright Moon Group's transformation journey to answer some of our questions.

Literature review

Affordance and critical realism

Critical realism is the general philosophy of science developed by Bhaskar, English philosopher. Critical realism combines realistic ontology with interpretive epistemology (Bhaskar, 1998a). This does not imply judgmental relativism; since a real world does exist where critical realism holds that some theories approximate reality better than others, and that there are rational ways to assess knowledge claims.

The concept of affordances comes from the field of ecological psychology (Gibson, 1986), defined as "action possibilities" that arise in the interaction between an animal and its environment.

In IS literature, it is described as emerging from the relation between IT systems and organizational systems (Zammuto *et al.*, 2007), and defined as "the possibilities for goal-oriented action afforded to specified user groups by technical objects" (Markus and Silver, 2008, p. 622) as the potential for behaviors associated with achieving an immediate concrete outcome and arising from the relation between an object (e.g., an IT artefact) and a goal-oriented actor or actors (Volkoff and Strong, 2013; Strong *et al.*, 2014).

Technology affordance

A renewed focus on the concept of affordances would provide IS researchers with an appropriate foundation for developing better theories of IT-associated organizational change. Specifically, we suggest ways affordances can be used as generative mechanisms to understand IT-associated organizational change (Volkoff and Strong, 2013). The techno-organizational context (i.e. structure) consists of networks of human, social, and technical objects, which in various combinations enable (or create the potential for) action (i.e. affordances) (Bygstad *et al.*, 2016). If the phenomena we study in the organizational sciences are changing due to the ubiquitous adoption of information technology by individuals and organizations, do we not run the risk of our theories and research becoming irrelevant unless they reflect the changes in those phenomena? IT is not simply a tool for automating existing processes, but more importantly it is an enabler of organizational changes that can lead to additional productivity gains. We try to capture the interplay between IT and organization using the term "affordances" in the sense that new combinations of technology and organizational features continually create possibilities that affect organizational form and function.

The definition suggests that the immediate concrete outcome in the empirical domain provides evidence of the existence of an affordance in the domain the real. Through observation and/or interviews with questions, such as "what did the technology enable you to do?", "what did it make more difficult to do?", "what did you use the technology for?", "what happened once you started to use the technology?", or "were there things you expected to be able to do that were not in fact possible?", the actual events that allow for reintroduction back to the affordances can be uncovered.

Innovation ecosystem

Ecosystem for innovation and foreign scholars studies are relatively flexible, they are generally based on case study, through research the role of innovation ecosystem is to explain its meaning: from innovation ecosystem, enterprises can get in order to survive the required environmental conditions as well as the need to establish the relation between markets because the innovation ecosystem plays a role in the process of production enterprises and can find an effective way to improve the value of enterprises and reduce the cost of production, resulting in the enterprises' core competitive ability getting promoted.

Through innovation ecosystem, different enterprises can also make products get a positive interaction with innovation, it can not only help companies quickly set into other enterprise study, but also can greatly enhance the value of the enterprise knowledge and resources. In the system at the time of innovation ecosystem, the enterprise can also help each other, support each other, and achieve common progress.

In China's domestic study, Yun-Sheng Zhang and Li-Fei Zhang studied the innovation ecosystem and mainly researched the high-tech industry, they thought of innovation ecosystem as a kind of a brand new innovation system, it is a high-tech enterprise on a global scale formation, and the natural ecosystems have some common features, and it is in the patent, the development of technology and cooperation with other enterprise common progress, to meet customer demand.

Zheng Xiaoyong proposed that innovation ecosystem around innovation and commercialization formed a kind of extensive connection between organizations. Huangmin argues that innovation ecosystem is the core of the organization and other related organizations of different levels, based on their common goal to build up a network organization form of innovation, in the process of innovation, core organizations frequently associated with other organizations such as contact, exchange of knowledge or information resources, and are based on the developed new systematic, network organization model. Innovation ecosystem includes innovation system, innovation network, and the environment. In addition to this view, some scholars, the government, enterprises, scientific research subject and intermediaries of elements such as the innovation ecosystem also think so.

While studying abroad, Adner (2006) thought innovation ecosystem is a collaborative and integrated mechanism, it will be in the system of each enterprise innovation together, thus forming a set available to customers that can be coordinated and planned. Luoma — aho and others will be defined as innovation ecosystems that boast of a skillful or temporary system, it can play the role of interaction and communication in the ecological environment, with a variety of the main body of innovation. Here, they can teach each other's ideas and promote the development of innovation.

Innovation ecosystem is formed by all kinds of relationships between coupling ecological networks, through various kinds of information flow in the system network and the elements of talent, to achieve the sustainability of common values.

Qingdao Bright Moon Group (BMG) transformation

Bright moon group introduced

Qingdao Bright Moon Group (BMG), founded in 1968, is one of the world's largest seaweed biological products enterprise and is also the world's largest alginate production base. Seaweed industry is an important part of the marine industry, its industry scale and characteristics belong to niche industry, but BMG is big business in this small industry. Although BMG's main alginate has made it to the world's first, in such an era, if just to increase production capacity, one has to continue to increase capacity, and not the research and development of innovation, enterprises will fall into a passive situation much sooner. Based on this consideration, BMG Chairman Zhang Guofang thought only of the development of science and technology enterprises to make the enterprise become strong. At the same time, scientific and technological personnel are the keys to prosper. Developing in recent years, BMG is committed to promoting products from intermediate raw materials to terminal consumer transformation, the original function of alginate, sugar alcohol on two big businesses successfully developed biomedical materials, marine cosmetics, functional food ingredients, marine microbial fertilizer for emerging four business sectors. Under the drive of Internet +, BMG used scientific and technological innovation and took the initiative to embrace the Internet, the Internet penetration of thinking to the management, marketing, manufacturing, research and development, sourcing and so on to each level for enterprise transformation.

Two important stages of development

BMG has experienced two important stages of development from the production process of sodium alginate. Functional sugar alcohol is a relatively single product line, and gradually developed into a product across the alginate, functional sugar alcohol, cosmetics, ocean Marine functional foods, Marine biomedical materials, seaweed biological fertilizer research and development and production of the six major industries of a large group.

Stage 1 (1998–2007): laying solid foundation for the seaweed biological industry

In 1998, Bright Moon restructured and established *Qingdao bright moon seaweed industrial co., Ltd*. In addition to the materials processing industry, the company's first food grade sodium alginate production line was put into production, the algae research center was established and the national pharmaceutical production of GMP certification was obtained. For the enterprise's innovation and development, the depth of using algae paved the way.

In December 2005, the Bright Moon Marine science and technology park was established, and was identified as "national industrialization demonstration base of marine science research center", the company headquarters to move to the moon marine science and technology park. In this phase, the BMG mainly developed two basic industries: alginate and functional sugar alcohol.

Research center was established to ensure that the Bright Moon Seaweed Group has a strong research and development base. Through the establishment of a multiple product line, the realization of mass production, therefore has a strong manufacturing capability. During this time, the BMG underpinned the seaweed biological foundation industry and provided a good foundation for subsequent emerging businesses.

Stage 2 (2007–2015): Upstream and downstream industry chain extensions, the formation of the big four emerging business sectors

BMG Chairman Zhang Guofang pointed out: "the seaweed industry is an important part of Marine industry, but industry development scale and industry characteristics belong to the niche, the specialization of

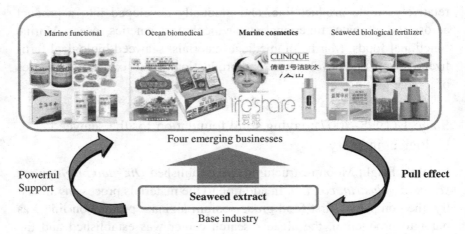

Figure 2. BMG's Basic Industries and the Four Emerging Industry Relations.

industry". Although BMG of alginate staples although are the world's first, there is still competition in the industry, resources and environment restriction. The low end of the present situation of excess production capacity made the BMG realize that if it continues to rely on increasing the production capacity, the old way of expanding the scale of this development and group will be passive soon. To survive, it is necessary to advance one step towards the road to development through transformation.

To expand the market and improve product-added value, from 2007, the Bright Moon fostered emerging industries, promoted transformation from intermediate raw materials to terminal consumer products, and successfully developed Marine cosmetics, Marine functional foods, ocean biomedical materials, seaweed biological fertilizer for four emerging businesses. Figure 2 shows BMG's basic industries and the four emerging industry relations.

Among the four emerging businesses, the Bright Moon will put most of the electricity resources into sea cosmetics. The Bright Moon plans to keep the cosmetics business occupied and then gradually expand to other business. The ultimate goal is to have Bright Moon on the Internet, which is a more comprehensive platform, and promote the Bright Moon seaweed way of life. With sea cosmetics business, on the one hand, and the company's e-commerce experience, on the other hand, the e-commerce resources cannot be used simultaneously and hence the performance of the cosmetics business e-commerce would be the first and the best.

In addition, the BMG in the supply chain also has achieved remarkable achievement, in the upstream, embodied in the Bright Moon to Chile to open subsidiary, and acquired the biggest local algae suppliers. In addition, the Bright Moon is also the largest supplier of algae and hence Peru's local cooperation, also helped him to become a shareholder to grasp the seaweed strategic scarce resources.

The BMG met so many unprecedented difficulties in the process of transformation. First, for the downstream industry chain extension, new business direction is hard to choose; second, it is hard to find a match with the emerging business sector of talents and support teams; Third, the enterprise to the upstream and downstream industry chain extensions, enterprise organization structure and business processes all need to change; Fourth, the intermediate raw materials have to be sent to the terminal consumer after transformation, the original concept of market and marketing model is no longer applicable, all need to be updated and reconstructed.

The future development direction

Looking into the future, the BMG will rely on the national Marine science and technology park, with seaweed as the core of the Marine industry ecosystem, and with "Internet +" building Bright Moon health life hall, through online and offline promotion of an healthy life through algae. In addition, the Bright Moon self-built electricity APP "community project", will build bright Moon 24 hours + 5 kilometer life circle through the mobile terminal. It will provide the moon 2 kilometer circle, sale of fresh vegetables through online order and immediate delivery, provide 24-hour groceries via online order, 2 hours door-to-door delivery services, products involving group in various industries, such as cosmetics, algae food, wine, band-aid, health care products, etc.

Dynamics analysis

As BMG has an industry leading status, it should develop through constant focus on research and development and, innovation. Since BMG moved from the traditional industries to the terminal four new industry transformation, it is aware of the need to change the process of thinking, and therefore, how to use the power of technology affordance to realize Internet + when faced with the problem.

In order to adapt to the transformation of Internet +, only in 2015, BMG modified the organization structure based on the four big adjustments: reduce the hierarchy, break the dissection, break the departmental boundaries, and further flatten the organizational structure. BMG attached great importance to Internet + and hence formed an independent Internet center integrating existing distributed Internet resources to accelerate the transformation of a new way of operating the Internet group, undertake network promotion, network marketing, design and planning, information management duties, and better services for the group and subsidiary. BMG, taking account of the enterprise information management system, the Internet's thinking, has implemented the VFP platform. The platform of a large company, mature ERP system, is now in the implementation and will improve the platform development, the reconfigurable ERP system, to satisfy the enterprise individuation requirement. At the same time, BMG also introduced the virtualization platform, through the construction of the Bright Moon private cloud: big data management, the management system of structured data collection, backup, analysis of the internal data, according to the requirements, management extraction, processing; keep collecting unstructured data, such as audio, text, backup and share. At one end of the production and operation are the main external data sources, data needed for the Internet and internal management, including the upstream suppliers, market information, and the downstream customers.

Other factors include Internet thinking management mode, the cloud management, through WeChat platform, implementation plan, daily, and project management, change time is working time. The office is not restricted by time and place. Management process is visible and controllable, improves work efficiency and the market competitiveness. At the same time, companies use the Internet for thinking and encouraging employees to start a business. A company was named science and technology business incubators in Qingdao and has hatched more start-ups.

In the management transformation in the above, the plan is for big data management to make up for the inadequacy of ERP further, strengthen the control and management business process to enhance the data interaction, realize the industrial data and ERP business by process by closely integrated comprehensive analysis of the data, multi-dimensional reports and intuitive display of global operational data.

From the marketing point of view, BMG through the Internet platform builds and manages customer information, improves the level of customer management, in addition to the traditional marketing way, via the Internet. BMG also increased the electric business platform through the establishment of the customer fan base, deep communication with the customer, collection of customer consultation, the customer for the product evaluation and opinion, timely feedback to the developers, optimization of product variety, improvement of the efficacy of our products and optimization of the product packaging to further improve the customer satisfaction of online.

In terms of product research and development, the Internet data analysis and market investigation, form guidance for product development and marketing through customer feedback and accurate assessment of the customer psychology. The seaweed industry innovation in algae active material as the center and state key laboratory based on the Bright Moon seaweed group of the existing technology platform, build algae biological industry science and technology innovation system.

The construction of innovation ecosystem

BMG, using their own resources and ability to build an Internet platform of their own, and other related enterprises, such as suppliers, research institutions, and customers, uses resources belonging to the boundary of the enterprise resources, through such a platform between the enterprises and the boundary of the enterprise resources. The running mechanism of innovation ecosystem is the innovation in the flow of resources. This kind of innovation ecosystem is divided into several steps:

First, BMG, through the establishment of the Internet platform for enterprises themselves and other various aspects, has carried on with the management. On the one hand is the enterprise management system, and on the other hand is big data management. Through such management, BMG determines the direction of enterprise innovation, and through this platform, production, suppliers, distributors and sales channels are introduced. This center of innovation ecosystem is also a starting point.

Second, through the Internet platform, BMG connects with other enterprises, suppliers through such system with BMG procurement work, scientific research institutions such as research and development of science and technology from BMG innovation in the direction of the Internet platform for research and development. These can also according to your needs request to improve the Internet platform; buyers and users also purchase products through the Internet platform. In this regard, BMG has successfully used the resources of the science and technology research and development institutions, these resources belong to the boundary of the BMG resources, make scientific research institution of research and development ability with BMG's own development direction and the existing research results in order to achieve the purpose of product development and upgrade.

Third, purchaser and user feedback to BMG can be done via the Internet. Such steps to make the enterprise of large data obtained perfectly also let BMG work according to customer demand for further innovation. The buyer and user feedback is also one of the boundaries of BMG resources, using the feedback information one can learn that BMG, due to the effect of product innovation research and development, product research and development, needs to move in the future direction.

References

Adner, R. 2006. "Match Your Innovation Strategy to Your Innovation Ecosystem," *Harvard Business Review*, 84(4), 98–107.

Bygstad, B., Munkvold, B., and Volkoff, O. 2016. *Journal of Information Technology*, 31, 83. https://doi.org/10.1057/jit.2015.13.

Gibson, J. J. 1986. *"The Ecological Approach to Perception."* Hillsdale, NJ, Lawrence Erlbaum Associates.

Markus, M. L., and Silver, M. S. 2008. "A Foundation for the Study of IT Effects: A New Look at DeSanctis and Poole's Concepts of Structural Features and Spirit," *Journal of the Association for Information Systems*, 9(10), 609–632.

Strong, D. M., Volkoff, O., Johnson, S. A., Pelletier, L. R., Tulu, B., Bar-On, I., Trudel, J., and Garber, L. 2014. "A Theory of Organization-EHR Affordance

Actualization," *Journal of the Association for Information Systems*, 15(2), 53–85.

Volkoff, O., and Strong D. M. 2013. "Critical Realism and Affordances: Theorizing IT-associated Organizational Change Processes 1," *MIS Quarterly*, 37(3), 819–834.

Zammuto, R. F., Griffith, T. L., Majchrzak, A., Dougherty, D. J., and Faraj, S. 2007. "Information Technology and the Changing Fabric of Organization," *Organization Science*, 8(5), 749–762.

Printed in the United States
by Bookmasters

Printed in the United States
By Bookmasters